How Babies Talk

How Babies Talk

*The Magic and Mystery of Language
in the First Three Years of Life*

**Roberta Michnick Golinkoff, Ph.D.
and
Kathy Hirsh-Pasek, Ph.D.**

A DUTTON BOOK

DUTTON
Published by the Penguin Group
Penguin Putnam Inc., 375 Hudson Street,
New York, New York 10014, U.S.A.
Penguin Books Ltd, 27 Wrights Lane,
London W8 5TZ, England
Penguin Books Australia Ltd, Ringwood,
Victoria, Australia
Penguin Books Canada Ltd, 10 Alcorn Avenue,
Toronto, Ontario, Canada M4V 3B2
Penguin Books (N.Z.) Ltd, 182–190 Wairau Road,
Auckland 10, New Zealand

Penguin Books Ltd, Registered Offices:
Harmondsworth, Middlesex, England

First published by Dutton, a member of Penguin Putnam Inc.

First Printing, June, 1999
10   9   8   7   6   5   4   3   2   1

CIP data is available.

ISBN 0-525-94455-9

Printed in the United States of America
Set in New Baskerville
Designed by Eve L. Kirch

This book is printed on acid-free paper. ♾

To our mothers, Joan and Anne, whose drive and determination we hope we have inherited. Good talkers themselves, they served as our role models for how to talk, and how to listen.

To our children, Jordan, Allison, Josh, Benj, and Michael, who gave us a bird's-eye view of what comes "out of the mouths of babes."

And to our husbands, Jeff and Elliott, whose constant encouragement and support made this dream a reality.

Acknowledgments

It is always the case that in an undertaking of this magnitude, there are many people to thank. First and foremost, we wish to offer special thanks to our colleagues from around the world. Their scientific discoveries made this book possible. Their inspired work paved the way for our understanding of language—the pinnacle of human behavior. Though their names cannot all be mentioned here, they stand with us in having contributed to the exciting story of language development. In that very real sense, this book is theirs, too, although they may not agree with all our interpretations.

Much of the research described in this book could not have been conducted were it not for the research support provided by government agencies, private foundations, and educational institutions. In our own case, our research has been supported by both the National Science Foundation and the National Institutes of Child Health and Human Development. In addition, Golinkoff has been supported by a James McKeen Cattell Sabbatical Award and a John Simon Guggenheim Memorial Fellowship. Hirsh-Pasek has held a number of grants from the Pew Foundation.

Having children who have mastered language is a great boon. Benj Pasek and Allison Golinkoff offered critical reviews of some of these chapters. With keen eyes and direct, no-nonsense commentary, they helped their scientific mothers learn how to write for a broader audience. Many thanks to our editors, Deborah Brody and

Jennifer Moore, who greatly improved our writing, and to our agent, Barbara Lowenstein, who had faith in this book. Thanks also go to Maryanne Bowers and Doris Davidson at the University of Delaware, who helped in preparing the bibliography. George Hollich, He Len Chung, Camille Rocroi, and Michelle McKinney also deserve our thanks. They kept our laboratories running so smoothly that we were able to concentrate on writing this book.

Finally, thanks to all the children and parents from around the world who participated in the research projects described here. Were it not for their participation, we would know much less about children's amazing ability to learn a human language. The parents, students, and professionals who read this book are benefitting, too, from the willingness of children and parents to allow scientists like ourselves to probe the workings of the developing human mind.

Contents

Introduction. Setting the Stage: The Magic of Language Development in the First Three Years of Life   **1**

Language Milestones   5
The Source of Our Knowledge: Scientific Sleuthing   7
    Theoretical breakthroughs   7
    Methodological breakthroughs   8
Scientific Sleuthing Pays off   9

Chapter 1. Watch Your Language! The Fetus Can Hear You: Development from Before Birth to Three Months of Age   **13**

The Fetus   13
    The Fetal Environment: Home Sweet Home   13
    Baby, Do You Read Me? Hearing Mother's Voice and Other Sounds   14
        Try This: Can my fetus hear? Can my fetus hear me?   16
    Does Fetal Learning Mean Fetal School?   17

Birthing the Baby: Will the Newborn Resemble the Fetus?   18
    Try This: Does the newborn react to sounds?   19
    Communicating Through Crying   20

Mother, Is That You? Newborns Prefer to Hear Mother's
Voice   21

Distinguishing the World's Languages   23
   Try This: Does your baby respond to foreign languages?   24

Face-to-Face: Love at First Look?   25
   Try This: Charting baby's smiles   28

Do Mouths and Voices Work Together?   28

Newborn Copycats   30
   Try This: Can my baby copy me?   30

The Roots of Conversation   31

Baby Talk Matters   31
   Try This: Do babies react to baby talk?   34

More Than Meets the Eye   34

Scientific Sleuthing Pays Off   35

Lesson 1. Silence is *not* golden   35

Lesson 2. New scientific methods can yield assessment tools   36

Lesson 3. Overestimate your baby's capabilities   37

**Chapter 2. Yada-Yada-Yada: The Babbling Period
Between Four and Eight Months of Age   39**

Babies Do Babble   39

How Babies Talk to Us   41
   Try This: Conversations from the crib?   42

From Coos and Goos to Babbling   43
   *Try This: Are "Mama" and "Dada" real words or just arbitrary
   sounds?*   44

Why Babies Babble   44

How We Babble to Babies   47

Widening the Topics of Conversation   47
   Try This: Finding objects near and far   48

Finding the Words (and Other Units) in the Stream of Speech   48

What's a Word Worth?   48

Use Your Head! The Headturn Preference Procedure   49
   Try This: Will baby notice disrupted speech?   51

Learn Your Handle: Lauren, Not Louise   52
   Try This: Does baby respond to her own name?   54

Once Upon a Time: Babies Recognize Words in Stories   54

How Do You Mean? Babies Grapple with Word Meanings   56

Scientific Sleuthing Pays Off 59

Lesson 1. Hear ye, hear ye: Watch for ear infections 59

Lesson 2. There is nothing wrong with small talk 60

Chapter 3. Point-ilism: Parents Become Tools for Babies Between Nine and Twelve Months of Age 63

Learning to Communicate Without Words 64

Finding the Causal Connection: My Signals *Can* Make Things Happen! 64

Try This: Can my baby communicate with intention? 67

How Do Babies Learn to Make Their Point? 67

Try This: When can baby follow a point? 69

The Negotiation of Failed Messages: You Just Don't Get It! 70

Try This: How does my baby negotiate? 72

Let the Words Begin! 73

Preverbal Communication: The Cradle of Meaning 73

Detecting the Patterns in the Language Stream 74

The Decline in Distinguishing Among the Sounds of the World's Languages 77

Whither the Words? 78

Try This: Playing games 80

Scientific Sleuthing Pays Off 80

Lesson 1. Honor babies' communicative attempts even *before* they are intentionally communicative 80

Lesson 2. Put my thoughts into words! 83

Chapter 4. First Words: Getting "Hi" Between Twelve and Eighteen Months of Age 87

What Does It Take to Learn a Word? 88

The Flowering of Vocabulary 88

The Stars and Stripes and Other Symbols 90

Try This: Comics in the crib? 92

The Fertile Path to Real Words 92

Try This: Creating a diary of protowords and first words 94

Communicating Efficiently 94

Try This: Tracking the use of the baby's first ten words 96

"Home Signs" and "Baby Signs" 97

Try This: Can my baby learn some baby signs? 99

Symbols, Categories, Meanings, and Emotions   100
  "Dog," Not "Dalmatian"; "Hat," Not "Baseball Cap": Why Babies
  Prefer Some Words over Others   100
    Try This: What kinds of words are my baby's first ten words?   102
  How Do Meanings and Words Come Together?   103
  Saying Your First Words: A Sobering Task   104
    Try This: Does my baby express emotion when she talks?   106

First Words Take Effort, More for Some Than Others   106
  A Tale of Two Toddlers   106
  Name Callers and Social Sophisticates   107
    *Try This: Is my baby a name caller or a socialite? What kind of
    parent am I?*   109
  Word Comprehension Exceeds Word Production   110

Scientific Sleuthing Pays Off   112
  Lesson 1. More baby talk = More baby's talk   112
  Lesson 2. There are big individual differences in the appear-
  ance of the first words   112
  Lesson 3. Picture book reading is a source of new words   112
  Lesson 4. When do you worry about a lack of words?   113

**Chapter 5. Vocabulary Takes Wing: Eighteen to
  Twenty-four Months**   **115**

The Vocabulary Spurt   115
  Finding the Vocabulary Spurt   116
    Try this: Catching the torrent of words in a diary   117
  Word Learning Is a Bear (Bare?)   118
  What Are Toddlers Talking About?   118
    Try This: Book reading as a classroom for word learning   122
  Babies Overextend Themselves: Misapplying Words for All the
  Right Reasons   123
    Try This: Looking for overextensions   127
  Does Sensitivity to Social Cues Lead to the Vocabulary
  Spurt?   127
    Try This: Is your child using social cues to learn new words?   130
  Do Mental Advances Lead to the Vocabulary Spurt?   130
    Try This: Categorizing objects and the vocabulary spurt   133
  Fast Mapping: Novel Names Go with Novel Categories   133
    Try This: Fast mapping and the vocabulary spurt   135

An Integrated View of the Vocabulary Spurt: It Takes Social Skill *and* Mental Advances   136

Individual Differences in Word Learning   137
Pronunciation: Saying It My Way   137
  Try This: Recording the baby's favorite mistakes   000
Boys and Girls: Early Sightings of Mars and Venus   139
Firstborn Versus Later-Born Toddlers   140
Social Class Differences in Word Learning   141

Scientific Sleuthing Pays Off   143
Lesson 1. The study of normal development helps in understanding language problems   143
Lesson 2. More language in = More language out   146
Lesson 3. Watching TV cannot make up for real communication   147

Chapter 6. "More Juice!"—Babies Understand and Produce Simple Sentences Between Eighteen and Twenty-four Months of Age149

What Toddlers Can Say   149
Two-Word Sentences Say It All   150
  Try This: Two-word sentences take off! But what do they mean?   153
What enables the Baby to Use Two-Word Speech?   153

What Toddlers Can Understand   154
Investigating Two-Word Productions: What Children Comprehend   154
  Try This: What are the cues my baby relies on to understand sentences?   155
What Does It Mean to Understand Sentences?   156
Babies find the units in the language stream   157
Babies realize that words in sentences describe events in the world   158
  Try This: Can my baby understand that language maps to unique events?   160
Different arrangements of the units in sentences change sentence meaning   161
  Try This: Does my baby understand that differences in word order signal differences in meaning?   163

Beyond Word Order: Children Attend to Grammatical Elements   164
   Try This: Is my baby sensitive to grammatical elements?   168
"With"—A Grammatical Element in Action   169
Comprehension Far Outpaces Production, but Why?   170

Scientific Sleuthing Pays Off   172
Lesson 1. Engage in rich interpretation but don't bother to correct   172
Lesson 2. Your baby's caregiver is your ally   174

Chapter 7. The Language Sophisticate at Twenty-four to Thirty-six Months: Why? Why? Why?   175

The Emergence of Grammatical Capability   175
Adding Glue to the Sentence: Function Words and Particles   176
   Try This: Finding grammatical function words and particles in your child's speech   178
Overgeneralizations: It Breaked!   179
Asking Questions   180
What's Up, Doc? Wh- Questions   181
Why, Why, Why?   182
Ifs, Ands and Buts: The Grammatical Spurt   184
Is It Really Grammar?   185

The Source of Grammatical Capability in the Human Species   187
Where Does the Grammar Come From?   187
A Language Instinct?   189
The Critical Period: Time Is Running Out   190

Scientific Sleuthing Pays Off   191
Lesson 1. When should you worry?   192
Lesson 2. What should we do or not do to promote language growth?   193
Lesson 3. It's never too early to start learning a second language   194

Chapter 8. "Please" and "Thank You": Using Language to Get Things Done Between Twenty-four and Thirty-six Months   199

Mastering the Uses of Language   199
Learning a Language Is Learning a Culture   202

What Are You *Really* Asking? How Toddlers Understand Requests　204
　Try This: How do I ask questions? Does my child make conversational inferences?　209
How to Ask: Getting What We Want　210
　Try This: Can my child consciously use polite speech?　213
Learning Social Routines　213
Conversations with Two-year-olds　215
　Try This: Can my child observe conversational rules?　219
Beyond Conversation: Telling the Stories of Our Lives Through Narratives　219
　Try This: Does my child tell coherent narratives?　221
Using Language for Fun: Jokes and Pretense　222
　Try This: Does my toddler make jokes?　224

Scientific Sleuthing Pays Off　224
Lesson 1. Constructing life stories with your child promotes narrative development　224
Lesson 2. There's more to storybooks than meets the eye　227

Epilogue. Tying It Up: Language Development from Birth to Age Three　**229**
How Far Have Children Come?　229
Where Is the Child Going?　232

References　**235**

Index　**251**

Introduction

Setting the Stage:
The Magic of Language Development
in the First Three Years of Life

Communicating through language is the crowning achievement of the human species. Dogs can't do it. Whales can't do it. Even our evolutionary cousins, the great apes, can't do it. Yet within every infant lies the potential to learn a language. Equipped with the power of words, every one of us can talk about a future and resurrect a past. With language we can mentally move through time and space unlike any other species.

Through human language we have transformed our planet and launched spacecraft to Pluto. Through well-chosen words a three-year-old can exclaim that she wants "the red cup with the giraffe on it, not the blue cup with the elephant." Language enables us to embrace an idea, to share our feelings, to comment on our world, and to understand each other's minds. Precisely because language is so pervasive, we fail to realize the remarkable capabilities that we take for granted. Trying to appreciate the complexities of language is somewhat like trying to appreciate the design of your eyeglasses while you are looking through them. With your glasses on, you gain a whole new perspective on the world—but you never stop to consider how your glasses actually work.

In the past several decades, specialists in the field have made enormous progress in understanding the intricacies of learning to talk. When you realize that you can chat on the phone for hours without ever planning what you are going to say or can generate a sentence that is as long as this one by stringing together a limited set of build-ing blocks like nouns and verbs, you begin to see the vastness of the system that young children have to learn. We have no problem turn-ing a sentence like this one into a question. (Do we?) And it is a commonplace assumption that a word like "window" can be widely applied to such instances as the stained-glass depictions in a church or the window opened on a computer screen. How do we know when to use the word "window"? What does window really mean? How do children ever learn to use words correctly?

As we begin to scratch the surface, we see that there is a great deal of extraordinary in the ordinary. The achievements of chess grand masters, musical virtuosos, and Olympic athletes hardly match what children accomplish in language learning by the tender age of three or four years. How do children do it? How do they learn to get their tongues in just the right place to pronounce a word? How do they learn those noun and verb building blocks that allow them to con-struct sentences? How do they learn the difference between "I eat to live" and "I live to eat"? These questions lie at the foundation of the mystery of language development.

Where can the answers to these questions be found? A common-sense approach was taken by our grandmothers. "How do children learn language, you ask? It's obvious. Parents teach their children to talk."

Grandma has to be partially right. It is no coincidence that French children learn French and German children learn German. Little two-year-old Harry down the street didn't just happen on his new word "parallelogram"; his mother the mathematician taught it to him. Yet parents don't explicitly teach children language in the ways that they are taught how to play chess, or to play the violin, or to run hurdles. We don't have grammar classes that teach our toddlers how to arrange their words. We don't even correct them when they use improper English. Imagine three-year-old Dennis who has come with you to Mr. Wilson's house next door. As you are standing in Mr. Wil-son's entryway, Dennis proclaims, "I goed to the bathroom," while standing atop a freshly made puddle. In situations like these no one thinks of correcting the child's grammar. You run for the nearest mop! And these moments are not the exceptions, but the rule. In most cases, if our children communicate the message, we are so over-joyed that we let the grammar slide.

These examples are not the only reason to doubt grandma's theory of language learning. Children all over the world learn language without any explicit instruction. From palaces to pitched tents, all children learn language in roughly the same way and at roughly the same time in development. Children become language experts even though they learn in radically different environments. They learn language when they are born into cultures that value conversation with infants. They also learn in cultures where parents don't talk to their infants. Though at first glance it seems obvious that we teach language to our children, language learning can't be explained solely by parental instruction.

So, how *do* children learn language?

The first to suggest that language was a function of nature was Egyptian King Psammetichus in the fourth century B.C.E. This king wanted to know which of the many peoples of the world were the first inhabitants. He ordered shepherds to raise two infants in isolation and to record their very first word. That word would provide the answer. The king started his experiment relatively certain of the final outcome. If the word was spoken in Egyptian, then surely the Egyptians were the first to inhabit the earth. Their language would be heralded as the original language.

As the king ordered, the shepherds raised the children, saying not a word in their presence. When the children were two years of age the experiment was complete. One of the toddlers said "*becos*." The shepherds immediately reported this to the king, to his dismay. It was not an Egyptian word, but the Phrygian word for "bread." His Egyptians were not the first inhabitants of the known world. Rather, they were second in line to the Phrygians.

King Psammetichus's experiment was based on the assumption that language is present in each child, just waiting for the moment to burst forth. The king on this point seems aligned with the popular writer Professor Steven Pinker, who recently wrote that just as spiders spin webs, humans learn language. It is in our very nature to learn language. Language is a product of the human mind.

So, is it nature or is it nurture? This question fuels a debate that has lasted for centuries, a debate that affects our roles as parents, teachers, and caregivers. If language is inborn, then we can stand back and watch the miracle unfold. If, on the other hand, we teach language, we must be active partners in our children's language growth. All of us need to know because children's language abilities are intimately related to many aspects of intellectual growth.

Those in the field of language development are finally in a position to answer some of these age-old questions. There has been a revolution within the study of language development in recent years. New methods can evaluate the language capabilities of the fetus (yes, the fetus!) and newborn. We can now see up close what newborns bring to the task of language learning (nature). New methods also permit an ever clearer view of the ways in which parents' teachings affect their children. It turns out that nature and nurture are involved in an intricate dance with each other. Children's minds are rich with language-learning resources. Even newborns have a proclivity to attend to certain sounds over others. Yet there is much that parents and caregivers can do to enhance children's language growth. We can now identify the environments that provide fertile ground for language learning.

These revolutionary findings have been widely published in the scientific literature. It is now time to share them with parents and caregivers who watch the miracle of language development every day. We serve as your scientific guides on a tour of language development. We begin with the fetus who is listening in on our conversations and then turn to the newborn who, in his own subtle way, is already taking part in these conversations. We will look at the four- to eight-month-old statistician who cannot say a word, but who accurately analyzes our speech for common sounds and patterns. Then it's off to the nine- to twelve-month-old who charms us with her points, her demands, and her questions—all without saying a word. Eventually, we work our way up to the knowledgeable three-year-old who talks in full paragraphs, rarely stopping for a breath.

On this journey we will take you to laboratories around the world as we see virtually every facet of early language development, from the fetus's first detection of speech sounds to the toddler's mastery of complex grammar. You will discover how infants easily solve language tasks that highly trained professional linguists who have studied language for years have been unable to completely understand. As researchers who have worked at the cutting edge of the field, we know what to look for. As mothers of five children we also know what a special experience it can be to watch as our children grow. Whether in the lab or at home, we continue to marvel at babies' monumental achievements as they learn language. With the scientists' tools in hand, parents can join researchers and watch their own children with renewed excitement and respect.

Each chapter of this book contains two broad sections. The first, "Language Milestones," explores what babies know about language and when they know it. We also examine the scientific techniques that allow us to uncover babies' burgeoning language knowledge. The second, "Scientific Sleuthing Pays Off," demonstrates how the scientific findings can be used to enhance our everyday interactions with our children. To help you further, we have studded each chapter with inserts called, "Try This." Using these sections, you can experience the phenomenon of language development in your own "home laboratory." All of these sections will enrich your understanding of your child's language development. Armed with this knowledge, you can facilitate your child's language growth.

Language Milestones

In this section is described what children at different ages can do. Using the latest scientific research, we will show the reader the milestones that children reach and the pitfalls they can meet along the road. Also described are the hidden capabilities that cannot be directly observed in children's daily behavior. In short, we examine what it takes to make language acquisition happen.

Milestones, such as when a child says his first word, are a constant topic of conversation and provide the yardstick for how children are faring compared to their peers. When parents compare two children in the same family or from different families, they invariably wonder if their child is "on target" or within the normal range. As experts who have tested thousands of children in our laboratories, we can reassure you that language develops at different times.

Consider the following typical scenario: Tommy is 19 months old and has not yet uttered his first word. Samantha, at the same age, is already talking in sentences. Tommy's mother, Lulu, is getting more and more concerned as each day passes (and especially on the days of play group, when Samantha's mother is quick to point out that Samantha can *say* what she wants while Tommy still has to grunt and point). Tommy is prone to tantrums when Lulu can't figure out what he wants, to the point that she is beginning to dread going to play group. Samantha seems so much more controlled and contained. Is this normal? Is it just a difference between boys and girls? Or is Tommy headed for the psychiatrist's couch?

Similar cases from the scientific literature show that both Tommy and Samantha are well within the normal range. While boys do lag behind girls by a few months, they soon catch up. Since Tommy is a second child, his mother speaks and reads to him less than she did to her firstborn. This is probably a factor in his slower development as well. Tommy's mother is experiencing needless anxiety, especially because it is clear that Tommy understands much of what is said to him even though he doesn't speak.

What is "normal" varies enormously in the area of language development. Some children speak their first words by 10 months of age, although most don't until 12 or 13 months. Others don't talk until they are Tommy's age (19 months). Almost all children who lag behind catch up.

Why is saying that first word so difficult? To illustrate, let's witness a scene with 11-month-old David and his mother in Cleveland, Ohio. David is in his high chair eating Cheerios. He's just finished with his turkey and sweet potatoes, and is wearing his dinner proudly on his face and arms. The floor around him shows the carnage of the "battle," since he is learning to feed himself. His mother, Wendy, is thoroughly exhausted from feeding David while trying to cook dinner for herself and her husband, Irving.

"Eh eh eh eh eh," David whines repeatedly as he points at the Cheerio he has just thrown on the floor. Wendy knows this is her cue to pick up the Cheerio. "I can't wait until you can talk," she says. David has been making sounds like "eh eh" and "gaga" for months now, but no words yet.

Their game is interrupted by the sounds of a car. David bobs up and down expectantly in his high chair. As the door opens and his father appears, David looks up and says, "Dada." In unison Wendy and Irving swivel their heads in David's direction. They smile proudly. There is no mistaking it! *This* is the first word. As if their son had just delivered the Gettysburg address, David's parents are now sure that their son is the genius they knew all along he'd be.

We rarely think of why this moment is so magical. After all, babies around the world perform this trick at approximately the same age, just as they all learn to walk. Yet consider what lies behind the making of a first word—even one as deceptively simple as "Dada." First, David has to notice the word "Dada" in the midst of all the speech he hears every day. David has to find where words begin and end in the cascades of speech that tumble over him. The problem David faces is not unlike what happens when an adult travels to a foreign country and doesn't speak the language. Finding sentences in the streams of speech all around—let alone words—seems hopeless. The words a tourist hears are not punctuated with commas or separated by spaces. People seem to speak so quickly. David, however, solves this problem and finds the word "Dada"—and many others—by the tender age of 11 months.

Of course, picking out the word Dada is only part of the solution. The second hurdle David faces is figuring out what Dada means. It could refer to Daddy's hair or to Daddy's clothes or to the peculiar way Daddy walks. Given how many babies call all males "Dada" for several months, we can see that this is no mean feat. Finally, David has to figure out just how to arrange his mouth and tongue to utter the word. Using your mouth is like playing a complex instrument. If you miss the mark—even by a little bit—you say an entirely different word. Emily Latella from *Saturday Night Live* designed an entire skit around words that were near misses when she made editorial pronouncements about problems with the "Deaf Penalty," "Violins on Television," and the "Presidential Erection." Or, consider tongue twisters such as "She sells seashells by the seashore." For David, all of language is like a tongue twister! Before David articulates that first word have come a host of accomplishments that paved the way.

Language milestones display the complexity and competency of the human mind. Our grandmothers would never believe what fetuses, infants, and toddlers can do. And why should they? Many language milestones can only be observed through scientific testing. In this book, we go well beyond what our grandmothers can see.

The Source of Our Knowledge: Scientific Sleuthing

The second broad issue concerns how researchers access what is going on in a child's mind. Scientific sleuthing is required to ask questions of babies who can't walk, talk, or follow directions. More is known now about how infants behave and think than in the prior fifty years. The reason for this leap in knowledge is twofold: First, there have been stunning theoretical breakthroughs, and second, new methods have been invented for studying babies.

Theoretical breakthroughs. Major advancements in the study of language development can be traced to one of the intellectual giants of the twentieth century: Professor Noam Chomsky of MIT. Chomsky was the first to posit that language is a window onto the human mind. He stated that language was an innate property of the human species. His work has given the field a way to talk about the complexity of language and to ask interesting questions. Chomsky appreciated the elegance of language structure, and realized that all languages are equally complex. By virtue of membership in the human species, infants' brains are prepared to learn language. This "language instinct," as Steven Pinker calls it, represents nature's contribution to language development.

Chomsky also recognized, though, that language learning is influenced by the language babies hear around them. Otherwise, as grandma rightly pointed out, all children would speak the same language. Many scientists have studied how parents talk to their children and how this affects language learning. *Both* the role of inborn factors—nature—as well as the role of the environment—nurture—are needed for language development.

Methodological breakthroughs. The theoretical breakthroughs influenced the kinds of questions that needed to be asked. If babies come into the world equipped with a language instinct, testing should be able to uncover evidence for it in *babies who could not yet talk.* This new viewpoint paved the way for the development of methods that investigate the hidden competencies of infants and toddlers. Because of these methodological breakthroughs, much new information about language development has come forth. Consider one of the popular methods that draw on a simple observation:

Babies suck.

This is a fact, not an epithet. Babies spend a lot of their time sucking, to obtain food and just because sucking satisfies a need. Put a bottle in their mouths and babies suck. Put a finger in their mouths and they suck too. Professor Peter Eimas at Brown University has invented a method that uses babies' sucking as a vehicle to tell what they know. He gives babies a nipple that is hooked up to an amplifier so the patterns of their sucking can be recorded. As the baby happily sucks away, Eimas plays the same sound over and over for the baby and watches what happens. When babies hear something new, they get aroused and show their excitement by sucking harder on the nipple. After they hear the same sound for a while, they, like adults, get a little bored and their sucking rate slows down.

This method has been used to find out if two-day-old babies can tell the difference between their own language and another language. After all, they have been hearing their own language for several months in the womb. Can newborn French babies tell their language apart from, say, Russian?

Imagine baby Jean-Paul, all dressed up in a Christian Dior outfit in his Yves St. Laurent stroller, being brought for a visit to a baby lab in Paris. Jean-Paul is given a brand-new nipple to suck on while he hears someone talking in Russian. He sucks like mad until he gets bored, and then his sucking declines. Then the researchers plays samples of French, said by the same bilingual speaker. With renewed excitement Jean-Paul starts sucking with a passion (*vive la France!*). Jean-Paul *could* tell the difference between French and Russian. Babies around the world can tell the difference between their "mother" tongue and a foreign language at just two days of age. Great headway in understanding language development has been made with the youngest of babies—even fetuses.

Scientific Sleuthing Pays Off

"Okay," you say, "it's interesting to chart the milestones of language development and to learn how scientists find these things out, but what does all of this newfound knowledge have to do with me?"

The last section of each chapter takes a broad look at language development during the age period covered by the chapter. Mining the scientific knowledge base, we can make informed decisions about everyday issues. When should we start talking to our children? Does "baby talk" help or hinder language learning? Equipped with knowledge, parents and professionals (such as speech therapists, pediatricians, and child-care providers) can become more astute participants in children's language development. They also are equipped to tell if something is wrong. Take a look at some of the advantages when you know what to look for:

On April 6, 1997, the lead story on all the major networks was about the results of the National Institute of Child Health and Human Development Study of Early Child Care. This landmark study, in which one of the co-authors of this book participated (Dr. Hirsh-Pasek), probed the effects of early child care on language development and intelligence from birth to three years of age. Since more than 70 percent of American women with children under the age of three are now in the work force, this issue is crucially important to the development of the country's next generation. The results of this massive study were that "above and beyond" the effects of children's home environment, what goes on at a child's day-care facility is critical for language growth. *Children in high-quality day-care environments have more vocabulary and more complex language than their counterparts in lower-quality care.*

This is important new information that can change children's lives. The study's findings describe not only what is meant by "high-quality day-care environments," but also help identify those kinds of day-care environments that enhance or impede children's language skills. In day care, silence is *not* golden. Other than at nap time, quiet rooms in which children are seen and not heard is a cause for concern. And rooms kept quiet by depositing children in front of a television are also far from ideal. With specific guidelines from the scientific data in hand, parents will know what to look for when they want to put their children into good day care that will stimulate language growth.

Scientific knowledge can also alert us to potential red flags. On July 23, 1997, *ABC News Nightline* with Ted Koppel ran a heart-wrenching story. Eastern Europe has become a fertile source for the adoption of white babies. Children in orphanages in these countries have minimal care and are often starved of stimulation. With too many children assigned to each caregiver, the responsible adults can provide only for infants' most basic physical needs. There is little time to touch, cuddle, or even talk to the babies in their charge.

It is into this setting that American families, having the best of intentions, have gone to adopt young children. What many of these families do not realize, however, is the nightmare of adopting babies who have had so little stimulation in the first year of life. Babies growing up in an environment where no one talks to them or plays with them are left with unseen scars. These children may never have the brain capacity to develop normally. When the desperate parents of these children were interviewed, they said that they never knew about the consequences of early profound deprivation. Recent research points to the effects of language stimulation and to the growth in brain pathways that are so critical to the first three years of life. With knowledge comes the power to make informed decisions—from which day-care center to select to whether to adopt an 18-month-old from a clean but psychologically empty orphanage thousands of miles from home.

Also in each chapter are sections called "Try This," which invite you to perform your own observations of language development. Your home becomes your laboratory as you look at your baby in a whole new light, attempting to have him reproduce some of the findings from the scientific literature. The only factor that limits you is the age of your baby—she may have to "grow into" the next set of mini-experiments.

Nature has exquisitely prepared infants (and even fetuses) with the tools for analyzing the language they hear around them. Yet it is through nurture—or the environments that we provide—that babies are able to bring these innate abilities to bear. As we explore the intricate dance between nature and nurture, we not only learn about the development of language, but also come to understand better what it means to be a member of the human species. What we are about to see is that nature and nurture are already at work even before the baby is born, preparing the baby for a dramatic entrance into the language-speaking world.

Chapter 1

Watch Your Language! The Fetus Can Hear You: Development from Before Birth to Three Months of Age

The Fetus

A game we used to play at the swimming pool approximates what it must be like to live in the womb. One person thinks of a word and then says it as loud as she can while she and her friend are submerged in the pool. Somehow, the friend is supposed to make sense of the noise and to guess what the word is. If you have ever played that game, you know that you can accurately report the number of syllables and the way the syllables are stressed in the word. It is extremely difficult, however, even with a lot of repetitions, to guess the correct word. Researchers believe that's what the fetus hears too. Apparently, the fetus is already prepared to hear the contours of our voice and the cadences of speech without ever hearing words the way that we do. Surrounded by water and with an inside rhythm section that thumps with each pump of the mother's heart, the baby hears only distant sounds beyond the uterine wall. The question is, what does the fetus make of the sounds she hears?

The Fetal Environment: Home Sweet Home

Jane, who works for a banking company, is 36 weeks pregnant. She has already discovered that her fetus can respond to sound. (In fact, hearing is only one of the senses that the fetus uses—along with sensitivity to brightness, taste, and tactile stimulation, all in place by the end of pregnancy.) When Jane is finished at work, she relaxes by listening to her stereo. As classical music crests or rock music pounds, she experiences firsthand her fetus's sensitivity to sound. When her fetus hears loud music, it seems to dance in utero as it is awakened from its repose.

Fetuses begin responding to sounds about six or seven months in utero. There is much to hear inside their cozy quarters. Using a waterproof microphone called a hydrophone, researchers can actually listen in on what must be "music" to babies' ears. Most of what they hear is the turbulence of rushing blood as it flows through the mother's system, a sound that is louder for the fetus than are most everyday conversations. A fetus also hears the constant rhythm of the mother's heartbeat; a pulse that rises above the background noise to provide a kind of soothing mantra. These sounds offer a consistent low-frequency baseline for the other noises that the fetus hears, those that are louder or of higher pitch. For this reason, Jane notices that her fetus responds only to loud music or to high-pitched sounds from passing ambulances or fire trucks. She also reports reactions to the loud booms of fireworks and the crashes of thunder, but not to birdsongs or other people's conversations.

Baby, Do You Read Me? Hearing Mother's Voice and Other Sounds

As researchers gain more knowledge about the internal environment of the womb and fetal reactions, they have come to the unmistakable conclusion that fetuses can hear their mothers. The technique used to discover this is called "heart-rate deceleration," and the masterminds behind the project are Professors William Fifer and Chris Moon from Columbia Presbyterian Medical Center in New York.

The professors started with the known fact that newborns, already out of the womb, show a curious reaction when presented with something new or interesting. Their heart rate goes down at first and then begins to return to normal. Show a newborn a bright red ball and its heart rate goes down. Play a whistle for the newborn and its heart rate goes down. Perhaps, they theorized, *fetal* heart rate might decline to interesting sounds in the same way that newborn heart rate does.

The professors invited a group of pregnant mothers into their laboratory. While the mothers lay down, the scientists recorded the fetuses' initial heart rates. Fifer and Moon then asked the mothers to repeat the sentences "Hello, baby. How are you today?" Sure enough, each time a mother asked this question, her fetus's heart rate went down. But how do we know that the fetus was responding to the mother's voice? Fetal heart rate did *not* decline when the mothers were silent. It also did not decline when the mothers were asked to *whisper* the same words. These results show that fetuses are attentive to the sounds of their mother's voice. Yes, baby can hear you.

Another experiment conducted in France asked if fetuses can hear the difference between sounds. Could they tell the difference between words that differ only slightly like "babi" and "biba"? Very patient and very pregnant mothers-to-be like Lisette, along with her fetus François (or is it Françoise?) came into the laboratory to find out.

After Lisette lay down, scientists placed loudspeakers just above her abdomen. When her fetus was in a quiet state, a loud and clearly articulated test word, "babi," was spoken through the loudspeakers. "Babi, babi," the voice continued. As expected, the fetal heart rate slowed down when this first word was presented. As the same word was delivered over and over, the fetal heart rate returned to normal.

At this point in the experiment, we already have learned something new. We have made contact with a foreign world, a world we all inhabited and yet no one remembers. What we don't yet know is whether the fetus just hears a *noise*, or whether François is actually responding to the specific *pattern* of sounds that occur in the word "babi." To test this, the scientists changed the word ever so slightly from "babi" to "biba." If François did *not* notice this change, it could have been because he was tired of the experimenter's game or because he simply could not distinguish between two similar sounds. If François did notice the change, and if his heart rate declined again when the new word was played, remarkable linguistic sensitivity in the unborn child would have been unveiled. If François could detect these differences, we were no longer eavesdropping on the fetus; rather, the fetus was eavesdropping on us!

The experiment continued. When the fetus was in a quiet, receptive state, the new sound ("biba") was played over the loudspeakers. The result? François responded as if it were a new sound; his heart rate declined. François and his fellow fetuses not only can hear loud noises, they can distinguish between *patterns* in the language they hear. The ability to detect such small differences in sound patterns is truly remarkable. It shows that babies are working on language while still in the womb. If babies can tell the difference between "babi" and "biba," *before birth,* is it any wonder that babies acquire language so readily after they are born? They enter our world prepared to analyze the language they hear around them.

Scientific methods such as heart-rate monitoring have opened new vistas for those interested in the discovery of fetal knowledge. And the findings uncovered in the laboratory continually cause us to re-examine long-held, commonsense beliefs about the unborn baby. No longer can fetuses and babies be regarded as unmolded blocks of clay. Such findings underscore the importance of good prenatal care, for they stress that fetuses are not only developing physically but mentally as well.

If babies can differentiate between sounds of language, can they also do so with music? To find out, researchers turned their attention to the study of musical recognition. In one test conducted in Ireland, fetuses who were between 29 and 37 weeks of gestational age heard a theme from a popular TV show. Both fetuses and newborns responded differently to this familiar tune versus an unfamiliar tune. Heart-rate changes can be detected when fetuses listen to hard rock versus Tchaikovsky. Studies in Italy and China report similar results.

Further studies have shown that the fetus is even sensitive to material read to them in the womb. Mothers-to-be recited a short children's rhyme to their unborn children every day between the 33rd and 37th week of fetal gestation. These same fetuses then heard either the old rhyme or a new rhyme that they had not heard before. The result? Using fetal heart rate as an indicator, fetuses could clearly tell the old rhyme from the new. These results suggest that fetuses have their favorite nursery rhymes picked out even before they are born.

Try This: Can my fetus hear? Can my fetus hear *me*?

It is not possible to monitor fetal heart rate in your own home. You can, however, experience the thrill of fetal responsiveness for yourself. To determine when the fetus responds to loud noises, bang a pot near the mother's abdomen. At what point in gestation does the fetus seem to jump or show any sort of response? Try to pay attention to which noises in the environment evoke a response from the fetus and which do not. If the mother-to-be has a particular musical piece she listens to frequently, you might want to see if the fetus reacts differently to loud, familiar music than to loud, unfamiliar music. And after the baby is born, does playing the familiar music soothe the baby more than music that was not heard in the womb?

You can also try to get a fetal reaction to the mother's voice. Mothers, try singing to your fetus and see what happens. When the fetus is active, does the sound of your voice slow the baby down? When the fetus is quiet, does the baby move in response to your voice? Does the sound of your partner's voice have the same or a different effect? When the fetus is inactive and you suddenly shout, does the fetus startle and jump? When your partner shouts, does it have the same or a different effect? You might have to try these things several times before you get a response, and it is possible that you won't get any response because you're not trying this in a controlled laboratory setting. Don't be concerned, however, if you don't get a response. But if you do, you can revel in the excitement of having made contact with your baby.

Does Fetal Learning Mean Fetal School?

Laboratories around the world are uncovering the first signs of language development. There are still few studies, however, compared to studies of later stages of language development, that have investigated the way fetuses respond to information from the outside world. For now, however, it is important to realize that headlines in the supermarket tabloids like READING TO YOUR UNBORN BABY INCREASES LITERACY are unfounded exaggerations of what the findings have shown.

It is intriguing that babies can hear and remember information before they are born, but we urge caution in the interpretation of this information. The studies were designed not to stimulate fetuses so that they would learn better, sing like Pavarotti, or memorize poetry, but rather to find out if a fetus could pick up any information at all.

Learning that a fetus can respond to sound does not imply that more sound is better. When babies are overstimulated, they turn away or close their eyes and block out the outside world. Thus, we must find a balance between our respect for the fetus's newly discovered capabilities and the impulse to offer more and more stimulation. It may be helpful to look to the animal kingdom to learn why fetal hearing is so important. Animal researchers have known for years that gestational learning is important for future survival. A classic study, for example, found that a duckling hears calls from other ducks while still in the egg. This head start gives ducklings a real advantage after they hatch: It helps them gravitate to members of their own species. Imagine the chances of survival for the poor duckling who has been prevented—for experimental purposes—from hearing its species' calls or its own calls while in the egg. It is born into a complicated world without knowing who is in the "in-group" (and will save it) and who is in the "out-group" (and might eat it). In the wild, a duckling is prepared to choose friend or foe before birth. Just before the egg cracks, the duckling makes its own species-specific calls. Because it hears its *own* calls, it can then use the model of its calls to guide it in finding like kind after it hatches.

Sensitivity to prenatal calls has also been found in newborn guinea pigs. Their heart rate slows down (an indicator of interest) to sounds played to them prenatally. Finally, research suggests that lambs too seem particularly attuned to the sounds of their own mother's heartbeat.

The key point here is that we are animals. If other species are sensitive to sounds during gestation, there is every reason to believe that humans are as well. Since sounds heard during gestation prepare different species for their entrance into the animal kingdom, it would be surprising if we were not evolutionarily primed as well. Indeed, it is probably because babies have already begun to learn from language and music while in utero that they are prepared to make sense of the language from the moment they are born.

Birthing the Baby: Will the Newborn Resemble the Fetus?

The fetal literature is rich with new information that is helping us to better understand the human experience. We know, however, a great deal more about humans after they are born. Here can be found a virtual explosion of research activity that shows how babies— even newborn babies—are preparing to be language users.

At long last, Jane's baby decides it is time to emerge. Stunned by bright lights, voices that travel through air and not water, and skin sensations that are more frigid than warm, Jane's baby has truly entered a brave new world.

Is there any reason to suppose that newborns capitalize on their experience in the womb? Do newborns' memories of things learned in the womb help them make sense of the new world around them? Or does the birth process itself—a traumatic process, to be sure— wipe out all that came before it? The answers to these questions may surprise you. Jane's baby has indeed brought with her memories forged from her experiences in her uterine world. Fetal learning forms the foundation for what babies do as newborns.

At the turn of the century, the famous Harvard psychologist William James surmised that the world of the newborn infant must be one of buzzing, blooming confusion. He reasoned that newborns do not know that sounds come from people who speak them, or that the hands holding them will support them (what *are* "hands" anyway?). A newborn can see only what is approximately 18 inches in front of him. To a newborn the world is a blur of lines and disjointed spaces. In this view, nothing would make sense and the newborn would much rather go back to sleep than attend to the chaos going on around him.

The last decade of research in the area of child development has greatly altered this picture of the unprepared and discombobulated infant. We now know that a newborn has a great many abilities and is predisposed to make order out of chaos. Infants are able to find human faces, to imitate human actions, and to process bits of human language. Infants are outstanding pattern seekers born with an ability to make sense out of the surrounding noise and to find those around them who can guarantee their survival.

Try This: Does the newborn react to sounds?

If babies are indeed primed in utero to make sense of their surroundings, and in particular of the language that will surround them, they should show this capability soon after birth. Try demonstrating this with a newborn. One way to tell is if they turn in the direction of a sound source. That is, if a newborn heard a sound coming from the side, would she turn in the direction of the sound, to figure out where it came from? This is exactly what newborns do. If you snap your fingers on one side of the baby's head (make sure the baby is awake and alert), the baby should localize the sound by turning in its direction. When you try this, approach the baby from behind so that she doesn't see you first. Then snap your fingers near one ear and wait and see what happens. You may need to snap your fingers more than once to get a response.

Communicating Through Crying

So babies can hear. You probably expected that from the discussion of the fetal literature. Once a baby is born, however, he not only hears. One of the first things parents notice is that babies cry . . . and cry . . . and cry. Nature has given babies a potent attention-getting tool in crying. Although deaf parents are at a disadvantage here, the facial expressions of a crying baby can also be used as a signal that the baby is in distress. Crying gets your attention. Newborns cry anywhere from thirty minutes to three hours in a twenty-four-hour day. The amount of crying builds until the baby is about two months of age and then declines.

For some time researchers have worked to identify different infant cries. Some argue that adults can perceive different types of cries—from hunger cries to tiredness cries to pain cries. Others say that only one type of cry stands apart from the others. Sometimes called the "biological siren," this cry alerts parents and caregivers that something is really wrong. Parents who have colicky babies probably have heard this high-pitched and seemingly never-ending cry. Current research, though, suggests that the ability to distinguish between various cries is a myth. Adults can distinguish the *level* of distress in a particular cry, but are rarely correct at guessing what the cry means. Is it hunger? Pain? Boredom? In one study, researchers asked parents to baby-sit a manikin baby that emitted various cries. They found that parents responded in the same way regardless of whether they played a baby cry that was triggered by pain or hunger. All the parents picked up the babies, talked to them, and patted them.

Scientists have also shown that cries have an interesting effect on the adult. Hearing a baby cry actually causes unpleasant physiological changes in the listener, whether male or female. Nature has designed it so well: Babies cry when they are in distress, and we are distressed as a result of hearing the cry. No wonder that parents will try anything to get the baby to stop crying. This does not mean that babies cry in order to communicate their needs to us. Babies have to understand a good deal more about the individuals who populate their world before they are capable—around 13 months—of using an abbreviated, "fake" cry for the purpose of getting attention. For this reason it is foolish to assume that babies cry to spite us or to annoy us. Babies cry simply because they feel bad (for whatever reason), and not because they think crying will lead to relief. Adults often interpret the baby's cry as an attempt to tell them something.

However, this is not a goal the baby is capable of formulating so early in life. Although crying isn't language, it is one of the first ways in which we interpret babies' feelings and needs. Crying (and smiling) therefore begin the dialogue between parents and their babies, a dialogue that will be refined and enriched as language develops.

Our newborns are telling us that they can hear and that they can cry. What they cannot tell us—at least explicitly—is that there was tremendous carryover from the fetal period. Their outward behavior, however, masks what they are doing on the inside. Thus, to gauge infants' ability we must again turn to clever methods that look beyond the startles and cries. As we return to the baby labs, we find yet again that babies are active, astute listeners, linking up what they have heard in the womb to the sounds they hear on the outside.

Mother, Is That You? Newborns Prefer to Hear Mother's Voice

We saw earlier that François could hear his mother's voice in the womb. Perhaps this is no surprise since her voice should be among the loudest of the sounds in that confined environment. Can he then recognize his mother when he comes into our world? The world François enters has very different sound properties from those that surrounded him inside his uterine home. It would surely be an advantage for François if he could find the person who feeds him and cuddles him.

To find out if newborns are able to find their mothers by their voices, a group of researchers tested newborns who were just 72 hours old. Babies heard samples of speech spoken either by their mother or by a stranger. Did the babies show a clear preference for their mother's voice over the stranger's? To answer this question, researchers relied on the sucking reflex described in the Introduction. Fast sucking means, "Hey, that's new!" Slow sucking means, "This is getting old. . . ."

Newborn baby Samantha hears a series of syllables like "pat-pat-pat . . ." delivered over a loudspeaker. Like most babies, she sucks when she hears these words (or virtually any other new words). As she sucks, the syllables are turned off, and a recording of speech from her mother is turned on.

Notice what happens in the next part of the experiment. Samantha now hears a new series of syllables like, "pst-pst-pst . . ." As she sucks on the nipple, these sounds are turned off, and a recording of a stranger's voice turned on. Now for the critical comparison. Will Samantha suck more when she hears the syllables "pat-pat-pat" or when she hears the syllables "pst-pst-pst"? Will Samantha learn that "pat" is followed by her mother's voice and "pst" by a stranger's? Samantha heard these various syllables along with her mother's or a stranger's voice for a total of 18 minutes. If Samantha can distinguish between these syllables *and* if she prefers her mother's voice, then she should suck more vigorously and more often when she hears the syllable "pat." Notice that to get this right, Samantha has to *remember* that one syllable is followed by the mom's voice and one by a stranger's.

The results showed that Samantha and other newborns wanted to hear their mother's voice, even when it was paired with a pleasant-sounding female alternative. Samantha could tell the difference and preferred her mother's voice. Clearly, she had learned something in utero about the quality of her mother's voice.

This study demonstrates that mothers have an advantage in capturing a newborn's attention. Perhaps this should come as no surprise, since the baby has been hearing the mother's voice from approximately 25 weeks of gestation. Unlike other noises in the baby's environment, a mother's voice need not travel through the abdomen to be heard. And most mothers' voices have a higher pitch, allowing them to be more clearly heard against the low and intense sounds in the baby's uterine environment. This may be one of the first ways in which babies find their mothers when they are born.

Developmental psychologists often engage in a hypothetical exercise that illustrates the potency of this finding. "If we were going to 'build' a baby, what would we build in?" Sensitivity to a mother's voice would be high on the list. It would help the baby find an immediate source of nutrition and nurture. From an evolutionary point of view, there would be a tremendous advantage in having babies orient to their mothers.

We must also realize, however, that it is only an advantage, not a necessity. Babies born to deaf parents haven't been given much verbal stimulation as fetuses. Babies who are adopted hear a different voice after they are born from the one that they heard in the womb. There are also very nurturing fathers whose voices do not naturally resonate in the uterus. Although the higher-pitched sounds of female voices and particularly mothers' voices are preferred, newborns would still rather hear a male voice than silence. Babies are known for their versatility and adaptiveness to any number of different environments. When nature builds a baby, she builds in multiple routes the baby can use for later growth and success.

Distinguishing the World's Languages

Nature also builds babies who are ready to learn any language. After all, the fetus doesn't know if it is to be born in China, America, or France. Getting a head start, fetuses hear the cadences of their native language, the one their mothers speak. As shown in the Introduction, even two-day-old French babies were able to tell the difference between French and Russian. French newborns can also tell the difference between Japanese and English, languages they rarely hear. How do they do this? The rhythmic properties of these languages differ greatly, and babies rely on rhythm, not on the *sounds*, to distinguish one language from another.

So, newborns are sensitive to the rhythmic properties of their own language and can distinguish between some foreign languages. By themselves these are very impressive findings. But there is more. Not only can they recognize rhythmic differences among languages, they can tell the difference between the sounds. By eight to ten months of age babies will focus on the sounds that are used in their own language, and the ability to recognize the sounds of other languages will fade away. Concentrating on the sounds of one's own language is a first step in learning it. However, at birth, newborns are ready to learn any language that they hear.

How do we know that? In a classic study conducted at Brown University in 1971, Dr. Peter Eimas and his students tested one-month-old babies in the laboratory. The researchers discovered surprising capabilities. Babies at just four weeks of age can distinguish language sounds as well as—and even better than—their parents.

Babies, of course, don't know where they are going to live. Thus, theoretically, they must be prepared to recognize all of the sounds of all of the languages so that they can learn whatever comes their way—whether it's the *b*'s and *p*'s of English or the click sounds that occur in certain African languages. Still, no one in the field knew if babies could actually do so. That is why Professor Eimas's findings represented such a breakthrough.

The initial test was performed with two similar but contrasting sounds, *b* and *p*. What is interesting about these two sounds is that

acoustically they are much alike, yet we perceive them as quite different. To gauge the babies' reactions, Dr. Eimas used the now familiar
sucking technique.

A month-old baby, Jody, was placed in an infant seat and fitted
with an electronically monitored nipple. Over a loudspeaker she
heard the melodic sound of the syllables, "pa,pa,pa . . ." She listened
carefully, sucked vigorously, and then let the researchers know that
she had heard enough as her sucking slowed down.

Now came the test: Could Jody tell the difference between p and
the acoustically similar b? "Ba,ba,ba . . ." was then played over the
loudspeaker. When Jody heard the new sound, she began sucking
again with enthusiasm, thereby demonstrating that she could tell the
difference.

But, you say, perhaps Jody would have started sucking again even
without a new sound. After all, babies are always taking breaks in
sucking. For this reason Dr. Eimas brought in another group of babies who heard "pa" (as Jody did) until their sucking slowed down.
Then, instead of following with the new sound "ba," this group of
control babies heard more "pa." The babies in the control group did
not start sucking wildly again. Jody and her peers really did hear the
difference.

From what has now become a host of studies like this, we know
that newborns who have never been exposed to languages other than
English show a remarkable ability to distinguish among the sounds
of all of the world's languages. Their sensitivity gives babies a big advantage in learning language, an advantage that anyone after puberty
struggles to regain, needing loads of repetition and practice, when
she learns a new language.

Try This: Does your baby respond to foreign languages?

Can you tell if a baby distinguishes your language from another by
watching the baby's response? When the baby is in an alert state, talk to
her. Then start talking in a foreign language. What does the baby do?
Does she widen her eyes and stop moving? Does she look at your mouth?
If you are not a fluent native speaker of another language, this probably
won't work, so you'll need to recruit someone. You just might be surprised to find that the baby already is sensitive to the fact that she is
hearing a language with which she's not familiar.

Along these same lines, should you hire that wonderful Hispanic or

Chinese or Korean nanny you just interviewed? Will it hurt your baby to have him exposed to another language from such an early age? To the contrary, it will enhance the baby's language and cognitive development to have access to another language. And it may well prove to be the case (research on this question is being conducted as we write) that exposure to another language very early in life enhances a person's learning of that language later in life.

Face-to-Face: Love at First Look?

Abundant evidence indicates that babies are prepared to learn language because they are sensitive to language sounds, even in the womb. Language, however, does not occur in a vacuum. Rather, it is the basis of social interaction. If babies are to learn to communicate through language, they must be prepared to use language within that social context. They must be able to find those humans in their environment who will talk to them and care for them.

Central to this quest would be identifying human faces. Arguably, faces are the single best cue to finding humans—and to finding particular humans. Researchers have already focused their attention on the social context of language learning, and what they have found is astonishing. Although babies can't see in the womb, they come into the world prepared to memorize human faces.

Let's take an example. Joshua is the firstborn son of two professional parents. When he first emerges, the baby looks startled from his long and dangerous ride down the birth canal. After a pat on the back, a thorough cleaning, and his initial "checkup," he sees his parents for the first time. Josh's father calls him by name and holds him 18 inches away, face-to-face. Without blinking, as if he too has waited a long time to see who his parents would be, Josh stares intently into his father's eyes. He seems to be studying his father's face, listening to each word that his father speaks, trying to make contact.

Is it our imagination that our babies are "connecting" with us? Perhaps we only think we see a baby's "human" qualities because of the joy of birth. Is this emotional connection we feel just a one-way street from parent to baby? Or is the baby actually predisposed to notice the kinds of features that beings like himself possess?

The past decade of research on infancy suggests that newborns like Josh are indeed "making contact." Research confirms that examining faces is a particularly important means of learning about humans. We communicate mainly through our voices and faces. Our facial expressions add dimension to our language, helping those around us to understand what we really mean. We can say one thing, but our faces and tone of voice can reveal something else. And within the face, the eyes are important too. They seem to provide a direct route to our thoughts. Even when no sounds are heard, we can empathize as we look into someone's eyes. Perhaps, then, we would expect infants to be predisposed to look at human faces.

But would we expect newborns to come out of the womb looking for faces? After all, fetuses cannot see in the womb. Yet the studies suggest strongly that Josh is not unusual. Newborns do prefer the sight of a human face. They enter into our world ready to look for faces that will communicate with them and feed them.

Babies' fascination with the human face was demonstrated in a remarkable study with newborns when they were only nine minutes old. Recall that in most hospital settings the medical staff's faces are covered by the masks worn in the delivery room, and during the initial "checkup," babies still haven't seen any faces. For the study, researchers waited until the babies were awake and attentive, then showed them drawings of faces. In some cases the faces were normal looking, with two eyes, a nose, and a mouth all in the correct anatomical position. In other cases the drawings were of scrambled faces in which either the eyes were at the bottom with the nose on the forehead or in which the eyes were arranged on top of one another, separated by a mouth and nose. All of these black-and-white drawings had the same amount of ink, the same characteristics, and were symmetrical. The only difference was in the arrangement of the facial features.

As the experimenters presented the faces to the infants, they watched the babies' responses. What they found shocked the scientific community. Nine-minute-old babies who had never before seen a face preferred to look at the drawing of the face that was anatomically correct. This result was also found by a different group of researchers with 37-minute-old babies. These experiments demonstrate that human babies are predisposed to seek faces just after birth. Josh really was examining his father's face!

It's comforting from an evolutionary point of view to know that babies are sensitive to human faces. What parents really want to know, however, is when babies first recognize not *a* face but *their* face! Several interesting studies have explored this very question and have revealed a surprising answer. They find that newborns prefer to look at their mother's face over that of another female. In one study, for example, researchers found that babies who are but 12 to 36 hours old will suck a pacifier longer to see their mother's face presented on a video than they will to see a stranger's face. How is this possible? Researchers suggest that newborns can quickly identify their mothers through the sound of their voice and through the smell of their milk. With these clear identifiers in hand, the baby seems to "lock on" to the particular features of the mother's face. They learn the visual association between face and their mother quickly because it is to their advantage to know what she looks like.

How can newborn babies learn so much visually in just 12 hours? The propensity to learn this information must be deeply embedded within the human species. This, it turns out, is not unusual. Studies throughout the animal literature suggest that animals quickly learn the visual characteristics of their mothers. Many people have been enchanted by the true story based on the work of the Nobel prize–winning ethologist Konrad Lorenz. In it infant ducklings follow the first moving object that they see after they hatch. They seem to learn instantaneously the visual features of that object, be it Konrad Lorenz himself, a watering can, a little girl (with geese) as in the movie *Fly Away Home*, or the ducks' real mother. If animals can do it, then why not humans?

Newborns' sensitivity to human faces allows them to learn patterns within human faces and specifically the features of the mother's face. Paying attention to faces and to high-pitched voices allows babies to look for just the right sorts of information in the environment to learn more about their world. This prepares babies for their apprenticeship in learning how to communicate with other humans. Once they have a starting point, babies quickly become expert in identifying faces or even languages. For example, studies have shown that newborns first look at the edges of faces and then come to look at the eyes to identify others when they are but five weeks old. They also know to look at our eyes most of the time when we are talking. They seem to know intuitively that the eyes are windows to the soul and to the meaning the speaker conveys. Finally, babies actually look more at our faces when we are talking than when we are not!

Communication is a two-way street, though. One of the expressions that is most engaging for us to track is an infant's smile. As soon as parents and caregivers are able to elicit that first smile, the seeds for communicative interaction are ready to grow. Researchers distinguish between different types of smiling. Newborns have what might best be called reflexive smiling, using just the corners of the mouth.

By week three, babies already grin and seem to pull their eyes into the smile, smiling when they hear voices. By weeks five and six visual movement will evoke a smiling response, and smiles are often accompanied by cooing. Finally, by weeks eight to twelve, babies will give a broad smile even to unmoving visual displays. These changes in smiling are not only interesting to watch but are also key to how we respond to our babies. We tend to become much more interactive as our babies stay awake longer and as they give us their enchanting smiles, smiles that seem to be just for us. Here again, babies play an active role in bringing us into a dialogue.

It's particularly interesting to look for the change that takes place in these communicative behaviors around two months of age. Professor Daniel Stern has argued that a shift occurs in the infant's ability to communicate at two months that is "almost as clear a boundary as birth itself." All of a sudden babies are spending more time in an alert state, using a social smile, starting to coo, and making more eye contact with us. As they coordinate all of these behaviors and direct them toward us, we feel like we are truly in the company of a social being.

Try This: Charting baby's smiles

To show that babies expect us to interact with them by this time, try a little experiment. Put yourself in the position you usually use to talk to the baby (probably about 18 inches away from the baby's face) but instead of starting to coo and talk, present the baby with a "still face" that shows no emotion. Research suggests that the baby will vocalize at you and try to get you socially engaged. When you fail to respond, babies will then turn away from you and avert their gaze if you try to maintain eye contact. To prove to yourself that the baby found your still, unresponsive face disturbing, or at least unpleasant, come back in a few moments and go through your usual routine with the baby. Watch for the difference in the baby's response. Babies crave social interaction, and they show you this by their social overtures. Already by the end of the first two months they are building up expectations about what to expect from people.

Do Mouths and Voices Work Together?

Newborns are quite adept at listening. They are also prepared to see our faces and to notice the language sounds that emanate from them. But at this point we have shown only babies that look at pictures of faces in silence and listen to voices delivered from loudspeakers with no mouths in view. Must the infant learn to put the two sources of information together? What enables infants to connect the mouth and the talk that comes from it? For us, this connection is so crucial that we are unnerved when mouths and talk are out of synch. We fidget in our seats when we see a dubbed movie and the language is delivered even a fraction of a second after the mouth moves. The connection between mouths and talk is so critical that many wondered if the telephone would actually be a successful invention since you couldn't see the speaker. Are young infants aware of the relationship of mouths to talking?

In a clever experiment, 10- to 16-week-old babies saw tapes of a woman speaking. Sometimes the sounds of the woman's voice were in perfect synchrony with the movements of her mouth. Other times, however, the sound came 400 milliseconds (almost a half second) after the appropriate mouth movements appeared. The babies were twice as likely to look *away* from the tape when the mouth and talk were out of synch than when the mouth movements and the talk came together. This is an amazing finding. It is not surprising that adults, having had years of experience watching mouths that talk and being able to move their mouths and create talk themselves, should be disturbed when the mouth and sound are not temporally coordinated. But who would have thought that babies as young as 10 weeks of age would show the same sensitivity? How can babies who do not yet speak know that the mouth and the sound emanating from it are out of synch?

Babies' achievements don't stop there, however. Babies also know—again, before they have produced a single word—when a mouth they are watching produces a *particular* vowel sound. This is tantamount to saying that by the time babies are 10 to 16 weeks of age, they can read lips. In one study, babies watched a pair of videotapes of a woman saying different things on two televisions. On one television she said the *a* (as in "ate") sound over and over again, and on the other television she said the *i* (as in "ice") sound over and over. The sound of her speaking was piped in from the middle of the two screens. When the woman said *a*, babies watched the *a* face significantly more than the *i* face. When she said *i*, they watched the *i* face more. How does a baby know what a mouth should look like when it says *a* and when it says *i*? We don't know. The evidence is clear, however. Babies can put sounds and faces together.

Newborn Copycats

Are babies merely passive listeners and analyzers of facial expressions? Not at all. They are, in fact, active participants, and their actions do much to drive your responses. Witness, for example, that these newborn students of language are studying your every move and (within their capabilities) can even imitate what you do.

Picture Karen lying in bed with her three-day-old infant, Saul. She is holding him and admiring his perfect miniature fingers and toes, the softness of his skin. Having read a number of parenting books, she has heard about the newborn's ability to imitate facial movements. It seems impossible, but she decides to try. Saul opens his eyes and looks at Karen's face. Then Karen starts her experiment. She rounds her mouth and sticks her tongue in and out, an action that she does repeatedly—up to ten times—as she looks into Saul's eyes. Just as she wonders what Saul is thinking of this bizarre activity, he begins to stick out his tongue too. Saul seems to know that he—like his mother—has a tongue (although he doesn't have a name for it) and that he can do whatever she can do.

Professors Andrew Meltzoff and Keith Moore first demonstrated imitation in newborns in 1977. Although this finding generated controversy when it was first reported, newborn imitation has now been replicated in many laboratories. It is a truly astounding feat when babies—some only 45 minutes old—imitate our behavior before they have ever seen their own face. How do they translate the movements of their mother's mouth and tongue into the motor movements of their own mouth and tongue? What they are doing is interacting instinctively with other human beings. Acts of imitation show the budding "intersubjectivity," or two-way engagement, of infants and their caregivers. At an implicit level, acts of imitation seem to show that infants assume that "no man is an island," and that they are related directly to the other humans in their environment.

Try This: Can my baby copy me?

See if you can elicit imitation from a newborn. Just stick out your tongue about ten times while looking closely at the newborn and see if she answers back by sticking her tongue out at you. If it works, this may be one of the only times that you will enjoy having someone stick their tongue out at you. Or, try opening your mouth wide about ten times and see if the baby can do that. It is exciting to know that the newborn is already able to mimic your actions, thereby communicating with you.

The Roots of Conversation

Imitation is a gift of nature and demonstrates how babies watch us so that they too can engage in social interaction. There are, however, many more subtle ways in which infants join into the conversation at a very young age. Nested in everyday routines like feeding can be found the very same interactive abilities, ones that emerge as parents provide a scaffold of support for the expression of social behavior.

It's 4:00 A.M., time for another feeding. Eight-week-old Trevor is wailing in his crib. As his mother, Angelica, stumbles into the room, she picks up the desperate youngster, cuddles him, and prepares for a middle-of-the-night feeding. She sleepily locates her rocking chair, holds the baby to her breast, and Trevor immediately finds the nipple and begins to suck. After what seems like only 30 seconds, he stops and falls back asleep. Angelica gently rocks him to awaken him, and the feeding begins anew. Trevor soon pauses in feeding, and again Angelica jiggles him to continue. After five minutes on one breast, Angelica raises him onto her shoulder and begins to pat him on the back. "Did you have a nice sleep, Trevor? You were really hungry, weren't you?" She continues to pat until Trevor burps and spits up a little bit on her shoulder. "Oh, that was a good burp. Do you have another one?" She pats him a little more, and he releases a little more air. "Very good. Now you are ready for the other side." Talking all the while—even in her dazed state—she finishes the feeding and then returns to bed.

What has happened in these moments is an interaction between a baby and its mother, a kind of "proto-conversation" in which parents guide the way and in which babies are passive participants. These moments provide the foundation for later communication and language development. In these quiet, ordinary times (such as feeding) we are showing the baby how to take turns and how to build a relationship.

Baby Talk Matters

Babies are not only taking turns with us, but we, as their parents and caregivers, unconsciously make it easier for our children to have conversations with us. Have you ever noticed how you talk to a baby?

That silly, high-pitched, singsong speech that we use assists babies in their language-learning tasks. That odd way of talking has been variously called "motherese" (although fathers do it too), "infant- or child-directed speech," or just plain old "baby talk."

Baby talk refers to the alterations we make in our language when we speak to infants, foreigners, and even to pets and plants. Around the world, people tend to change the way they speak when they are conversing with babies. Even young children change the way they speak when they talk to babies. It's great fun to watch a four-year-old talking to his younger sister while using a squeaky version of our child-directed speech. In English, baby talk is very different from the way we talk to other adults. To a baby we say, "Gooood mooooorrrrn-ing" while to an adult we would say simply, "Good morning." As the example shows, we greatly lengthen our vowels and produce exaggerated pitch swings. We also use shorter sentences and place longer, clearer pauses between utterances. More subtly, we also tend to put words we judge as unfamiliar to our babies at the ends of sentences, where they receive stress ("Aaammmy! See the dooooogggie?").

Baby talk aids in language development for a number of reasons. For one, it says to the baby, "This talk is for you." One-month-olds and even newborns prefer to listen to infant-directed speech over adult-directed speech. Another reason is that baby talk reveals the emotions of the speaker, thereby serving as the first way in which language expresses meaning. Studies have found that parental sounds of comfort, prohibition, and praise are remarkably similar around the world. For example, if a baby is doing something dangerous, parents will use sharp, clipped utterances, as in the English "Stop that!" or the French *"Arrête!"* that instantly get the baby's attention. On the other hand, if parents want to comfort unhappy babies, they are more likely to produce longer, more modulated utterances such as "Ooooohhhhh." Perhaps the emotional timbre of baby talk gives babies insight into the content of the message, serving as a first avenue into linguistic communication.

Does it make any difference if infant-directed speech is used with infants? As researchers, we are often asked if baby talk is bad for babies, retarding their development. To the contrary, there is evidence that baby talk helps babies make discriminations between sounds and words. For example, at around five months of age, babies can tell the difference between the made-up words "malana" and "marana"—but only when they hear them pronounced in the singsong patterns of baby talk. Since baby talk exaggerates sounds babies seem to more easily hear the differences.

Baby talk helps babies figure out how the vowels in their language work. A study using mothers from America, Russia, and Sweden compared how mothers produced vowel sounds in infant-directed and in adult-directed speech. Mothers were far more likely to exaggerate vowels in infant-directed speech, making them clearer for their babies.

Is it really so surprising that babies hear the sounds of language more clearly in baby talk? Consider how we talk to each other. A typical conversation between parents with a school-age child (John) and a baby sitting in her infant seat on the kitchen table might go something like this:

Mother: I . . . I . . . I . . . I need to go to the— Put that back, John! I need to go to the store and—

Father: (*interrupts*) Which, uh, what time did you say I need to be home tonight? My meeting's late.

Mother: It's your mother's birthday. Are you buying a gift or—no, John, you can't wear that thin jacket today. It's thirty degrees outside. (*turning to Father*) How about by seven?

John: (*said at the same time as Mother speaks to Father*) Watch me, baby! (*He jumps off his chair.*)

How is a baby supposed to learn language in this situation? The speech adults use is full of errors, interruptions, and false starts. Topics change all over the place, and there are no exaggerated pronunciations as in baby talk to make the words stand out in any particular way. Nor are there clear boundaries between the utterances, since overlaps and interruptions (even by oneself) occur all the time. Yet babies are pattern seekers, continually looking for the regularities in the language they hear. Infant-directed speech may ease the baby's burden and make finding the words and phrases of speech a simpler task. Samples of adult-directed speech like that above would be difficult even for adults to follow if they were living with a family in a foreign country and learning the language. Babies are learning a foreign language too—even though it is to become their native language with time. New research from a number of laboratories, including our own, suggests that the use of infant-directed speech may confer an enormous advantage on the infant and toddler.

Try This: Do babies react to baby talk?

It is easy to demonstrate that babies prefer to listen to infant-directed speech. Compare what the baby does when you use baby talk and when you use adult-directed speech. Try to say the same things in both ways. One of the things you may notice if you watch someone else try this is that the speech is not the only thing that changes. When we use baby talk, our facial expressions become exaggerated as well and therefore very animated. If we used these same facial expressions in talking to an adult, we would be considered a bit strange. Our faces are much less expressive when we address other adults. So if the baby shows a different response to being addressed in baby talk, you won't really know to which aspect (the talk or the facial expressions or both!) the baby is responding. In any event, it is worthwhile seeing if baby talk elicits more vocalizations, excitement, and eye contact than adult-directed speech.

Recall that scientists have discovered that babies attend to the rhythms of speech. This is one of the reasons why baby talk, with its singsong properties, is so attractive to babies. Try saying something rotten to the baby in your nicest baby talk, something like "You were so bad today!" Then try to say something kind in a rotten voice, such as "You were so good today!" You will get a chance to see the baby respond to the cadence of the speech and not the message.

More Than Meets the Eye

As newborns, babies eat, burp, eliminate waste, and sleep (up to 75 percent of the time). Our job feels largely custodial and we are constantly on call. But things are changing. The gurgles and vegetative sounds dominant in the first two months give way to coos. A range of cries develop that seem to indicate clearly whether a baby is mildly or seriously upset. The baby's eyes appear to grow wider as they mature into three-month-olds and can stay awake longer. Finally, at four to six weeks, comes the first smile, which the scientific literature now shows is truly a social smile, and not, as old baby-care books suggested, just gas.

Hidden in the everyday routines of parenthood are the shining moments that scientists have used to reveal the linguistic capabilities of fetuses and newborns. Babies do more than just notice that we are here. They engage us and mimic us; they analyze what comes out of our mouths.

As we look at newborn milestones through the scientific lens, we have a new respect for what babies can do. They come prepared to learn language. It is seen in the ways babies respond to language, in the ways they notice faces, in the ways they piece together sound and sight and in the ways they interact during conversations.

Scientific Sleuthing Pays Off

There are three important lessons to be gleaned from the recent scientific discoveries that have been discussed, lessons that are already being taught by professionals and used by parents and caregivers.

*Lesson 1. Silence is **not** golden.* Not so long ago, child-care specialists might have recommended that babies be kept in pristine white environments and visitors be silent in their midst. While the scientific literature would not advocate that we now take babies to rock concerts or mow lawns with them on our backs, we know that even the youngest of babies benefit from both visual and auditory stimulation. Formerly white nurseries have been replaced by colorful rooms alive with patterns and music boxes. Parents and caregivers are told to chat with infants and to touch and cuddle them so that they get sufficient tactile stimulation. This move toward more stimulating environments provides babies with the material they need to make sense of their world. With this natural stimulation babies thrive. Without it—as in the extreme conditions found in orphanages in poor countries—babies do not do as well. Articles about such adopted babies report that they have behavioral and academic problems as toddlers and beyond.

While stimulation in general is important for development, linguistic stimulation—whether audible or visible sign language—is crucial for language development. Case studies of children indicate that language does not develop fully in the absence of linguistic stimulation. Parents, caregivers, and professionals can all help by talking to young children.

Knowing the importance of language interaction can shape parental behavior and decisions. When infants are alert, it is vital to interact with them and to respect that they are interacting in return and working on finding meaning in what we say. One way to do this is to acknowledge their contributions (however meager) to the conversation. Parents might also look for evidence that caregivers and baby-sitters engage in this kind of interaction. It is not unusual for sitters to watch television when they are with infants or to spend a lot of time on the telephone even when babies are awake. More than a bottle and a clean diaper is needed. The new view of the interactive infant means that caregiving involves more than custodial care. The new job description for caregiving might add "caregiver stimulation required in the form of sensitive and responsive behavior." Parents should look for empathic and encouraging caregivers who are eager to converse with babies. Research shows that language stimulation from a television set does not prepare infants for language learning. Only conversations with people will.

Scientific data shows that early interaction with babies increases later communicative ability. Moreover, that early interaction can come from anybody. In many cultures around the world, infants are tended to by other children as well as by adults. Extensive studies of language learning in these cultures reveal that infants learn their native tongue at the same place as their American and Western European counterparts. The key is engaging the baby in conversation, or at least the baby hearing their actions described.

Even babies born deaf should not live in a "silent" world; they should be exposed to sign language as soon as possible. The visual movements and facial expressions that compose sign language are every bit as expressive as words spoken orally. For some hearing-impaired babies, however, lack of stimulation remains a problem. This is largely because parents and professionals have such a difficult time detecting that babies are deaf or hard of hearing. Thus, the scientific discoveries noted in this chapter have another application—they can be used to assist in the early detection of hearing loss and can lead to earlier interventions for children who need them.

Lesson 2. New scientific methods can yield assessment tools. Irene was born deaf, with a hearing loss of 85 decibels in her better ear—a loss that suggests she will hear nothing spoken within the normal range. Her hearing parents were elated by their first baby and had no reason to suspect that Irene could not hear. She looked like all of the other babies in the nursery, attentive to the sights around her and startled by the vibrations of loud noises. She carefully examined her parents' faces when they first met and went on to cry and gurgle in the same way that other babies do. Irene was different, however. She loved to watch her mother's mouth movements as her diaper was changed, but she never heard the words that were spoken at those special moments. She could feel vibrations when her mother entered the room, but never hear the sound of an approaching voice. Irene was at a disadvantage and would continue to be at a disadvantage until her deafness was detected.

In some hospitals new methodologies can identify deaf babies at birth. In these forward-looking hospitals, babies' brain waves in response to auditory stimulation are monitored and can reveal congenital deafness. Unfortunately, without the use of these innovative assessment techniques, deafness is often not detected until babies are 12 to 18 months of age. Early on, however, there are some behavioral cues that a baby might be deaf. For example, babies who are alert respond to sounds even when they do not see the source of those sounds. When a door slams behind the baby or when a loud sound like the dropping of pans is heard in the kitchen, babies usually respond by crinkling up their faces or by acting startled. Sounds created by unseen sources provide a much better test of deafness than, for example, clapping your hands in front of the baby's face. With hand clapping, the baby could be responding to the visual event or even to the gush of air created by the clap. For parents who do suspect a problem—or who just want to be reassured—it is worth having a brain-wave assessment done so that the diagnosis of deafness is not put off until later behavioral techniques can be reliably used.

Lesson 3. Overestimate your baby's capabilities. Perhaps the main point of this chapter has been to dazzle you with the capabilities that fetuses and babies have. Armed with these facts, you are in a position to counter the naysayers who tell you that this or that experience could not possibly matter to the young baby. Just let "sleeping babies lie," Aunt Gertrude may tell you. "Don't go all gushy on the baby, talking to it and getting it all excited. It's not good for the baby." To the contrary, we have learned that Aunt Gertrude is wrong. Not only can babies see and hear (not a known fact until the late 1950s!), newborns are analyzing and remembering the experiences they have. They are eager to engage you socially and to hear you talk. The fetus and the newborn are far from being blobs, just lying there in a semiconscious state. They are already learning in the womb, and once they graduate to the outside world, they are capable of learning all you have in store.

Chapter 2

Yada-Yada-Yada: The Babbling Period Between Four and Eight Months of Age

Babies Do Babble

Heidi, a six-month-old baby, is lying on her back in her crib, having been put down for a nap by her father. She holds her little hands up in the air and forms little gestures with them as she laughs quietly to herself. In another few minutes, Heidi is asleep.

Rachel, also a six-month-old, has also just been put down for her nap. She rolls over onto her back and makes little noises like "babababababa" and "nuhnuhnuhnuh" until she drifts off to sleep.

What do these babies have in common? On the surface, it looks like their age, sex, and circumstance—that is, they're both awaiting the arrival of the sandman. But Heidi is a deaf child who has been born to parents who are also profoundly deaf and who speak in sign language. Rachel is a hearing child who was born to hearing parents who talk to her almost incessantly when she is awake, although they don't really expect her to reply in kind. For Rachel's parents, even a burp from Rachel is an acceptable conversational contribution.

What these babies have in common is that they are both babbling. You have no trouble believing that about Rachel—after all, she is producing the usual combinations of meaningless vocalizations associated with babbling. But Heidi? How can she be said to be babbling? Dr. Laura Pettito of McGill University in Montreal has done some fascinating research on babies born to deaf and hearing parents. Although all babies move their hands (and feet) in novel ways, only the infants of deaf parents use their hands in ways that approximate the sign language of the deaf. Just as hearing babies produce vocalizations that sound like language but are meaningless, deaf babies produce hand shapes that look like sign language but convey no meaning. Dr. Pettito's results suggest that language is almost irrepressible in the human species. Language seems to burst forth through any available avenue.

In this chapter, we look at babies' burgeoning language skills. They didn't say much in the first three months, but that is about to change. Between four and eight months, we can chart the typical course of sound making that babies go through before they say their first word. Not surprisingly, the change in the baby's abilities to produce sounds is tied to biological changes in her sound-producing apparatus. This partly answers the implicit question that many may have had when reading about babies in the first three months: If babies are so capable, why don't they talk sooner? Researchers have found that the infant vocal tract is not simply a miniature version of an adult's. Rather, it resembles the vocal tract of nonhuman primates. This prevents babies from using the mouth as an instrument in the ways necessary for speech. Not until the end of the first year of life, when the oral cavity has lengthened and expanded, are babies able to produce language sounds.

After looking at the early precursors of language production through babbling, we go on to ask just what babies are hearing. Even if they can't talk to us, we do a superb job of talking to them! How do we talk to them and what do they hear from our chatter? This chapter goes beyond the young children's meager productions to their comprehension of language in the world around them. Do babies understand what we say? A wonderful Gary Larson cartoon suggests one answer. A dog owner might say: "Okay, Ginger, I've had it! You stay out of the garbage! Understand, Ginger?" *What the dog hears* might be more like this: "blah, blah Ginger blah blah blah blah blah blah blah blah blah blah blah blah Ginger." Does this cartoon capture the human experience as well?

One thing is for sure: Most middle-class American parents talk to their babies all the time. Babies don't have to say a single word for parents to take every opportunity to share gobs of useless information with them. Listen in for a moment as Rachel's mother comments on her newfound interest in the thermometer that hangs outside the kitchen door:

> Oooooooooooh, Rachel found the thermometer. Yes, that tells Mommy how hot or cold it is outside so I know how to dress Rachel. Does Rachel want to go outside later? Well, when that little arrow goes above thirty-two degrees, we can go out. Would you like that, Rachel?

As Rachel's mother does, we all talk in a very different way to our babies (and to our pets) than to our friends and acquaintances. We talk in a high-pitched, singsong way that seems to grab the infant's attention. This "baby talk" is not only used by hearing parents, but by deaf parents who use sign language as well. We'll look more closely at how we talk to our children and how we modify our speech in this chapter.

But is all this talk useless? Do babies hear only strings of sounds in a stream of speech? Do they just hear blah blah blah? In this chapter, we'll discover that babies listen carefully and figure out things about their native language's unique properties. They are analyzing and comparing adult language in ways that are preparing them for their dramatic entrance into language. Rachel and Heidi are like little scientists, using their mothers' talk and other language that comes their way as grist for their language-learning mill.

Even though Heidi is deaf and Rachel can hear, they have a tremendous amount in common as they enter the dawn of language learning. What lies beneath the surface of our language (be it oral speech or visual signs) is a rich system that is at the very core of what it means to be human. When the coos and gurgles of the first three months give way to babbles in months four to eight, the system really starts to take off.

How Babies Talk to Us

In the beginning, babies like Rachel (and Heidi) make sounds reflexively, to express their feelings. Fussing noises as well as vegetative sounds associated with eating make up their repertoire. In the first month speech-like sounds are rare. Instead, as any new parent can report, cries are the most frequent expression. By the time Rachel is three months old, her parents can look forward to some relief: the amount of crying seriously declines. Rachel is awake more and her vocal apparatus is growing, so she can now make sounds that have variously been called "gooing" or "cooing." Roughly in the second month, she produces open-mouth vowel-like sounds as in "goooooo" or "gaaaaah." She also develops a hearty laugh. It may not be language, but there is nothing more delightful than hearing a four-month-old laugh irrepressibly.

With these developments as a backdrop, let's look at Rachel's progression in vocal play between roughly four and eight months of age. At four months, Rachel now sounds as if she is manipulating her vocal apparatus purposefully—sometimes shouting, sometimes whispering. She is clearly having fun making noises. It is in this period that children first produce raspberries and snorts. Vocal play occurs both when Rachel is alone and when she is interacting with an adult. Studies show, however, that Rachel's vocal responses sound *more* like language when she is interacting with an adult than when she is alone. Perhaps she is listening to the adult's sounds and attempting to match or reproduce some of the qualities of what she hears.

If research shows that four-month-old babies vocalize more when an adult is present, what is the crucial factor that stimulates this vocalization? Eye gaze! When an adult looks Rachel in the eye, she babbles more. This research goes on to show just how conversational Rachel is. If the adults around Rachel talk to her by *following* her vocalizations rather than by speaking *during* her vocalizations, the pattern of her babbling changes. When Rachel is interrupted, she tends to vocalize in bursts. When we wait until Rachel has finished and then start our part of the conversation, she pauses, looks attentively at the adult, smiles after the adult's vocalization, and then starts the cycle again. Although Rachel doesn't understand the meaning of what is being said to her, she vocalizes only after the adult is finished. By just four months of age, Rachel already enjoys talking to adults and taking conversational turns.

Try This: Conversations from the crib?

Test these conversational abilities in your own baby by trying an experiment. When your baby is alert and making sounds, hold the baby facing you but do not make eye contact. (The fact that this is terribly hard to do shows what compelling conversational partners babies are.) Now listen to see how much the baby "talks." In the next step, change your strategy by looking into your baby's eyes. You'll probably find that your baby starts to talk even more. See if you notice the difference. You should also notice that your baby talks more when he can see you than when you are out of view.

If you are an adventurous parent, you can try to replicate the research on turn-taking that we just discussed. While looking into your baby's eyes, wait for him to talk and then add your own commentary when he is finished. Now try to interrupt him by talking when he is "talking." Do you get a different pattern of vocalizing? Does your baby look happier when you wait until he has finished what he wanted to say?

From Coos and Goos to Babbling

A four-month-old's coos and gurgles represent only the beginning. Starting about six or seven months of age, infants around the world begin to make real, language-like sounds. They begin to sound somewhat like Bam Bam in *The Flintstones*. When this occurs, parents are sure they hear patterns that approximate the first words. What parents are hearing is *babbling*. This kind of sound making heralds a big step forward in the progression to language. Indeed, babbling in this period sounds like standard syllables repeated over and over again. "Dadadada" and "mamama" are premier examples. Before calling all the relatives to say that Rachel or Heidi has produced her first words, however, parents need to observe when these sounds are made. If Rachel says "dada" whether her father is present or not, it is unlikely that she means dada. It is striking, however, when true babbling begins because it does so suddenly. Even babies like Heidi will babble orally at this stage. Amazingly, deaf babies babble in both oral speech (as if exercising their vocal cords) and through their hands. Without any feedback from their own speech, however, Heidi's oral babbling quickly drops off in favor of visually rewarding signed babbling.

Toward the end of this period, around eight months of age, Rachel engages in a different, even more advanced kind of babbling. She no longer produces merely the same syllables over and over (as in "mamama") but begins using different syllables strung together, such as "mada" or "dele." The technical name for this kind of babbling is "variegated," since the parts of any given babble vary. Some children even string together long "sentences" of babbles, with the rhythm and intonation of real English sentences. Rachel produces "jargon," as it is called, and it is hilarious to hear. She sounds as though she is really talking, but she makes absolutely no sense. She even ends some of her "sentences" with the intonation of a question, making the adults around her feel compelled to respond. It is as if babies who use jargon (and not all do) are imitating the way entire sentences sound even before they know that sentences have meaning.

Researchers used to assume that children went through a period of babbling, variegated babbling, and jargon, and then became silent just before they uttered their real first word. Extensive observational research, however, has shown that babbling, jargon, and real words exist side by side. Rachel can babble away while introducing what may sound like some real words into her jargon. Parents often give babies the benefit of the doubt, although at this age it's wishful thinking to think that these are real words.

Try This: Are "Mama" and "Dada" real words or just arbitrary sounds?

During the early babbling period, chart the kinds of babbling patterns your baby uses by writing down the sounds your baby makes and also the context in which you hear these sounds used. Are any found regularly—are certain sounds used more often in certain kinds of situations?

When do you hear the first "mamama" or "dadada"? Are these true words for the baby or just sound play? If the baby says "Mama" mostly when Mommy is present, or "Dada" mostly when Daddy is present, you might be hearing real words. More probably, babies are just engaging in sound play at this stage. By keeping records, you will see for yourself how the baby begins to use the vocal instrument of the mouth and how certain syllables are practiced over and over again. You will probably discover why languages around the world have chosen the sounds of "mmm" and "dddd" to represent Mom and Dad. Languages seem to have capitalized on the sounds that babies can produce in abundance early on.

Why Babies Babble

All this talk about babbling raises a curious question. Why do babies babble in the first place? If they can make the sounds, why not move directly to words? And what is the link, if any, between babbling and later speech? Perhaps the way to think about this is to remember back to when we were children and struggled to put a puzzle together. Grown-ups around us would have called our activity "play" and relegated it to a category of things less important than, say, brushing one's teeth or learning to say "please" and "thank you." Yet consider what a child is doing when he puts that same puzzle together over and over. He is practicing the skills of finding pieces that fit into the puzzle, of seeing spatial relationships, and of comparing and contrasting puzzle pieces that look very much alike.

Babbling is analogous to putting a puzzle together over and over. Just as children learn a good deal about how puzzle pieces differ in small but significant ways, so do babies learn how to manipulate the pieces of sound that make up the puzzle of language. Rachel is learning how to move her lips and tongue to replicate the sounds she hears around her. She is learning that placing her tongue in a slightly different position has the effect of producing a slightly different sound. She is learning as well how to modulate her voice—how to yell and how to whisper.

How do we know that babbling helps babies practice forming the sounds of language or modulating the volume and intonation of their voices? Every now and then a child who can hear perfectly well is unable to babble because of medical problems. John Locke of Harvard University found a child he referred to as "Jenny" who had a tube inserted into her trachea (windpipe), which bypassed her larynx (voice box) because she had various respiratory abnormalities. The tube was not always present but inserted intermittently. Jenny was normal in all other ways. When the tube was removed for good, she was 17 months old. Her vocalizations immediately increased in number when the tube was removed. However, the quality of her vocalizations was not up to par. Even by the end of her 21st month, Jenny had still not begun to produce well-formed syllables in her babbling. Furthermore, Jenny produced only five different sounds. Children who have had an opportunity to practice their babbling produce nearly *thirty* unique sounds by 18 months of age. Jenny also produced sounds in a quiet monotone with very little variation in volume and tone. This too is far from typical. Since Jenny was normal in all other ways, the only explanation for the poor quality of her sound production is that she had missed out on hearing herself make playful babbling sounds.

So babbling is not just play. If a baby cannot hear herself make noise, she will eventually lag behind in the quality of the sounds she makes. She will produce fewer true consonant-vowel-consonant or consonant-vowel syllables. The baby will also lose the opportunity to practice "playing" with the volume and intonation of language. Much of how we communicate with each other rests on our manipulation of these variables. Volume can transmit urgency, anger, or interest, among other emotions. Intonational changes can give an entirely different meaning to the same exact words. Try saying "I love your tie" as though you mean it and then say it sarcastically. Babies who can't babble (like Jenny) or hear themselves babble (like Heidi) lose out on important practice in being able to manipulate these factors to suit their communicative needs.

Proof that babies are practicing the sounds of their language when they babble comes from much careful research. One way to test if babies' babbles resemble the language they hear around them is to have native speakers of a language—people who are not linguists—make judgments from audiotaped recordings. That's exactly what several French scientists decided to do. They appointed judges who were asked to listen to 15-second segments of babble before deciding whether the babies were French or not. By and large, the judges *could* identify which babies were French just from their babbling. How did they do this? The researchers determined that the judges' decisions were based on the *sounds* the babies used along with the *rhythm* and *intonation* of the babbles. For instance, English-reared babies babble mostly with a falling intonation. That is, their voices go down at the end of a string of babbles, just as an adult's voice does at the end of many sentences. The babble of French babies, however, end on an up note about half the time, just as sentences in French often end in a rising intonation. This finding shows us that the intonation pattern of a language is one of the first aspects babies identify.

Researchers have also found that babies produce different *proportions* of the same sounds when they are reared in different countries. For example, Rachel, hearing English, produces more vowels like the *i* in "ice" and the *e* in "easy" while Jing, a Chinese baby, produces more vowels like the *a* in "ask" and the *u* in "use." By ten months of age, just as a baby is on the verge of producing words, his variegated babbles come to take on the sound patterns of the language in which he is being reared. It's almost as if the syllables a baby produces in variegated babbling are frames that are being set up to accept what will soon be real words. But even after real words are used, babbling will persist into the first year of life.

How We Babble to Babies

Widening the Topics of Conversation

Even in the newborn period, babies interact socially with their moms, dads, grandparents, and siblings. Up to four months of age, however, they focus only on the people who come into close view during their interactions. Research has shown that adults position themselves roughly 18 inches away from the baby's face in an attempt to make eye contact. Babies don't seem to notice other interesting objects off in the distance. If you show babies an object while you are playing with them and you hold the object close enough, babies will look at it. If you hold the object too far away, they won't give it a glance. Some of this has to do with their vision. Although babies can see at birth, their visual acuity is only about 20-200. However, about four or five months of age, the picture literally changes. Babies start to focus on objects that are *not* right in their faces. Parents often notice when this occurs, because babies become less willing to engage in the eye contact and face-to-face interaction that they so enjoyed before.

At this stage parents rush to buy mobiles and play toys for the crib. More important, they also begin to incorporate talk about "faraway" objects into their playtime with baby. Heidi's parents do this in sign language and Rachel's parents do it in spoken language, but the effect is the same. Parents follow their infants' gaze to objects outside their own relationship. The conversation becomes exponentially more interesting. Instead of talking about how cute Heidi and Rachel are or what they had for lunch, parents can talk about the interesting sound that baby Rachel made with the rattle or even about the toy that baby Heidi is looking at on the changing table. By following a baby's gaze a host of new conversation pieces enter into the dialogue. No longer content to look at their immediate surroundings, babies reveal another human characteristic—active exploration. And their parents are thrilled to tell their babies all about what they are seeing, filling them in on details they won't need for years!

That's Mommy's pocketbook, Rachel. Would you like to see what's inside? Look, we have sunglasses that prevent the glare from hurting our eyes and keys for Mommy's car. Can you see the keys? Look, see the keeeeeeys?

Try This: Finding objects near and far

Watching babies as they first explore the world beyond is really quite dramatic. You can actually see this process as it develops. First, experiment with whether or not they see you. At the beginning of this period (at four months), try standing about 10 feet from the baby and calling to her. If she can't locate you, don't be surprised. Keep moving in and calling the baby's name until she can see you. How close to the baby's face did you have to get before she could find you? Trying this at the end of the period (around eight months) will elicit a totally different response. The baby will find you on the first try, probably even farther away than 10 feet. No wonder the range of conversational topics broadens during this period. A baby's perspective on the world widens and parents tend to follow the baby's lead.

Now test if the baby finds a stuffed animal or interesting toy at various points during this period. First place it in front of the baby. She will undoubtedly focus on it and try to reach or swipe at it. Now move the toy away slowly. How far can you move it before the baby loses interest? The distance should increase—dramatically at first at four months—but still some even after. In general, the older the baby is, the farther she will be able to search "faraway" places to find the object. Older babies also have more strength in their neck muscles so that they can look with greater precision and determination.

Finding the Words (and Other Units) in the Stream of Speech

What's a Word Worth?

Finding a word in the language stream is much harder than you would think. Imagine yourself in a foreign country with people speaking all around you. The analogy between language and a fast-moving body of water is quite apt. You are awash in this new language, unable to make heads or tails of it, feeling as though the new language is flooding over you and offering you no anchor point. So it is with babies. Speech is not punctuated with commas, periods, and question marks. Instead, like a continuous flow of stream water, language seems to move along quickly with no breaks in the flow.

Six-month-old Sylvia is lying in her crib, having just awakened from a nap. Delighted to see Sylvia awake, Mom notices her looking intently at the stuffed animals. She says, "HelloSylvie!DidSylvie haveanicenap?"

There are no spaces between the words when they are spoken. Someone invented the convention of spaces between words for written material. When we talk, however, words run into each other, and even the familiar words can sound somewhat different depending on how they are said. How does a baby find words in the quick-flowing stream that is speech? Perhaps he doesn't start out looking for words at all.

Instead of knowing about words or any other language elements, babies come into the world biologically prepared to look for regularities and patterns in the language they hear. Babies seem to start out finding larger units (sentences) and then move onto smaller ones, eventually getting to words. An oft-used scientific method allows researchers to peer into the infant's mind and to see just what they are doing as they listen in on their parents' conversations. The method is called the Headturn Preference Procedure, and it has been widely used to gauge the mental abilities of infants.

Use Your Head! The Headturn Preference Procedure

Barry, a beautiful brown-haired, blue-eyed four-month-old, and his mother, Sheila, are greeted at the laboratory by a friendly graduate student who explains the purpose of the study. After Sheila signs a consent form, Barry is placed in an infant seat with his mom sitting right behind him. They are in the midst of a three-sided testing booth, which is open in the back. Sheila is asked to wear earphones that are playing loud music so she can't influence Barry's responses in any way.

Barry sees a green lightbulb at the front of the booth. On the two sides of the enclosure, at approximately the height of Barry's head, are two small red lights. Below each of these lights is an audio speaker. Since Barry is facing forward, he will have to turn his head to see the lights on the sides.

Barry is first trained in the way the procedure works. First the green light begins to flash at the front. Then the red light on one of the sides of the booth begins to blink. After Barry turns to look at the blinking red light, both that light and the green light stop blinking.

Now one of the audiotapes plays. When the tape segment ends, Barry is beckoned back to the front with the flashing green light again. Then one of the side red lights begins to blink, and Barry is offered another passage to hear. After eight trials just like this, he has learned how to turn in response to the lights and has become familiar with the audiotapes that play on each side. The fact that Barry can follow this procedure in so few trials is impressive all on its own.

The audiotapes Barry hears are of a real mother reading a story to her own 18-month-old daughter. Although the words in the story heard on both sides are identical, the tapes were artificially doctored. Using advanced audio equipment, the researchers removed any pauses longer than a half second and added uniform one-second pauses. How the audiotapes differ is on *where* in the sentences the pauses are placed. You can roughly duplicate what these two versions sounded like by reading the two stories below out loud. Pause briefly at the spots indicated by an asterisk.

Version 1. Once upon a time, a lady and a witch lived in a big house.* The house was very old and messy.* It had a big garden and six windows at the front.*

Version 2. Once upon a time, a lady* and a witch lived in a big house. The house was* very old and messy. It had a big garden and* six windows at the front.

In version 1, the pauses are where they'd be expected—at the ends of clauses. In version 2, the researchers purposely avoided the natural clause or sentence boundaries and put the pauses within clauses in places where they do not occur naturally in speech. This made the voice on the audiotape sound choppy.

The question is, are babies such as Barry sensitive to this choppiness and do they prefer to hear their pauses at the ends of clauses? It could be argued that Barry should hear no difference in the two speech samples. After all, a four-month-old may not know a natural-sounding string of speech from an unnatural one. Further, the experiment is misleading, for both samples have pauses. Thus, both should sound equally good.

On the other hand, Barry has had four months of hearing language—along with several months in the womb. Maybe he has already noted where pauses are likely to occur in the speech he hears. Notice, for example, what changes when the pauses are inserted within units. For example, your voice usually goes down at the end of a clause. When a pause is inserted in the middle of a clause, however, the voice does not go down. There is an incongruity in the less natural sample of speech. Pauses do signal breaks between units, but—and this is a strong but—so does a drop in pitch and the lengthening of the final syllable in a clause. These cues that ordinarily work together in normal speech are working here at cross-purposes: one (the pause) is saying, "This is the end of a unit," and the other two (voice raising and the absence of syllable lengthening) are saying, "This is *not* the end of the unit." If Barry and other four-month-olds are sensitive to the alignment of cues in speech, they would prefer to listen to version 1.

In the test phase of the experiment Barry sees the green light go on. This is now followed by red lights that blink on *both* sides of the booth. Barry gets to make a choice. What does he want to listen to and how long will he listen to his selection? He will show which version he prefers by how long he keeps his head turned to the side he chooses. As long as Barry looks in the direction of the light from where the story is emanating, the story will continue to be played. When Barry turns away from that side, the story will stop playing. The green light in the middle will then flash, and the cycle will start all over again.

In twelve trials in which both sides are played equally often, researchers discovered that Barry listened longer to version 1. The test shows that babies as young as four months of age can distinguish normal from abnormal versions of a simple story.

While these findings are fascinating, readers should be clear on what they mean. Babies do not understand the *meaning* of the story they are hearing at four months, nor do they know what a clause is. Indeed, in many preliterate societies around the world where no one explicitly teaches the art of diagramming sentences using formal grammatical concepts, everyone still learns a human language. Yet from having heard lots of speech addressed to them, babies expect to hear pauses and voices going down at certain places. In other words, babies during this period (four to eight months) understand the way language *sounds.*

Try This: Will baby notice disrupted speech?

You may be able to get a different response from babies in this period when you read them version 1 and version 2. Wait until the baby is happy and alert. Then facing the baby, read version 1 twice and observe what she does. Does she vocalize? Listen attentively? Smile? Then after a few minutes have elapsed, try doing the same thing with version 2. When you read both versions to the baby, use equally animated infant-directed speech. This will take some practice because the pauses in the wrong place disrupt your reading, as you may have noticed above. Does the baby respond any differently to the disrupted version? Is there a furrowing of the brows? Fewer vocalizations? Turning away? To do this experiment correctly, you really should try it again the next day or so reading the disrupted version first, followed by the natural version. Do you get the same results?

Learn Your Handle: Lauren, Not Louise

To learn a language, however, babies need not only to hear the sounds, but to remember them. Babies, just like adults learning a new task, start with the "bigger picture" aspects of language rather than the details. However, there does seem to be an exception to this rule. There is one word that infants hear a good deal, depicted in the Larson cartoon. Amid the blah, blah, blahs, Ginger did hear her own name. A remarkable set of studies provides evidence that even four-month-old infants can recognize their own names.

Although no one has counted, a baby's name is used much more frequently than other words. Parents constantly use the baby's own name ("Does Jordan want to go out?") instead of using pronouns ("Do you want to go out?"). Scientists hypothesized that if a baby recognized his own name he should have a different response to it than to other names. For example, hearing one's own name over and over again might get a baby's attention more than hearing someone else's name repeated. After all, you probably know from experience that even if you are actively involved in a conversation at a party, you can hear your own name if you are being discussed in another conversation. This has been called the "cocktail party phenomenon." It is as if our own name "pops out" from the surrounding talk. Perchance babies experience a kind of cocktail party phenomenon of their own.

In order to test whether babies recognized their own names, researchers had to decide what name to pair each baby's own name against in the Headturn Procedure. Babies' memories of their own names could be gross rather than detailed. Would they just as soon listen to a name that had the same number of syllables and the same stress pattern as their own name? This is what speech experts think Ginger does when she is taken out for a walk. Ginger could be as easily excited by hearing, "Want to go for a walk, Michael?" Ginger would come bouncing forward in anticipation. Names like miCHELLE are stressed on the last syllable, as are names like louANNE. If all babies detect about their own names at four months is the *stress pattern,* baby Michelle might be just as happy to listen to her own name—miCHELLE—as she is to listen to the name louANNE which shares the same stress pattern. And baby JAson should not distinguish between his name and CORey.

On the other hand, if by four months, babies have more than just a broad notion of their own name, then they might be expected to listen to their own name (say, miCHELLE) more than they would listen to the same-stress name (louANNE) or names with the opposite stress pattern (JAson and CORey). So which is it? Are babies like Larson's Ginger or do they really know the details of their own names?

To find out, a female speaker who did not know what the study was about was asked to say each baby's name fifteen times on tape. This speaker also recorded another name fifteen times. Some of the names had the same stress pattern as that of the baby to be tested, and some names had the opposite pattern. In the Headturn Preference Procedure the baby's own name (miCHELLE) was paired with both different kinds of names (that is, with louANNE and CORey).

What did they find? Babies prefer to listen to their own names above both kinds of other names. That is, Michelle preferred to listen to her own name most, followed by the name with the same stress pattern (louANNE), followed by the name with the opposite stress pattern (CORey). The researchers were stunned to learn that babies preferred to hear their own names over names with identical stress. Does this mean that babies *know* that they are hearing their own names? Do they understand that this is what *they* are called? Experts think this is doubtful. It is more likely that before babies know their own name, they recognize the sounds that compose their name. A better test of whether babies know that their names refer to them is having them turn in the direction from which their name is being called. If they turn and look expectantly, this may mean that they are aware that the name refers to them. In babies we tested, we saw this response at six or seven months. But no one really knows when babies first have this realization.

Try This: Does baby respond to her own name?

See if your baby knows her own name. Sneak up on the baby when she is awake and alert. Stand to one side so that she has to turn to see you. Say her name, "Corey!" Does she turn to you? If she does, it isn't yet proof that she knows her own name. You have to try the test again with names that have similar (JAson) and different patterns of stress (louANNE). At what age does the baby turn only if you use her own name and not others?

Once Upon a Time: Babies Recognize Words in Stories

The fact that babies can detect and remember their own names is but another example of their ability to detect patterns in the stream of speech. Without realizing it, the baby is working toward breaking down the speech stream into words. Detecting her own name is a stepping-stone in this process.

To duplicate an infant's experience, imagine four-month-old Sally hearing "DoberayrayboSallyyada." None of the words mean anything to Sally, but one familiar element stands out: "Sally." Notice that the element to the right of Sally ("yada") now stands alone. Finding one's own name in the speech stream, therefore, gives a baby an advantage. It may help her segment or break apart the stream of speech into words. The effect presumably "snowballs," in that once the baby has found the word "yada," she has yet another word available to help in segmenting the speech stream.

Although finding the words is not the same as knowing what they mean, think of the progress the baby has made. What started out as a mass of undifferentiated sounds bombarding the baby is slowly separating into clause-like units, phrase-like units, and even some words. Even at four months of age, a baby can exploit the patterns found in the language stream and find elements like words in sentences. Babies still have a long way to go, though, before they can be said to be in possession of a human language.

If by four months babies can recognize their own names, by the "ripe old age" of seven months they might be expected to find and remember other words. To test to see if they could, researchers used the Headturn Preference Procedure once again. This time the scientists used the procedure to see if seven-month-olds could recognize words they were hearing in a story. The reasoning was, if the babies heard these words read from a list first, they might recognize the words when they were embedded in a story.

Enter our veteran Barry—now all of seven months old—who happily returns to the baby lab. Barry repeatedly hears the words "cup" and "dog." (Other babies heard the words "feet" and "bike.") After Barry is familiar with his pair of words, two stories are presented. On the left side, he hears stories containing either the word "cup" or the word "dog." On the right side, he hears two stories each designed around one of the unfamiliar words, "feet" and "bike." By way of example, the story containing the word "cup" went like this:

> The cup was bright and shiny. A clown drank from the red cup. The other one picked up the big cup. His cup was filled with milk. Meg put her cup back on the table.

Would Barry prefer listening to the stories with the familiar words ("cup" and "dog")? By maintaining his head turn to one of the sides over repeated exposures of the stories, Barry would show his choice. Why wouldn't he want to hear the unfamiliar stories? Because in studies like these, babies seem to go for the tried and true. Familiarity breeds "content"; babies who are trying to make sense of a complex system—language—seem to want to find some familiar anchors they can hang on to.

Barry again cooperates beautifully while he hears the word lists, looking all around, trying to figure out where the disembodied voice is coming from. Then he is trained in the Headturn Procedure and hears a story with an unfamiliar word ("bike") on the left side. He gets bored pretty fast, perhaps because none of the words sound like the ones he just heard. Barry turns away from the unfamiliar story to look at the middle again. The light on the right side of the booth now blinks, and a story with a familiar word ("cup") plays. As Barry listens to this story, he realizes that he's heard some of these words earlier. He is excited to find something familiar in the stream of speech and looks to the side with the familiar words for about two seconds longer than the side with the unfamiliar words.

In effect, Barry (and many other seven-month-old babies who participated in the same procedure) "told" the scientists that they could remember words in a list when they later appeared in a story. Does this finding suggest that babies now understand what these words mean? That is not likely. Attaching meaning to words does not happen until the baby is about ten months of age. What this research does show, however, is that by seven months of age, when most babies have just discovered babbling, they are already analyzing the language stream. This skill paves the road to language learning. By creating a storehouse of familiar sounds, babies are stockpiling what they will need when they eventually learn how to pair words with meanings. By memorizing what they hear, they are building a foundation for language.

Babies can remember words *before* they have a clue as to what they mean. To understand what this is like, harken back to the French classes you took in high school. You could recognize many words but not know what they meant. Of course, in French the textbook provided word lists with the English meanings next to the French words. For example, the list might have contained the French word *la main* and next to it the translation "hand." The poor language-learning baby has no list to consult. Somehow the baby—who can't yet use utensils, or make a phone call, or cross the street—has to figure out both *where* the words are in the speech stream and *what* they mean. Returning to the French example, it would be as if you learned French without a textbook. All you had to rely on was hearing your teacher blather on in French. How would you figure out what the words she was using meant? You'd need to develop some strategy to dope out the meanings of the words you could find in the stream of speech. You'd also need to be bathed in words, to hear them, to internalize them, to find out how they "hook up" with meaning.

Indeed, the finest programs for second-language learning espouse that immersion is the *only* way to learn a language well. Research with babies helps us to understand why. Long before you even have the words on the tip of your tongue, long before you can put the words together in the packages we call sentences, you are creating a mental dictionary of sounds that pave the way for future learning. Your next task will be to somehow hook up these familiar sounds with the objects, actions, and events that they come to represent.

How Do You Mean? Babies Grapple with Word Meanings

If babies are learning lots about the sounds that make up their language, and if they can remember sequences of sounds that for us are words, why don't we see evidence of word learning sooner than the end of the first year of life? One possibility is that the ability to associate a word with an object is itself an arduous task. According to some interesting research "hooking up" a word to an object may at first require special circumstances. To illustrate what we mean, consider the last time you learned a new word. As adults, this happens continually although we may not notice it. In the last ten years for example, how many people have begun to talk of "faxing" each other or "e-mailing" friends? Perhaps the last time we learned a novel word was at the car repair shop when we were shown a greasy-looking metallic object that we were told had been removed from our car, and told that the "_____" (fill in the blank) had broken and needed to be replaced. For us as skilled language users, to learn the name of the new engine part, we would only need to hear it once. We would not need to see the new object in motion, or hear its name repeated multiple times. We would have probably no difficulty remembering the new name and recalling it to our spouse that night in explaining why the car repair bill was more than the public works budget of a small country. For babies, however, the situation is very different. Not only do babies require many, many repetitions of a word paired with an object to learn it, but they may only learn a word under very special circumstances. Research suggests that for babies around seven months of age, the circumstances in which the new word is offered really matter.

Consider for a moment that the relationship between an object and its name is completely arbitrary. We could call a chair "chair" or "rup" or "dax" or anything we wished, since there is no way in which a word sounds like what it stands for. In fact, this is exactly what happens when someone invents a new product: Madison Avenue decides what to name it. Shakespeare captured this best when he wrote that "a rose by any other name would smell as sweet." Names are arbitrarily linked to what they stand for. We can't rely on the way a word sounds to help us figure out its meaning.

A tantalizing finding from a number of different laboratories suggests that babies are first capable of learning the arbitrary relation between a word and an object only if the name is said as the object *moves*. Before word learning can begin in earnest, babies need words to occur in predictable coordination with the objects they stand for. Until they recognize the arbitrary association between words and their objects, babies need to have a tightly locked coordination between word and object that they will not need later on.

How could we possibly know that babies need to hear a word and see its referent move at the same time to learn it? In one experiment a team of researchers created three sets of videotapes to show to three different groups of seven-month-old babies in the lab. On all the videotapes a hand holds first one new object (a plastic crab) and then another (a plastic lamb chop) and moves each object across the surface of a black table in a slow, random pattern. For example, the crab is moved five inches forward and held stationary for a few moments. Then the crab is moved six inches to the left and held stationary, then eight inches to the rear, and so on. The lamb chop is moved around in the same way. A pleasant female voice "names" the crab by making the vowel sound "aaahhh." The same voice "names" the lamb chop by making the vowel sound "eee." The only thing that distinguished between the three videotapes was how the objects moved when the vowel names were said.

Allison, a curly-topped seven-month-old girl, is in the *synchrony* group. She is placed in an infant seat with her mother blindfolded behind her and waits for the show to begin. Each time the crab is set down, the friendly voice says "aaaahhh," and each time the lamb chop is set down, the friendly voice says "eeee." The "name" of the object is said just as the object is moved. Allison watches the videotape until she gets bored.

Michael, a blond seven-month-old boy, is placed in the *asynchrony* group. As he watches his videotape, the sound "ah" is said at all different times—not just as the crab moves. The same is done with the lamb chop: there is no relationship between when the name "ee" is said and the movement. Thus, in the asynchrony condition, the names of the objects are heard at *unpredictable* times in relation to the movements.

Seven-month-old Melissa watches her videotape, the third version. She does not see the crab or the lamb chop move at all but hears the names of the objects ("ah" or "ee") spoken in the same friendly manner and for the same number of times. The same hand still holds the objects on the table, but they don't move. Melissa is in the *stationary group.*

Melissa, Michael, and Allison are all tested on the same videotape after this initial training. After they get bored with the training tape, they are all shown a tape on which the *opposite* sound is paired with each object. Now the crab is called "ee" and the lamb chop is called "ah." Only if the babies have learned that the crab was called "ah" and the lamb chop called "ee" should it bother them that now the names of the objects have been switched. How do they show that it bothers them to have the names switched? If they start paying attention to the tape again, researchers can infer that they noticed the switch. If they don't notice that the names have switched, they assume the same boring game is still being played and don't watch the test tape for much time at all.

Only Allison, the baby who heard the name just as the object moved, noticed the switch. She alone watched the test videotape longer, as if to say, "Hey, what's going on here?" Allison, the scientists reasoned, learned to associate the name with the object because she saw the object move in synchrony just as the name was said. This finding shows that babies really are making a lot of progress in word learning as they move from four to seven months. They can find words in the stream of speech, they can remember these words, and they can even hook up a word with an object. While these are all significant accomplishments, there is still a great deal left to achieve.

For the seven-month-old baby, a word may be nothing more than a familiar sound that "goes with" an object, an action, or an event in the same way that a bark "goes with" a dog or a beep "goes with" the microwave. These accumulated words may have no real significance as words. They might not even symbolically represent the things they go with. Yet these accomplishments represent the very first steps on the road to language mastery. What we see as we watch four- to seven-month-olds work through the process of word learning is that it is a Herculean task; much mental preparation goes on to prepare them for the magical day when they utter their first words.

Scientific Sleuthing Pays Off

Lesson 1. Hear ye, hear ye: Watch for ear infections. The research reviewed in this chapter gives clues about what practices might be useful in promoting language acquisition. Comparisons between deaf babies who can vocalize, hearing babies who cannot vocalize, and babies (the vast majority) who both hear and vocalize teach the importance of babbling for language development. These studies also show that hearing one's own vocalizations is critical for normal language development. Herein lies a clue for what parents can do to promote language learning. Make sure your baby can hear. This sounds so straightforward and easy. Yet in this period of development there is a menace that often prevents children from hearing clearly. During this period babies start to get ear infections. In some cases, mothers stop breast feeding, and the immunities they had been transmitting to the baby wear off. In addition, many babies (approximately 70 percent) enter into some form of child care where they are exposed to other children's germs. The result is not surprising: Babies in child care get more ear infections than babies at home. Most babies get their first ear infection during these months, and about 30 percent have continuous episodes of ear infections.

Ear infections are often accompanied by fluid in the inner ear. This fluid prevents the membranes of the ear from vibrating in the way that they should, preventing children from clearly hearing all of the sounds of language. Children who suffer from recurrent ear infections hear intermittently, and this impeded access to sounds may have lasting effects. What can you do? You can be more vigilant about this fluid and better monitor your children's infections. While most parents take the child to the doctor when they suspect an ear infection, most also fail to return to the doctor for a two-week follow-up to see if the ears are clear of fluid. This fluid generally remains in the inner ear for 14 to 30 days, and infections can recur for months on end. While the research is still accumulating, studies show that long-term fluid in the ears can hurt language development. Fluid in the ears may even have long-term effects on older children's ability to stay directed in school and to tell a coherent story.

Research also points subtle cues to infection that your infants might show. Children who tug at their ears or who have continuous runny noses may be giving signs that they have an ear infection, even if they are not screaming from pain. Thus, let the reader beware. It is important to look for subtle signs of ear infection and to be aggressive in treating these infections.

Lesson 2. There is nothing wrong with small talk. Research has shown that babies' babbles improve in quality when they are babbling back and forth to an adult. It may seem silly to carry on conversations with your baby that mean nothing at all. Yet research shows that it is far from silly. Nor is it silly to use baby talk or infant-directed speech. Parents who engage their babies in such small talk are probably helping their babies by emphasizing sounds and silences that are used to form the stream of language. Aside from having fun connecting with the baby, these sounds and silences are also indirectly teaching the baby about the joys of communicative exchange.

A common way to engage very young children in the conversation is to accompany caregiving activities with talk. This is easy enough to do and provides babies with more data about how language works. If these little monologues are delivered in infant-directed speech, babies are likely to pay attention to it. Saying the same thing over and over to a baby—as we do when we change that diaper over and over again—probably helps him learn how language can separate the day into familiar routines. Some of the first meanings that babies figure out are undoubtedly embedded in the context of these routines. Words said repeatedly in well-structured routines provide the grist for the mill of language learning.

Researchers who study teenage pregnancy and how teenage mothers interact with their children have found that these babies are sometimes delayed in their language development. One possible reason is that, as the researchers discovered, teen moms don't routinely talk to their babies. Instead, they are more likely to engage in their caregiving tasks silently and without telling the baby what his role is: "Now lift up your leg, Irving, and let me put on your pajamas. That's right." Perhaps teenage mothers are not sufficiently far removed from childhood themselves and still too much in the grip of adolescent self-consciousness to be able to use baby talk without feeling foolish and worrying about how their baby talk looks to others. Remember, though, silence is not golden! Talking with your child is critical to development—not only for language learning but for a host of abilities like reading and storytelling that will not emerge for years.

By the end of this period, babies are capable of remembering individual words, including their own names. Clearly, babies are busy looking for patterns in the language stream wherever they find them. They are also computing (believe it or not) statistics on the sounds to which they are exposed. Babies simply cannot do the calculations if they don't hear enough language. Talking to babies provides them with the data they will need to find the patterns. Babies are not waiting around like passive blobs for you to "teach" them language. Instead, they are actively analyzing the language stream and teaching themselves language on the fly!

Chapter 3

Point-ilism: Parents Become Tools for Babies Between Nine and Twelve Months of Age

Although he now knew of something beyond languagelessness, he didn't have enough symbols to convey a complete thought. . . . Nor could his primitive acting and pointing ask the questions he had puzzled over all his life. From Ildefonso's perspective, however, he now possessed the great secret, the magic formula that had always eluded him, and he wanted to use it. . . . With all my concentration and imagination I could not understand more than one communication out of ten.[1]

What would it be like to have thoughts, feelings, observations, and desires, and be unable to communicate them to other people? Yet, from observing others, you knew that there was a way that people got their ideas across to each other. This passage describes a 27-year-old man who was born deaf and never given an opportunity to learn sign language or lip reading until he met Susan Schaller, a teacher of American Sign Language.

The passage above could easily describe how a baby between nine and twelve months feels: "I have these things I want to communicate, things I want others to know, things I want others to do and show me, but the resources at my disposal are too few for the task." At this stage babies struggle to express their ideas and feelings first by using

1. Susan Schaller, *A Man Without Words* (London: Ebury, 1992), 70.

points, grunts, and whines, and then by the beautifully streamlined, far more efficient sound waves known as *words*.

Why are people so excited by their children's language achievements? One major reason is that parents have spent their child's first year desperately trying to find the meaning behind their infants' burps, whines, and babbles. What *does* she want? How many parents have vainly searched through the refrigerator or the cupboard attempting to satisfy the imperial point and whine of their hungry (?), thirsty (?), or bored (?) infants?

Chapter 3 explores what babies do to manipulate their world (translate that as their parents and caregivers) even before they can talk. By the end of the first year of life, babies' communication skills have undergone a transformation. They become members of the human community. They initiate games and routines that only the parent or caregiver started before, and they are extremely social and very communicative. This is the age when babies become charmers, capable of stealing the scene with their social overtures.

Learning to Communicate Without Words

Finding the Causal Connection: My Signals *Can* Make Things Happen!

Six-month-old Angela is sitting in her high chair during lunch and sees her bottle on the counter. She's pretty tired—it's been a tough day!—and Angela wants her bottle. She looks at it as her mother, Sophie, feeds her and gets more and more frustrated. Eventually, she turns away from her mother's spoonfuls, arches her back, gyrates around in her high chair, and vocalizes as if she is about to cry. Sophie is clueless about what Angela wants. When Sophie just happens to look at the counter for another reason, she notices the bottle on it. "That's what you want," she says, and gives Angela her bottle. Success at last!

Eleven-month-old Angela is in the same situation. Seeing her bottle on the counter, she looks at her bottle, looks into her mom's eyes, and then looks again in the direction of the bottle. When Mom follows Angela's gaze to the bottle, Angela vocalizes loudly ("eh eh eh!"), points at the bottle, and looks at her mom again. Sophie quickly surmises that it is the bottle that Angela wants and gets up to give it to her. Success at last!

Consider the difference between six and eleven months. Although Angela achieved her goal in both vignettes, the means she used were drastically different. At six months all Angela could do was *look* at the bottle. She had no other communicative signals. Her actions also suggest that she was not capable of formulating a plan for getting what she wanted. When she couldn't, all she could do was arch her back and gyrate in her high chair. Angela had not yet realized two important insights: First, things don't just come to you by magic. Second, Mom can be a tool for getting things done.

By eleven months Angela is a far more sophisticated baby. She sees the bottle and seems to realize instantly that Mom better be recruited to help with this plan. She *looks into her mother's eyes* twice, trying to get her to follow her eyes to the counter. She also *vocalizes* and *points*. Just in this one episode—and these happen every day—Angela is showing all the signs of using communicative signals. The hallmarks of "intentional communication" include many of the things Angela did—making eye contact, waiting for a response, and persevering in the face of initial failure. Only within the past week has Angela begun using her "eh eh eh" vocalization consistently in situations when she wants something. She also adds to or changes her signals when she doesn't meet immediately with success.

The communication that goes on before this time in such situations depends upon the mind-reading skills of the parent or caregiver. At eleven months Angela's behavior still requires that the adult make inferences, but much more is spelled out. What is responsible for Angela's transformation into a baby who now can use communicative devices? To begin with, she needs to understand the cause and effect—that her communication to mom can cause her to act. Following the lead of the brilliant developmental psychologist Jean Piaget, one of us (Golinkoff) with Professor Carol Harding from Loyola University came up with two simple experiments to see whether a baby's understanding of cause and effect was related to his ability to communicate.

To test the communicative ability of babies who can't *talk*, we had to set up a situation in which the baby has to appeal to someone to get something done and see what happens. Have you ever sat next to a baby in a high chair while you were reading a book or were absorbed in a conversation? What did the baby do when it wanted to get your attention? Did the baby vocalize? Make eye contact? Grab your arm? Let's follow eleven-month-old Irving and his mother, Shiffra, as they came into the laboratory to participate in our experiment—an experiment in frustration, designed to get babies to communicate with their moms.

After Irving was settled in a high chair with Shiffra beside him reading a magazine, we brought out an intriguing toy. It was a little like a carousel encased in plastic, and when wound, it moved. We placed the carousel just outside Irving's reach on a little table. How would he try to get it? Some babies never even looked at their mothers, acting very much like six-month-old Angela. But some babies vocalized and tried to make eye contact, as if to say, "Hey, Mom, I need your help!" This test demonstrated how advanced each baby's communication was. If, like Irving, they vocalized and made eye contact with their moms, we decided that they were communicating on purpose, with the *intention* of contacting mom to help them out. If they only jumped up and down and whined or grabbed her arm with no eye contact, we knew that they hadn't yet figured out that their vocalizations and eye contact could set their moms into motion on their behalf.

In another text, one of us gently blew into Irving's hair a few times and waited to see what he did. Babies love this game. Not surprisingly, Irving wanted the adult to do it again. The question was how would he get the adult to blow again. At six months of age, Irving would only have been able to wiggle and jump in his high chair, hoping that the blowing would start again, unaware of what made the blowing happen. At a higher level, say, at eight or nine months of age, Irving would have touched the adult's mouth but made no eye contact. It's as if Irving is saying, "Maybe this will turn the lady on again." This level is analogous to the "just do something" response people often have when a soda machine fails to deliver. We somehow convince ourselves that kicking it, talking to it, or pulling the change lever will prompt the machine to give us the soda. After all, we know that there must be some cause for the effect; we just don't know what to do to make the effect happen. So, we just do something!

Finally, at Irving's age babies look into the adult's *eyes* and place their head expectantly into the position where their hair can be blown again. They may not be using formal language, but it is as if the baby is saying, "I have to contact you—by looking into your eyes—to tell you to do that fun thing again." This baby understands the causal connection between their communications and the actions of another. Although Irving had this realization by 11 months, other babies who came into the lab were sometimes as old as 13 months of age before they understood cause and effect.

How does an understanding of cause and effect relate to early communication? Our original hunch was that only babies who understood cause and effect would be able to use their vocalizations with the intention of contacting their moms. Babies who weren't yet using vocalizations along with eye gaze probably did not "get" the causal connection between communication and making things happen. We were stunned at how clearly the results came out. Every child who used vocalizations with intention (that is, with eye contact to the parent) was also capable of the highest level of causal reasoning in the hair-blow game. This means that babies who use communicative signals to accomplish their goals understand something about cause and effect. They know that events do not just happen; rather there are causes for events in the world.

Try This: Can my baby communicate with intention?

Try the hair-blow test just described. Does the baby look you in the eye to restart the interesting hair-blow event? Aside from being good clean fun, and perhaps the start of a repetitive game that the baby will like, you can see if your baby has an understanding of causality sufficient to use communication intentionally.

Try the other part of the test as well. Perhaps during a play time or a mealtime, put an object the baby is interested in just out of reach. Pretend to read and ignore the baby. What does she do? Does she just grab at your magazine, or does she use non-cry vocalizations and eye gaze to try to get you to retrieve the object? Does the baby point at the object, checking your eyes to see if you are looking at it, too? Or does the baby respond in a less mature way, by jumping up and down and arching her back, for example? Try the same little game several times, say, once a month, to see the differences in your baby's development.

How Do Babies Learn to Make Their Point?

One of the advantages of words for babies is they can single things out in the environment. Irving at age two says, for example, "I want the big cup, not the little cup." In such a situation, sometimes pointing

can serve Irving as well as talking can. But even pointing has to develop. How babies come to understand and produce the deceptively
simple pointing gesture is an interesting story in itself.

It starts during the last quarter of the first year. The "imperial"
point sends parents and caregivers hither and yon to satisfy baby's
every demand. From here on out, life will never be the same. Babies
like Angela become merciless at controlling their parents' behaviors.
But where does this gesture come from? Is it really an abbreviated,
failed reaching toward an object, or is it an attempt to gain an adult's
attention and to control him?

Learning to point is actually a slow process that begins as early as
one month. The very first index finger extensions are seen when
the baby is attentive to an interesting display (say, a new object).
There is, however, little evidence that this early point is used to communicate. For one thing, one-month-old babies do not attempt to
make eye contact when they point; for another, they are unlikely
to extend their arm. In a way, the early, uncommunicative point is
analogous to babbling—not a way to communicate but clearly a
precursor.

The next stage in pointing occurs around six months of age, as if
to direct their own attention to an interesting object that they are ex-
ploring. It does not seem to emerge from actions related to grasping
out-of-reach objects but from a desire to direct attention, at first
their own, and later that of another. Ironically, though babies point
for themselves at around six months of age, they don't understand
what it means when others point. Even at nine months, they have not
caught on. When you point to an object in the distance, the baby will
look at your finger and not at the distant object!

Parents don't give up, though. They will try anything to get their
babies to follow their points to an interesting sight. We snap our fingers, tap on the far-away object, and even manually turn our babies'
heads to the sight. Why? We do it because we want to share information with our babies. We want to have a "conversation." For most of
the first year of life, parents work hard to keep the conversation going. And, by the end of the first year, the hard work pays off. Babies
start looking at the appealing sights we indicate with our points. At
the same time, babies join in the conversation by using pointing and
eye gaze as they work their way toward language.

How do babies get the idea of following a point between nine
and twelve months? Probably because when they look by accident
in the direction in which we are pointing, they are rewarded by

an interesting sight. Little by little they learn that the point of a point is not the pointing finger. Instead, the "point of a point" is what they see when they follow it. Acquiring this skill is a leap in early language development. Babies find there is a world of sights they might not have discovered on their own. And once a point is *produced,* the baby can comment on and single things out in the environment. The point gives babies another tool to use with the more powerful people in their lives who can help them realize their goals.

Is there a relationship between when children point and when they talk? Scientists have noted differences in when babies first start to point, and those who point early also seem to acquire their first words early. Why? Perhaps understanding how pointing works helps the baby direct adults' attention to objects and events whose names they'd like to hear.

Try This: When can baby follow a point?

It is interesting to trace a baby's understanding and production of the point. If you start early enough, you will probably find a time (around nine months) when babies will look at the end of your finger when you point. When does the baby shift to looking off in the general direction of your pointing? When does the baby look at the object of the point? When you try this, be sure not to direct the baby's attention to something in the field that is making noise; the baby might be following the noise rather than your point. Can you catch the baby producing points? Remember that babies start to point for themselves, only pointing for the benefit of others later.

You can also try the same process with eye gaze, a communicative signal that is the hallmark of the baby's ability to use intentional, as opposed to accidental, communication. See if you can direct a baby's attention merely by shifting your gaze. Try this with a baby while you are sitting directly in front of him, no more than two feet away. Look into the baby's eyes and then shift your attention to one side. Does the baby follow your gaze, or does he keep looking at your face? Early in this period it is unlikely that the baby will shift their eye gaze to your focus of attention. However, toward the end you may well get the baby to look where you are looking. If not, make sure to capture the baby's attention first ("Oh, Irving!) when you look at him.

The Negotiation of Failed Messages: You Just Don't Get It!

Once intentional communication occurs, and prior to the appearance of much language, babies go to town trying to convey their complex thoughts and feelings. Consider the following vignette (which actually occurred to one of us):

Jordan:	(*vocalizes repeatedly until his mother turns around*)
Mother:	(*turns around to look at child*)
Jordan:	(*points at one of the objects on the counter*)
Mother:	Do you want this? (*holds up jelly jar*)
Jordan:	(*shakes head no*)
Mother:	Is this what you want? (*holds up spoon*)
Jordan:	(*shakes head no and jumps in frustration in his high chair*)
Mother:	How about this? (*shows him cheese*)
Jordan:	(*shakes head no, leans forward as if pointing with his whole body*)
Mother:	This? (*said incredulously, as she picks up sponge*)
Jordan:	(*leans back in high chair and puts arm down; tension leaves body*)
Mother:	(*hands child sponge*)

At first blush there does not seem to be much going on here—a whiny, determined child who has an agenda of some sort and is driving his parent crazy. The beleaguered parent is playing along. Through the scientific lens, however, this vignette is a treasure trove of wonderful advances in the child's ability to get his message across— even without saying a single word. Pointing was merely one of the communication signals Jordan used. When the parent or caregiver fails in their initial attempt to figure out what the baby wants, they then engage in a surprising number of "conversational turns" without the baby ever using language. Babies modify their communicative signals by repeating them, refining them, and adding to them.

Dr. Golinkoff wondered if such lengthy and complicated interactions were typical of other mother-child pairs. In an informal test, she hid behind a cardboard screen with a video camera and taped three mother-infant pairs intermittently during lunchtime in their homes. There is really no better time to see these exchanges than at mealtimes. Babies who are eating have clear objectives, especially when it comes to their choice of food. What she found was that babies who were barely talking (if at all) were nonetheless carrying on lengthy communicative exchanges, using perseverance and creativity to make themselves understood.

How often do these exchanges occur? Don't mothers always understand what their babies are trying to get across? The answer is definitely no. In half of these the mothers initially failed to understand what their babies wanted. Imagine, from the babies' perspective, what it must be like to be misunderstood 50 percent of the time? Yet babies don't give up. They—and their moms—usually persevere until the mother understands. Interestingly, very few (less than 5 percent) of these episodes ended in complete failure. More often than not, if the mother couldn't figure it out, she offered the baby a substitute, such as an object the baby was not asking for, in an attempt to mollify her infant.

What happened the other 50 percent of the time? Babies were understood immediately, as the following example with Betty (age 12 months) indicates:

Betty: (*looks at clock and points and vocalizes, then looks at Mom*)
Mom: (*looks at clock, at Betty*) That's a clock.
Betty: (*looks at Mom and stops pointing*)

Here Betty appears to be "asking" her mother to notice and perhaps comment on the wall clock. When she does so, Betty is quite happy to accept her mother's interpretation of what she wanted.

What do these communication episodes tell us about a child's progression to language? Once pointing, vocalizations, eye gaze, and other signals are used for the purpose of intentional communication, babies have a wealth of "conversational" tools at their disposal. These episodes are also "hot spots" for vocabulary learning. Since mothers often put their babies' intentions into words ("Oh, it's the *cheese* you want!"), babies are hearing words for precisely what they are focused on at the moment. We too would learn a new word in a foreign language in just such a situation (*"Ah, c'est la plume vous desirez"*), since the emphasis highlights the very object we were thinking about.

Of course, there are limits on what a preverbal baby can convey. From studying early episodes of communication before the babies can talk, experts know that babies are capable of signaling three broad types of intentions. The first is *rejection*, and this comes in very handy. As with Jordan's head shake of no, rejection can negate what someone has just said, get the listener to stop doing something, or get rid of an object you're being offered. Babies can also formulate *requests*. They can "ask" the name of something (as Betty seemed to be doing in her vignette), ask that we do something, ask for an object, or just ask for us to interact with them—all before they say any words. Finally, even before babies can talk, they can *comment*. They use nonverbal communicative devices to share an adult's attention with an object or event. To do this, babies sometimes show or offer an object to an adult and hand it to them with a vocalization and eye gaze. This is the time when the "giving game" becomes a favorite. The baby gives something to you, and you say "Thank you" and perhaps comment on it or name it. Then you give it back, and the baby gives it to you yet again. You comment again. Think of all the language information you are offering the baby just at the point when the baby is most interested in your response. In fact, babies whose mothers routinely name objects for them have enhanced vocabularies a few months later.

Try This: How does my baby negotiate?

At mealtime (or any other time) see if you can notice the kinds of things your baby does to get his point across. This is not easy to do because you are so busy trying to please the baby that it's hard to observe his behavior at the same time! One thing you might do is to feign that you don't understand. That way you can plan your observation. Wait for the baby to request something using his nonverbal communicative devices and watch what happens. How does the baby respond? Does he use eye contact, pointing, or vocalizing? Does he keep signaling as you keep failing? Does the intensity of the signals (and the volume) increase as the baby keeps trying? Does he use postural cues such as leaning forward in his high chair? Of course, give the baby what he was really asking for at the end. When you do, does the baby sit back and relax in the high chair when you finally hit what he wants?

These negotiation episodes should be very different at the beginning (around nine months) and at the end (around 12 months) of this period. At the end, there should be more diverse signals and more obviously intentional communication. By the end of this period, there may also be some words in the mix!

Let the Words Begin!

Preverbal Communication: The Cradle of Meaning

Babies are now grappling with ways to express their ideas and thoughts and feelings—just like Ildefonso in the opening vignette. When they start to talk, there will be no limit to the intentions that they can express to accomplish their ends. Think of all the delicate situations in which adults use language, albeit some more artfully than others. We can find out information that our friends may be reluctant to share, tell a story but not reveal too much of our motivation, or frame a delicate request to someone whom we know may not wish to comply. All these more subtle, adult intentions have their origins in the three broad kinds of intentions babies started out with at the end of the first year of life. The meaning expressed in *preverbal communication* turns into the meaning expressed in *language* interactions. But before children can learn words to express themselves, they go through a period of using nonverbal devices to do the job.

Why are babies motivated to engage in such communicative exchanges? Is it just because they want to get something? Achieving material ends is only part of the story. Babies do not communicate, or later talk, simply to get what they want. They communicate and talk because they want to share what's on their mind. The little child desperately tries to share her thoughts, feelings, and perceptions with others. As a child's worlds expand and she comes to understand more about events she observes or creates in the world, her motivation to share information increases. Babies want us to notice the ants that are crawling by their feet as we hustle them forward to the car. Babies want us to say the name of the bird-like thing they see moving across the sky. Babies want to hear us talk about what interests them. They want us to put into words the sights and events they have experienced—even when there is no material payoff. Parents do this all the time with children as they add words to interpret everyday experiences. Take this from our diaries when Jordan was 20 months old, although similar episodes occur between nine and 12 months as well.

Jordan was riding on his wooden giraffe on the porch. He bumped the back of his head on a chair as he got off the giraffe. He kept touching the back of his head and vocalizing, "mmmm." I didn't know what he meant. Then he touched the back of his head and the chair while still vocalizing, "mmmm" and looking at me. Finally, I figured out that he wanted me to say, "Oh, Jordan hit his head on the chair!" Once I did this he was happy.

Using nonverbal means, Jordan was quite insistent about his goals. He wanted his mother to put his experience into words. Why? Surely, it was not for the satisfaction of obtaining some material end. It may be because he wanted to know that his mother knew what happened to him. If his mother verbalized his experience, she would allow him to share the contents of his mind with her, to comment on the event that he could not comment on himself. Babies start to communicate and then to talk because they want us to understand what they are thinking. Babies want to create a "meeting of minds."

Detecting the Patterns in the Language Stream

Before babies can learn to talk, they have to be able to find words in the speech stream. This daunting task is known as *segmentation*—finding the breaks in the language stream that correspond to clauses, phrases, and words. If babies were aware of the properties of words in their native language, they could find the words more easily. But what *are* the properties that distinguish possible from impossible words? Segmentation is a problem because words (or phrases or clauses, for that matter) don't come with labels. They are not even neatly displayed in the speech stream: no commas or blank spaces show us where the words are. What is a baby to do if she wants to find more conventional words and learn how to use them?

Even without the pauses and commas, there are three rather subtle cues that babies could use to find the words in the language they hear. First, at some point babies come to distinguish between the kinds of sounds that are used in their language and the kinds of sounds that are not. For example, English, unlike Kikuyu (spoken in Africa), does not have words that contain clicks. (Try making a click by popping air with your tongue on the inside of your mouth or making the click sound associated with a horse trot.) Babies reared to speak English recognize that clicks are not used to segment the speech stream. Second, babies become sensitive not only to the types of sounds but also to the possible *order of sounds* in their native language. Polish words, for example, can start with "kto" while English words cannot. Finally, after sufficient exposure to language, babies become sensitive to the typical *rhythmic patterns* used in their native language. English speech has a kind of cadence that is different from that found in Italian or Hebrew. English has an alternating stress pattern of strong-weak syllables as in "TAble" and "REcent" and far fewer words that have a weak-strong pattern, as in "inCLUDE" or "obSERVE."

Dr. Peter Jusczyk decided to test if babies really used these cues to segment the speech that they heard. Not surprisingly, the method of choice was the Headturn Preference Procedure. The study asked whether babies could tell the difference between the sounds of two different languages. After seeing the center light blink, the test babies heard words from either English or Dutch. Why Dutch? Because its cadences are similar to those of English. Therefore, if babies could tell the difference between Dutch and English words, they must be doing so based on the *sound segments* that make up the words. Hearing Dutch would sound strange to adults because some Dutch sounds are not permissible in English. For example, Dutch uses the *r* sound very differently from the English *r*. Sometimes it sounds like a trill, sometimes like gargling, and sometimes like gathering phlegm. Also, in Dutch words may start with sound sequences like *kn* and *zw*, and English does not. At what age do babies become sensitive to such differences?

By nine months of age Harry and his Dutch counterpart Hans could already distinguish between English and Dutch. Harry turned his head more to listen to the speaker that played English words while his Dutch friend Hans preferred to hear Dutch. At six months of age, babies are still clueless, showing no preference for words pronounced in their native language. These are impressive capabilities, since the average nine-month-old is babbling and producing no words.

The skeptical reader could say, however, that Dutch Hans and American Harry are just making a gross analysis of the languages. Perhaps they are listening for sounds they've heard before. What would be even more impressive is showing that Hans and Harry are also sensitive to the *sequences of sounds* that are possible (or not possible) in their native language. Answering this question would address the second point raised above: Do babies notice the order of the sounds in their native language?

How was this more refined ability tested? Researchers came up with words in English and Dutch that did not include "illegal" sounds in either language, yet included *sequences* of sounds that are permitted in only Dutch or English. That is, the sounds were all the same but the *order* of the sounds was different. Could nine-month-olds isolate the sound patterns of their native language?

Yes, indeed, Hans, Harry, and other nine-month-old babies went beyond merely noticing sounds to noticing the sequences of sounds. A further study showed that Hans and Harry were *really* listening to the sequences of sounds and not simply distinguishing between English and Dutch based on differences in the cadences (however slight) of the two languages.

Why are these findings about the capabilities of nine-month-olds important? Knowing the many possible sound combinations that can occur in her language gives a baby a leg up in finding the breaks between the words. The nine-month-old pattern detector has an enormous advantage over the six-month-old in finding words in the stream of speech. Experts can now say with some conviction that by the time babies are all of nine months old, they are performing *statistical analyses* of the language they hear. Through this knowledge they can figure out that "bigbaby" must be two words, "big" and "baby," and not three words, "bi," "gba," and "by." The sounds "gba" never occur together in English. By knowing the possible sequences of sounds, infants discover where words begin and end.

A remarkable study carried out at the University of Rochester substantiates this claim. Picture Emily, using the Headturn Preference Procedure, listening for two minutes to a meaningless, continuous sequence of sounds said in a monotone like, "bidagola." She is then given a chance to listen to new sequences of sounds, some of which conform to the sequence of sounds possible from the original sequence and some of which do not. Does Emily prefer to hear the new words that preserved the probabilities she heard before? Indeed, Emily and her peers preferred to listen to new "words" that conformed to the original sequence. With a mere two minutes of exposure, she had performed enough statistical analysis to accomplish the task.

The question then becomes: can babies use the third cue for finding words—stress patterns? English uses what is referred to as a strong-weak alternating pattern, as in the noun version of "RECord." Maybe infants recognize that in their language most of the words have a strong-weak pattern. If they do, they might assume that words start with the strong syllables that they hear in the flow of speech. Would nine-month-old babies prefer to listen to two-syllable English words that followed the predominant strong-weak stress pattern (as in "LOOny" and "PLIant") or would they be just as likely to listen to the less frequent weak-strong stress pattern as in "aBLOOM" and "comPLY"? In one study, English-reared Harry and his nine-month-old American peers preferred to listen to the list composed of strong-weak words, the predominant stress pattern of words in English. However, at six months of age, Harry and his younger friends didn't care which list they heard.

Taken together, these findings reveal remarkable sensitivity in nine-month-olds to the cues that reveal words. These findings also show the lower limit of this ability. Some important development between six and nine months of age allows infants to analyze speech into the language units called words. They attend to those cues—the sounds, the order of the sounds, and the stress patterns—to locate the building blocks of language. Babies are also storing the words that they find so that they can put them to use later on. It's as if babies are working hard to create a store of words that can later be infused with meanings.

The Decline in Distinguishing Among the Sounds of the World's Languages

As noted in chapter 1, babies must be prepared to learn any language. Adults no longer have this capability, as those who have studied a second language after puberty can attest. Native speakers can hear distinctions that you cannot. After much practice, these distinctions may become clear to you, but you still make mistakes. For example, adult Japanese who are learning English have trouble distinguishing the *r* sound in "rate" from the *l* sound in "late." They make many mistakes on this because Japanese does not use this distinction, just as English does not use the three different kinds of *d* sounds in Hindi.

Shortly after birth, Japanese babies can tell the difference between the sounds *r* and *l*, just as American babies can tell the difference between the three Hindi *d* sounds. Around nine or ten months of age, however, as Hans and Harry are analyzing their own languages' sound, sound sequences, and stress patterns, they become less sensitive to sounds not found in their native language. By ten months Japanese babies no longer notice the difference in our words "rate" and "late" because these sound differences have no significance in their language. This loss of sensitivity to the complete menu of sounds in the world's languages is a robust finding. In fact, this loss of the ability to tell the difference between (and then produce) non-native sounds is one of the main reasons that babies are better language learners than we are as adults.

It makes sense that just as babies are mining the statistical regularities in their native language, they lose some of their sensitivity to sounds they do not hear spoken. One explanation is that the statistical computations they do result in noting that non-native sounds occur with zero frequency. Why hold on to information that is useless? Holding on to all the possible sounds in the world's languages might interfere with looking for the regularities in the native language.

Another explanation goes under the term "neurological imperialism." Baby brains are overpopulated with neurons that continue to grow rapidly until children are around two years of age. The newest literature suggests that what happens in brain development resembles pruning rather than construction. That is, we are born with more than we need, and the brain is then sculpted by experience so that neurons that are not used become dormant or are pared away. Such may be the case for language sounds. Babies might initially have neurons that respond to sounds from all the languages of the world. Experience shaves away the neurons that respond to sounds that are not heard. This helps to organize the brain around the sounds that are heard.

All of the abilities that babies demonstrate in this period seem directed at one goal—finding and learning words. Words are central to allowing babies to share the contents of their minds in more conventional ways. How close are babies to using words?

Whither the Words?

By nine to twelve months, babies have many nonverbal meanings *they* want to convey. When do they figure out that the units called words can be used to convey these meanings? When do they start to remember words and their *meanings* and not just the *sounds* of the words? By eight months of age babies are probably finding more and more words in the language stream, as they use their computational tools to segment the language stream and decipher where words begin and end. Through their sensitivity to sound patterns they can at least *find* the words in the language stream, even though they may not know what many of them *mean*.

The period from nine to twelve months is when all the excitement begins to unfold. Babies have discovered meanings they want to share; babies can remember units that for us are words. During this period babies start to put these together and find that words are receptacles for meaning that can be used as tools. Once these are put together—putting meaning into the "words" they recognize—the "words" become true words, not just sound patterns.

The child's ability to form mappings between meanings and sounds doesn't happen all at once, however. A further piece must enter the picture. Babies must not only be able to recognize and store words and their meanings, they must be able to *pronounce* them.

Getting your mouth to produce the words you wish to say is no easy task. It is not uncommon for only immediate family members to be able to understand what few words (if any) babies this age are saying. An analogy to the difficulty of pronunciation can be made with any athletic skill. In tennis, you can recognize a great backhand when you see one, but you can't necessarily produce one yourself. Years of practice are needed to produce a good backhand, especially one that can be counted on in a tough spot. So it is with producing the sounds of language; they have to work for you even when you're under emotional distress because your parents just left you with a new babysitter.

Not surprisingly, therefore, babies' ability to analyze and comprehend language greatly exceeds their ability to produce it. Every parent knows this. Ask a 12-month-old, "Where's your bunny?" and she quickly scans or crawls to the place where her treasured object is found. Scientists have been investigating to see just what babies understand at this early age, a subject addressed in detail in the next chapter, but suffice it to say that by 12 months of age, the average baby understands about fifty words! As might be expected, many of the earliest words babies understand are embedded in their familiar routines, such as feeding, bathing, dressing, and going for a walk. Words such as "drink," "eat," "kiss," "kitty," "bath," and "shoe" are early favorites, for example. Babies also understand the words that signal the little games adults play with babies. A popular game around this age is "identify the body part" and, for some reason, it seems to start with "Where's your nose?" "Nose" is among the earliest words understood, as are "patty cake" and "peek-a-boo," the openers for two other games. Things they can manipulate (such as "car," "ball," and "Cheerios") are also popular. Babies also understand words their parents and caregivers say in an attempt to avoid unfortunate situations ("no," and "don't"—often said with great urgency) as well as words that signal that the situation occurred anyway ("uh-oh").

Try This: Playing games

When babies are on the brink of talking, this is the time (as well as the last period from four to eight months) to play those repetitive games that babies so enjoy, games like "peek-a-boo," "ride-a-cock-horse" while bouncing baby on your knee, and "How big is Irving?" "Identify the body part" is another way to help build the baby's vocabulary. Toward the end of this period, babies will enjoy the attention and the language they hear in the "Where's X?" game, in which family and friends are continually mentioned by name and Irving has to point or look at each person in turn.

Of special interest in this period is that Irving will start to initiate these games, throwing a blanket over his own head, for example, to initiate the game of peek-a-boo. Babies who are capable of intentional communication can take both roles now—initiator and follower. They are beginning to feel like true conversational partners. Watch for when baby takes the lead. This will be a wonderful moment!

Scientific Sleuthing Pays Off

Lesson 1. Honor babies' communicative attempts even **before** *they are intentionally communicative.* Babies cry a lot in the first year of life. Some baby books used to recommend that babies be allowed to "cry it out," lest they become spoiled if their parents respond to every whimper. This belief was put to the test by Drs. Silvia Bell and Mary Ainsworth. Two competing hypotheses were evaluated. On the one hand, babies who get a response whenever they cry are more likely to cry since their behavior is reinforced by attention. On the other hand, babies who live in a responsive environment move on to mature forms of communication more quickly.

To test which of these views was correct, babies were followed over the course of the first year of life, and the results were quite clear. Babies whose cries got a response more frequently cried less in the last quarter of the first year of life than those who did not. What does this mean? It certainly suggests that trying to interpret babies' signals, even before they are using them intentionally to communicate, has a good effect.

Although these data are fascinating and help justify the behavior of parents who jump at their babies' every whimper (and dampen the arguments of in-laws who threaten dire results), explanations for these findings were in short supply when this study first appeared. Now, after discussing the development of intentional communication in this chapter, we have gained some insight into why babies who are responded to cry less. Responding to babies' pre-intentional communicative attempts helps them move more rapidly to intentional communication.

All babies cry some of the time, more when they are little. The difference in how much they will cry at nine to twelve months may well depend on how their parents have responded to their cries all along. Babies whose parents hear a cry and try to change the situation probably come to believe that the world responds to their distress, and that a full-blown cry is not necessary. These babies may also come to feel in control of their environment.

Some parents, in contrast, believe that all of this crying is designed to drive them nuts, to control them and to take over the house. These babies are learning that their world is not terribly responsive to their needs. Thus, the baby might believe that more subtle expressions of distress don't work. This has the paradoxical effect of reinforcing the infant's cry as a way of relieving distress. These infants will be slower to develop alternative means of expression that are at a higher level, such as eye gaze, vocalizations, and gestures as a means of obtaining their goals.

The transition between pre-intentional and intentional communication can be seen in a study on twelve mothers and their first-born infants from six to eleven months of age. The research helps show the factors in the mother-infant relationship that help babies use their vocalizations, eye gaze, and gestures as means of obtaining their goals.

First, most mothers in the study reported in the diaries they kept a number of their infants' behaviors. Eye contact, gestures such as reaching and pointing, crying, whines, screams, and babbles were all interpreted as attempts to communicate. Infants' vocalizations were particularly noted. Second, mothers' diary entries were fairly accurate in gauging their babies' level of communicative development. Mothers were shown to be fine observers of their babies' behaviors and to have a good sense of what their babies were up to communicatively. Finally, and of most relevance to our main point, mothers who imputed intention to their babies' behaviors reported that their babies engaged in intentional communicative behavior sooner than reports of babies whose mothers did not think their baby was using intentional communication. Why? Because if we interpret a behavior as communicative, we will probably respond to it differently. In other words, the attributions mothers make about their babies' behaviors influence how they respond to those behaviors. Thus, mothers are reinforcing their babies' attempts to communicate with them.

The power of attributions can be illustrated with a homespun example. What if someone you knew well ignored you on the street? If you think that the person ignored you on purpose, you would act differently the next time you saw her. You might avoid her or be very cold and subtly convey your resentment. But if you thought the person ignored you *accidentally* or because she was preoccupied, you would probably be friendly the next time you saw her. The attributions made about another's behavior—even if not always correct—have the power to influence behavior.

The babies whose parents respond learn to manipulate their parents in other ways than crying. British researcher John Shotter captured this process quite well when he wrote:

> At first, an infant clearly has little power to satisfy his own needs. But to the extent that a mother can interpret her infant's behavior as having an intention to it (no matter how vague and indefinite it may be on his part), she can help him to complete or fulfill it, and in the process "negotiate" a satisfaction of his needs with him. The child's action is thus made to eventuate in a consequence that is at least intelligible to her; and she does it by rendering herself available to him as an "instrument" or "mechanism" acting to produce a result which she feels may be "intended" in his activity.[2]

In other words, acting as if the baby's behavior is intended to communicate may ultimately make it so.

The same point can be made about parents' willingness to negotiate with their babies once intentional communication comes on the scene. When parents are willing to negotiate over the babies' "vague and indefinite intents," they implicitly send their babies two important messages. They are "telling" their babies that "yes, I believe that you really are trying to tell me something, to tell me about the contents of your mind." It is as if they are legitimizing the baby's

2. John Shotter, "The Cultural Context of Communication Studies: Theoretical and Methodological Issues," in *Action, Gesture, and Symbol: The Emergence of Language* (New York: Academic Press, 1978), 68–69.

communicative attempts. Parents are also empowering their babies to learn even better communicative devices (like words!) because babies' attempts at establishing meaning are honored and rewarded.

Crediting a baby's vocalizations and actions with meaning is the way in which parents model communication for our children. That does not mean you must now run to satisfy every need or be at the beck and call of your nine-to-twelve-month-old. Kaluli babies learn language even though their parents do not attribute intentions to them. Thus, many kinds of environments assist language growth. Within our culture, however, attributing meaning to a baby's behaviors can have important consequence for the baby's communicative development.

Lesson 2. Put my thoughts into words

Clarissa, a happy nine-month-old, has been fascinated with the realistic pictures her parents have on the walls, pictures of animals and people and country scenes. As Clarissa is carried around the house during caregiving activities, her father—attuned to Clarissa's behavior—notices that she often gives lingering glances to the pictures. He stops in midstream and talks about the pictures that Clarissa looks at. Sometimes they spend ten minutes circulating around the house moving from picture to picture.

Will Clarissa become a museum curator? Or will she just learn the names of the items in the pictures, leaving art history to someone else? It makes sense that if Clarissa's dad talks about what she is interested in, she is more likely to learn the names for these things.

Reginald likes trucks. His mother, Lynne, is certain he is obsessed. He has a fair number of cars and trucks in his toy collection, and this is always what he gravitates to first. Lynne has purchased some new toys that she intersperses with the toys already on the floor. As Reginald moves an umbrella along the floor as though it was a vehicle, she says, "No, Reginald, that's not a truck. It's an umbrella and it opens like this." She removes the umbrella from his hand and demonstrates. Reginald ignores her. He next picks up another of his trucks and begins zooming it around. Lynne ignores this activity. When he continues to play with the truck, she takes it away and tries to shift Reginald's focus to a plastic cube with cutout shapes. As she demonstrates how the shapes fit into the cube, she reprimands Reginald for trying to put another of the miniature trucks into one of the holes.

A group of researchers studied episodes like these with Clarissa and Reginald in children's homes when the babies were nine months of age. They divided mothers' behaviors with their babies into several categories. They first looked for evidence of maternal responsiveness to the baby's behaviors and whether mothers would continue to talk about what their babies were interested in. Does the parent, for example, follow up on the baby's vocalizations or exploratory acts with a verbal response, as Clarissa's father did when he labeled the pictures for her? Does the parent follow the baby's lead and comment on the baby's focus of interest? This is just what Clarissa's father did on his little art tour; as long as Clarissa wanted to see the pictures, he would stroll around the house talking about them to her. Clarissa was, then, initiating the "conversational" topic, and showing her interest in maintaining it. Dad was happy to follow her lead. The researchers first recorded and later counted up the number of times such behaviors occurred during ten minutes of free play between the mother and the baby with a set of toys they brought along.

The researchers also looked at some other parental behaviors. When the baby did not seem terribly focused on anything, did the mother attempt to engage the baby's attention on a toy by talking about it? So, if Clarissa seemed a bit tired, would her father say something like, "Oh, look, Clarissa, it's a shoe like you have!" They also looked for times when mothers failed to respond to the focus of the baby's attention as when Lynne above ignored Reginald's truck play. And they counted up the number of times mothers tried to shift the baby's focus of attention (as when Lynne tried to interest Reginald in the plastic cube). They also counted the number of times mothers gave prohibitions and restrictions, as when Lynne corrected Reginald's umbrella play.

They had mothers fill out a language inventory when the babies were nine months old and when they were thirteen months old. Even though babies don't say much of anything at nine months, and not much more at thirteen months, they usually do understand a few words and gestures like "bye bye." The question asked was if the way mothers acted with their babies at nine months was related to the size of a baby's comprehension vocabulary at thirteen months.

The results were clear. Babies at nine months whose mothers followed the baby's lead, who responded to what the baby was interested in, had larger comprehension vocabularies at thirteen months. These mothers also attempted to focus the baby's attention through language when the baby had no particular focus and who were willing to talk about the same subject for as long as the baby seemed to want to listen. On the other hand, babies at nine months whose mothers engaged in more intrusive behaviors (such as topic switching or prohibiting the baby from playing in particular ways), or who missed out on using babies' focus as an opportunity to use language, had smaller comprehension vocabularies at thirteen months.

These results suggest that parental responsiveness, in the form of following the baby's lead and honoring the baby's communicative focus, contributes to language growth. This is not surprising. Imagine that you were interested in obtaining information about a vacation spot. However, for some reason, the person you were talking to kept switching topics on you. Each time you brought up Virgin Gorda, your interlocutor found something else to talk about. Perhaps they had a painful experience at Virgin Gorda they didn't want to discuss. In any event, you would walk away having learned a lot less about Virgin Gorda than you wanted to and having heard information in which you weren't terribly interested. When what we hear coincides with what we want to know, we are more likely to remember what is being discussed. It's just the same with babies.

A note of caution: All mothers are by turns responsive and intrusive, and even intrusive mothers are not ruining their babies' lives and destining them to school failure. The differences we find in our research, though statistically significant, are really small. Sure, talking about what your baby is attending to is a way to help babies learn new words. But these behaviors are unlikely to be the difference between attending a community college and attending Harvard.

So we leave babies in Chapter 3 as they are just about to speak. They have made tremendous progress on the route to language and without showing much on the surface at all, we are now aware of all the work they are doing in analyzing the patterns of language they hear around them. They have also made tremendous progress in understanding how communicative behaviors can be used to express the contents of their minds. Now they need to harness these capabilities to start to produce the words they have found in the language stream to express the meanings they wish to convey.

Chapter 4

First Words: Getting "Hi" Between Twelve and Eighteen Months of Age

There was not a moment to lose. Miss Sullivan placed Helen's other hand over her own. Rapidly she spelled w-a-t-e-r. Again she pumped cold water from the well, causing it to pour over Helen's hand. Once more she spelled w-a-t-e-r for the child. A sudden light dawned on Helen's face. She seized the pump handle from Miss Sullivan. This time she herself pumped the water from deep in the ground. When it fell on her hands, she moved her fingers with purpose. "W-a-t-e-r," she spelled. "W-a-t-e-r," she spelled again. The teacher's face was as happy as the child's. "Helen understands!" she cried. "Before she has only copied me, but now she understands." [1]

Katharine Wilke offers a dramatic rendition of Helen Keller's accomplishment. She captures the feeling that many people have when their children break through the language barrier. The triumph of learning a first word is one of the crowning achievements of human development. Armed with a word or two as they begin their second year of life, children are ready to enrich their conversation with us. They are preparing to share the contents of their minds with us through language, no longer relying exclusively on nonverbal communication.

1. Katharine Wilke, *Helen Keller* (Indianapolis: Bobbs-Merrill, 1969), 75.

In this chapter, we lay the goundwork for the momentous appearance of the first word. Children have spent a year preparing for this achievement. They will spend many more before they reach the 52,000-word vocabularies of the average adult. With the help of scientific tools, we will chart how they begin to build their repertoire of words. At age one, children are working hard for every word that they add to their budding vocabularies. Though the average age of the first word is around 12 months, the normal range is very wide, starting about 10 months at the low end to 24 months at the high end. Once vocabulary learning starts, progress is slow and measured. At the end of this period most children have amassed about 50 words and vocabulary learning takes wing. From 12 to 18 months, children support words with gestures and abandon idiosyncratic words for more conventional forms. They, like Helen Keller, show a clear intention to communicate and learn that all things have a name.

What Does It Take to Learn a Word?

The Flowering of Vocabulary

On a warm day in the beginning of May, 12-month-old Josh and his parents were gardening in the front yard, planting azaleas and impatiens. Crocuses had just pushed through the ground along with daffodils. Josh had his own plastic tools and was bringing over each separate flower and laying it in front of his mother. The conversation was rich with discussions about where to put the flowers, how to plant the flowers, when to get the flowers. "Where should we put that flower? That is a beautiful flower, isn't it, Josh? That's right, put the flower here. Get the flower. The flower. Thank you." Josh ran to and from delivering plants to the desired location.

Amid his babbling, Josh provides an unexpected moment that brightens this already beautiful day. Josh, admiring the newly planted flowers in the garden, utters his first word—"flower."

What is it about a first word that is so enthralling? After all, children around the world learn their first word at approximately the same time. Is it really so amazing if everyone does it? In many ways, yes, for it shows what it means to be human. Even as infants, children can do something that no other animal can.

Understanding and producing first words are parts of a very complicated process. People use words so effortlessly that they often fail to realize the enormity of their accomplishment. Adults rarely see the difficulty of the task unless they are learning a foreign language, or are sitting at their computer frozen by the failure to retrieve a word that is on the "tip of my tongue." Thirteen to 18-month-old children, on the other hand, face these hurdles every day. Somehow they plow through the mass of language coming at them to find the words in the stream of speech, and to figure out what these words could possibly mean given the vast array of objects, actions, and events that are present when the words are said.

> Curly-topped, vivacious 16-month-old Allison has about ten words to her credit. She notices her older brother is wearing slippers one night. She looks into her mother's eyes and points at her brother's feet. Her mother is more than happy to oblige, "Yes, those are Jordy's slippers." Then Allison points at the plastic toe-capped feet of her Dr. Denton's. Her mother again rises to the occasion and says, "No, those aren't slippers. They're pajamas." Now whenever Allison hears "pajamas" she points at her plastic toe-capped pajama feet!

There is so much going on when a word is heard and so many opportunities for misinterpretation. These errors can be charming—worth an entry in the baby book—and we often fail to notice them. Consider, for example, all the pitfalls that Josh avoids, or to put it more positively, all the things that Josh knows when he uses the word "flower." He knows that the word "flower" goes with a particular object in the world. He also knows that "flower" refers only to the flower and not to those things that are seen with the flower like the shovel and the dirt that always occur with the flower. Josh could have easily assumed that the word meant the entire scene. Josh also interpreted "flower" to mean the entire flower, and not just the green leaves that surrounded the flower or the stamens in the middle of the flower. Josh used the word "flower" for other flowers of different colors, differently shaped leaves, and less visible stamens, as shown in the next example.

At twelve months and one week, Josh took his word to new heights. He walked into the living room, and atop the piano he saw a bouquet of dry beige flowers that were part of the decor. Josh pointed toward the piano and said, "flower." His mother thought he was incorrect and was straightening him out in a gentle way. "No, honey, that's a pian—" when she noticed that the bouquet was there. "You're right!" she quickly added as she went on to repeat the term. "Flower, that's a flower!"

Later that week while in the bedroom, Josh pointed at a tissue box and said "flower" when he noted the floral pattern on the box. He then said, "flower" when he saw pictures of flowers that made up the pattern on the bedspread. And even more impressive, "flower" was uttered at night when he looked out the window toward the garden— even though in the dark he could not see any flowers. "Flower" became his favorite expression used while reading the *Pat the Bunny* book, which invites readers to "smell the flowers" and while cruising in the car and looking out on suburban lawns. Josh's new word set the theme for play group as he meticulously pointed out every flower in anyone's home. Never before had his parents realized that there were so many opportunities to use but a single word.

In this example are several key characteristics of what scientists have defined as "real" word learning. First, Josh said "flower" with clear intention and purpose. He said the word as he pointed at the flowers. This was no off-the-cuff casual imitation of a sound pattern he heard his parents say. Josh had actually computed that "flower" referred to something specific in his environment.

Second, if we could hear Josh, we would notice that the term "flower," although not perfectly pronounced (in fact, it sounded more like the word "flare"), was the best rendition of the term that Josh was capable of uttering given his limited ability to produce all of the sounds of English.

Third, and finally, scientists would consider Josh's word "real" because it was used consistently and was no longer bound to a single context. Josh applied his word widely and used it often. Once Josh can use a word with intent, with good pronunciation and consistently without context he has entered into a new era in language learning.

The Stars and Stripes and Other Symbols

"Flower" is a symbol. It sounds so fancy to say that a baby who can't yet be trusted alone in a room for more than 15 seconds learns to use *symbols,* but that's exactly what real words are. A symbol is something that stands for or represents something else. A country's flag is a symbol since it stands for that country. In the same way, the golden arches have come to stand for McDonald's. Symbols are used all the time in film and literature. As we watch two characters becoming more and more cozy on screen, and the camera pans to a roaring fire in the fireplace, we know we're missing out on a hot love scene. The roaring fire is the symbol for the passion that follows.

Obviously, these are not the kinds of symbols babies will come to appreciate for a long time. But language's stock and trade is in symbols, and this is exactly what Josh is learning to use. He is becoming aware (unconsciously, of course) of the fact that a sound sequence ("flower") symbolizes a concept (the concept of a flower). Josh is learning that by saying "flower" he can call up the concept in another's mind even when they can't see a single flower (as when he looked out into the garden at night and said "flower"). Josh is also learning that a word does not sound like what it stands for. Other than onomatopoeic words like "buzz" or "swoosh"—of which there are only a few in any language—babies have to learn that *arbitrary* sound sequences stand for concepts. Interestingly, many babies' first "words" are animal noises (such as "woof woof") that are often used by adults and babies as though they were names for these animals. Since animal noises *sound like* what they stand for, they are probably easier for babies to learn than words like "dog" which bear an entirely arbitrary relationship to what they represent.

Around the time that Josh and his peers say their first words, they are showing evidence that they are beginning to use *nonlanguage* symbols. One of the first ways babies act symbolically is when they reveal a sense of humor. When babies make "jokes" by pretending to do something, they are distancing themselves from the real activity. Activities done for pretend, with a twinkle in the eye, are showing that they can do an action that stands for something else. For example, the psychologist Jean Piaget noted that at around a year of age his daughter Jacqueline saw a fringed cloth that reminded her of her blanket. She immediately grabbed the cloth, put her thumb in her mouth, lay down laughing hard, and blinked her eyes as if alluding to sleep. Jacqueline was making a joke! She was using the props and actions of sleep as a symbol for sleeping. The second means of symbolic activity is when babies use familiar objects in pretend ways in their play. So when Dagmar feeds her stuffed dog a truck, or Jamie uses a stick as if it were a telephone, holding it to his ear and chattering to grandma, they are both acting as if the pretend object is a symbol for the real one. In this period, babies are just beginning to do pretend play, and behaviors like these mean the symbolic use of words is not far off.

Try This: Comics in the crib?

Now that you know that babies can use symbols in their play even before they have any words, it's time to keep your eyes open for just such episodes. The humorous episodes will probably jump out at you because, after all, the baby is doing them for your benefit, trying to make you laugh with their "joke." The episodes in which the baby substitutes one object for another are more subtle since they occur during the baby's quiet play to fill a need the baby has to call up some concept for which they don't have the correct prop. But you will notice these now because you are prepared to look for them. It will be interesting to see how the appearance of such symbolic activities predicts the age of the baby's first words.

The Fertile Path to Real Words

Word learning is part of a continuum. By the time Josh learned his first word, he had already experimented with linking sounds to meanings. The first real words, however, are different than the protowords that have come before. Protowords are idiosyncratic, invented words, even if used with a consistent meaning, and are recognized only by the baby's immediate circle. Parents or caregivers know that when Josh says, "nuhnuhnuh," it means that he wants something. Protowords, linking sounds to meanings, represent a breakthrough in Josh's recognition that sounds can be used to convey specific meanings.

Existing alongside protowords are *context-bound words.* These look and sound like real words, and anyone who speaks the language has a chance of understanding them, but they aren't real words either. Why? Because they are bound to a specific context. It would be as if you learned the word "carburetor" but you could only use it to name your own carburetor as the car's hood was being lifted. Did you really learn the word if you could use it only in one specific circumstance?

This is exactly what children do with some of their earliest words. Twelve-month-old Adrienne, for example, used the word "duck" only in a single situation: when she put the duck on the ledge of the bathtub. When she saw a duck in picture books or among her playthings, she never used the word. Was "duck" really naming the object, or was it naming the entire event of putting the duck on the ledge? Early in word learning, before babies understand that words label categories of objects, they may have to hear "duck" used to name more than one type of duck in more than one type of situation. Once children have learned some words, however, they figure this out for themselves and start using words in a contextually flexible way.

As the diagram below shows, children move into real word use slowly. Unless the process is studied systematically, it is easy to miss the steps along the way. What starts out seeming like a single event ("Josh said 'flower'!") is actually an accomplishment that Josh has been building up to over the course of the entire first year of life. Josh first started with babbling—word-like sounds with no obvious meaning at all. He then proceeded to protowords, idiosyncratic words with consistent meanings, to context-bound words. Simultaneously with protowords and context-bound words, babies are also starting to say some real words—because they are making important discoveries about how words work.

No Words → Protowords → Context-Bound Words → Real Words
(invented;   (bound to a single   (context-free;
consistent meaning)   context)   label categories)

The path to word development is now clearer, but some cases still are unclear. Josh's mother sees a cow and says, "What does the cow say?" Josh proudly announces, "Moo!" Did he say a real word? How about the sound that a car makes? Every time that Josh sees a toy car or truck he goes, "vrrmmm vrrmmm." Clearly, "moo" and "vrrmmm" meet some of the criteria for a word. Unlike protowords, they are not totally idiosyncratic and only understood by those the child interacts with; everyone knows a cow says "moo." They are used in a context-free way (that is, to a range of cars and trucks and to a range of cows) to label categories of objects. They also have a consistent meaning.

Researchers agree on four characteristics of real words. A word is real when:

1. The same word is used consistently to signal the *same meaning*. In other words, a baby can't use "shoe" to mean "shoe" one day and then call a shoe "chair" the next day. Names for things must remain constant.

2. The word the baby uses approximates the sound of the *conventional word* used by the family (protowords such as "mmmmm" to mean "I want food" no longer count).

3. The word is spoken with the *intention to communicate* and not just as something the baby is immediately imitating.

4. The word is used in a *variety of settings* to name items of the same type that the child had not heard anyone name before. In other words, the word is no longer bound to a single context.

Whether babies express language using their hands (sign language) or using their mouths, these criteria for the use of the first real words apply.

Try This: Creating a diary of protowords and first words

This is a good time to begin a diary of your baby's vocabulary. Capture the special moments when your baby first begins to say *protowords* and then words. Protowords don't last too long, but they will bring back fond memories as your child grows up. You'll enjoy watching how, as your child develops, he turns these protowords into real words. Just keep the diary in an easily accessible place and jot down the protowords as they emerge. You'll want to write down the context too so that you can pinpoint the meaning of these protowords. However, not all babies develop protowords; some start out using real words. If that's what your baby does, you'll be ready with your diary to catch that first real word.

What advantages are there to saying real words, aside from the obvious fact that now the baby can more easily express his wants and ideas? What do real words enable Josh to do that he couldn't do before?

Communicating Efficiently

When a baby masters her first real word, she makes an enormous mental leap. She shows us that she has learned that language has two purposes: to communicate *and* to represent objects, actions, and events in her mind. We are the only species on this planet to have one system—language—that accomplishes both of these goals. This is not to say that other species cannot communicate or form mental concepts of their world. They can. The difference between humans and other animals is that animals don't communicate *about* these representations. That is, even without language, other species have the ability to remember the things, events, and spatial terrain they encounter in their world, and to form categories of these instances. These abilities are essential for survival. If a rat didn't remember where the hole to its nest was, it would wander aimlessly and its pups would die. If the giraffe didn't form a category of inedible plants, it would poison itself. If the warthog didn't remember the smell and sight of a leopard, it would be a leopard's next meal. While these species can form mental concepts of their environment, and while each has a way of communicating to other members of the same species, only humans can use their communication system to talk about their environment. In other words, humans can talk about what's in our heads. We can tell someone how to get to the next tree, where to find the best wild berries, and the importance of avoiding the red-ant hill to the left of the path. And language frees us *temporally*. Language allows us to talk about what we might encounter in the future or the past. It frees us spatially by allowing us to communicate about what we might face down the road. Most animal communication systems allow animals to comment only on the present.

Bees may be the exception. Despite the fact that they appear to be in chaos milling around in their hives, bees are not moving randomly at all. They are using dance to communicate with their hive mates about where to find the next source of nectar. Orienting their bodies with respect to the sun as they dance signals direction; the speed of their tail waggle signals the richness of the source of nectar; and the length of the dance signals the distance from the hive. This research, which garnered a Nobel prize for Karl Von Frisch, shows that bees are remarkably accurate in interpreting their hive mates' dances. Nonetheless, as astounding as this communication system is, it is really quite limited. Bees cannot point out landmarks, or comment on the lateness of the hour, or suggest that yesterday's nectar will not compare in taste to the present batch. We can do all this and more.

Real words give babies great power to talk about the categories of objects and events they have formed from their interactions with the world. Language therefore offers great economy. "Flower" allows us to communicate effectively and efficiently without knowing the names of all the individual types. Perhaps this is why children in this period sometimes call all men "Daddy." They surely know that the man walking down the street is not their father. Yet they see that these "daddies" have something in common and that a word ("daddy") can be used to represent an entire category (large males).

Pointing out and talking about categories affords humans an

enormous advantage. We can name things that we have never encountered before, just as Josh did when he said "flower" of the flowers on the tissue box. We can say that we are sitting on a "couch" in our friend's house, even though this couch looks nothing like the first couch at grandma's house when we learned the word. A little later in development, language allows us to make quick inferences about novel things we encounter or are told about. If I tell you that a "zorch" is a kind of flower, you already know all kinds of things about zorches without ever having seen one—it is probably a color other than green, it uses photosynthesis, and it grows in the ground, among many other things.

Also observing the way your *culture* uses words provides access to categories you wouldn't have without these words. For example, the Eskimos have over a hundred words for snow, given its importance in their environment. A child sorting out the differences that these hundred words capture is surely learning a great deal about the features that distinguish different types of snow. In another culture, some Aborigines in Australia use the language Dyirbal, which has a category including "women, fire, and other dangerous things." Think of the insight children gain into the way their culture thinks by learning which items language classes together!

Try This: Tracking the use of the baby's first ten words

The most celebrated method for watching the process of language development up close is to keep a diary of your baby's first ten words and how they change in use over the course of development. This is truly the period in which to do this since once vocabulary takes wing, it becomes difficult to keep up with the number of words that your child will acquire. If you revisit these entries every month, you will be able to chart changes in your child's progress.

For each word you enter, answer the following questions: What is the word? How is it pronounced? Just write what it sounds like—no fancy phonetic symbols are needed. Did your child intend to communicate through the use of the word? If so, what was the baby trying to tell you? What was the context in which the word was used? Is it a protoword—with a wholly idiosyncratic form? You will not be able to tell if the word is context-bound or a real word until you hear your child use it several times. Then record whether the word appears only in a single context or is a real word, used to label a category of objects in a context-free way. It is interesting to see how and whether your baby's use of these words changes month by month.

Make sure to do this for all your children because it will allow you to look at the individual differences within a single family. It is truly remarkable that we can have children who come from the same parents and yet who develop so differently.

"Home Signs" and "Baby Signs"

Astonishingly, first words emerge even when babies find themselves in a language desert. A project at the University of Chicago studied a group of ten deaf children who were born to hearing parents. Because these children could not hear, and because their hearing parents did not know how to use sign language, these babies had no language models. Furthermore, these families were discouraged from using sign on the theory that these children could be taught to rely on lip reading once they were enrolled in a deaf school with an oral approach. Nonetheless, language burst forth from these children in the form of "home signs" in the midst of a language vacuum. Children spontaneously developed two kinds of signs: "Indicators" (such as pointing) that the child used to refer to people, places, and things in the immediate context; and "characterizing" signs, used to refer to actions and properties of objects. An example of a sign for an action is holding a fist to the mouth and making a chewing motion. The child uses this sign to mean "eat." An example of a sign for a property of an object is holding the index finger and thumb in the air while forming a circle. The child who invented this sign used it to mean "round." In combining an indicator sign with an action sign, a child might point to the food on the table and sign "eat." When the researchers examined the kinds of signs parents used, they found that the parents could not have taught their children signs since they were not as good at producing them as their children! What do these amazing findings mean? They imply that language is irrepressible in the human species. Just as spiders spin webs, humans develop language—even if they hear no language themselves.

If babies can invent their own signs, perhaps we should expect that babies can use signs for concepts even before they can say much at all. This is exactly what Drs. Linda Acredolo and Susan Goodwyn have argued in their book called *Baby Signs*. While in a doctor's waiting room, Dr. Acredolo's 12-month-old baby Kate spied an aquarium.

She toddled over to it, pointing excitedly, and made a blowing gesture with her mouth as if she were blowing out candles on a birthday cake. It seemed that Kate was using blowing as a sign to stand for the fish in the tank. Linda couldn't figure out why blowing would stand for the concept of fish until later that night. She then realized that she and Kate took turns each night blowing the fish on a fish mobile over Kate's crib as Linda commented on how the fish were swimming.

Kate also used a sniffing sign for "flower" and a finger-rubbing sign (from the "Itsy Bitsy Spider" song) for "spider." When her parents realized what she was doing, they decided to play along and found other gestures (such as wiggling a finger for "caterpillar") that Kate could use. When they saw how easy this was for Kate, and how her language was blossoming right alongside the use of these signs, Drs. Acredolo and Goodwyn conducted a full-scale research project with 140 families to see if other babies could also be taught signs, and whether it would hinder or promote their word production. The researchers found many advantages to teaching babies these kinds of signs. For one, parents reported that it was wonderful to be able to communicate with their babies and that the babies seemed less frustrated because they could get their ideas across. When language skills were tested, babies in the families who had been encouraged to teach their babies signs were advanced in language, in intelligence tests, and in their play. Moreover, the babies who had been taught baby signs on average knew about fifty more real words at the age of 2 compared to their nonsigning peers.

Why did learning signs accelerate babies' language development? You might think that having a sign for a concept and being able to communicate about that concept would slow down the baby's progress toward words. Or, perhaps the adults who knew the signs the baby was using would use language to them less. The researchers found that parents and caregivers always accompany their signs with language or use language to comment on the baby's use of a sign. Imagine a mother and toddler on a springtime walk in the park and the baby noticing some flowers in bloom. As the baby makes her "sniff-sniff" sign for flowers, it seems natural for the mother to say, "Oh, yes, see the pretty flowers!" Babies who have signs have a way of calling attention to things they want to talk about. Therefore, teaching babies signs gives them a way to express their thoughts and to hear the conventional words that adults use to say the same thing.

It is important to say that these baby signs are not the same kind of signs that deaf speakers who use a sign language employ. Real sign language signs do not look like what they stand for, or resemble the actions performed with the objects (like the baby sign "sniff-sniff" for "flower"). Real sign language signs are much more abstract, and you'd have a hard time figuring out what they mean by watching them being performed. In addition, real sign language has an entire set of grammatical rules which the deaf child must learn to convey meanings that are longer than a single word. Baby signs are not a substitute for language at all. They just help the child ford the transition between babbling to speech and real words. And, because they are more likely to resemble what they stand for, they are intermediate between protowords (invented words) and real words (or real signs) which bear no resemblance to what they stand for.

Try This: Can my baby learn some baby signs?

If you are serious about teaching your baby some baby signs, you really should buy the book *Baby Signs*. In that book, the authors suggest that you start introducing baby signs as soon as she seems to want to talk about things. An increased interest in people and things around her is the signal that she is ready. Introduce a small number of signs. Bye bye and nods for yes and no are good introductions that may already be in your baby's repertoire. With that minimal start, you can then move to what the authors refer to as "surefire winners," the signs for "hat," "bird," "flower," "fish" and "more." They make the following recommendations for the parent who wants to try teaching their toddler baby signs:

Hat	Pat the top of your head with your hand open and your palm down.
Bird	Flap one or both arms out to the side like a bird's wings
Flower	Make a sniffing gesture with a wrinkled nose as if smelling
Fish	Open and close your lips, smacking like a fish does
More	Tap the index finger of one hand into the opposite palm

Remember that the more often the baby sees the signs, the more likely she is to learn and use them. See if your child picks up on these signs. If she does, you can go on to add new ones that spring from the natural gestures that you and your baby use.

Symbols, Categories, Meanings, and Emotions

"Dog," Not "Dalmatian"; "Hat," Not "Baseball Cap": Why Babies Prefer Some Words over Others

What are the kinds of words that appear first? You will not be surprised to learn that words such as "drink," "eat," "kiss," "kitty," "bath," and "shoe" are early favorites. Why? One reason is that these are objects and activities that the baby frequently encounters and hears adults saying. Another reason is the way that adults talk to babies. Consider the following dialogue between Nancy and her 13-month-old son Keith as they flip through a zany baby book with no words:

> See the *doggie*, Keith? Oh, he's so cute! He looks like the dog that Mr. Owen has, doesn't he? And there's a *car*! The doggie is driving a *car*! What is the doggie wearing? A *hat*! The doggie looks funny, doesn't he, Keith? The doggie is driving a *car* and wearing a *hat*!

Typical? Absolutely. However, if Nancy were to describe this picture to another adult, the description would be very different. Nancy would say something like, "A Dalmatian is sitting in the driver's seat, driving a jeep. He's wearing a baseball cap put on backward." For Keith she emphasized the key words, often putting them at the end of the sentence and saying them with heavy stress. This makes these words stand out for Keith and easier to remember.

Also different is the level of specificity she used when speaking to another adult, referring to the dog as a "Dalmatian," the car as a "jeep," and calling the hat a "baseball cap." Why didn't Nancy say these words to Keith? Nancy, like other adults, uses words to babies that are at the "basic level." The famous Berkeley-based psychologist Eleanor Rosch came up with the idea that concepts can be talked about at three different levels of specificity: (1) the *subordinate* level (for example, "Dalmatian") is the most specific because it names a subtype of dog; (2) the *basic level* (for example, "dog"); and (3) the *superordinate* level (for example, "animal"), which groups all kinds of animals (dogs, cats, worms, etc.) together with a single word.

Basic-level words have several unique properties compared to words at the other levels of specificity. Basic-level words emphasize the *commonalities* of items in a category as opposed to their differences. For example, dogs around the world have a tremendous amount in common. They all have four legs, a face, eat meat, run and jump, and most have fur. "Dalmatian," on the other hand, names a type of dog that has a particular characteristic (its black and white coloration) that sets it apart from other types of dogs. Doesn't it make sense that a baby needs to learn the word "dog" before we teach them the word for the subtype at the subordinate level ("Dalmatian")? On the other hand, calling a single dog "animal" is too broad and doesn't capture the uniqueness of the dog category.

Basic-level words capture those categories that are easiest for babies to carve out of the flux and flow of events in the world. Furthermore, basic-level words are shorter. Words that are more specific—like "baseball cap" or "Dalmatian" are usually longer than basic-level words and sometimes have phrasal names (as in "baseball cap") composed of more than one word. Simple intuition (and research!) tells us that it is easier for babies to learn shorter than longer words.

Basic-level words also capture commonalities in *function* for inanimate objects. Basic-level words depict the general things done with all members of the category. For example, we put *hats* on our heads. We drive in *cars*. We put our *shoes* on our feet, whether they are sneakers, boots, or high heels.

How conscious are parents of introducing basic-level words to babies before using words at other levels? Consider the following episode: In the supermarket with 15-month-old Amanda, Elaine saw a policeman and was about to say "See the policeman?" when she decided not to. Why? Because Elaine remembered that Amanda still couldn't say "man." Without knowing anything about the different levels of words just described, Elaine made a decision about introducing a subordinate-level word ("policeman") to Amanda before Amanda had learned the basic-level word ("man"). Parents, at least some of the time, think about what it would be best to call something to their language-learning baby. Scientific study tells us that among the options, basic-level names win hands down.

Not only do babies start out with basic-level words for objects. Around the world, babies' early vocabularies contain predominantly object words. Object words are easier for babies to get a "hand on"— literally!—than words from other parts of speech. Although objects can look different under different lighting, the fact that they can be touched and manipulated seems to make them easier for babies to understand. Frequently encountered liquids which can be seen in containers and carted around by the baby in bottles and sippy cups also have an advantage. "Juice" is an early favorite. Few, if any, babies acquire adverbs early, even easy ones like "fast," although children do learn "more" very early. Babies acquire a few adjectives (like "yucchy" or "dirty") among their first words as well. Overall, though, adverbs and adjectives capture concepts with vague boundaries compared to object and liquid words. They name concepts that are relative. How soiled does something have to be to be called "dirty"? How fast is "fast"? But a dog is a "dog" whether it's a Dalmatian or a chihuahua.

Babies may also have some action words like "run" and "dance" in their first word vocabularies. How do babies learn words like these? Although they are not relative concepts like adverbs and adjectives, they still require some thought to apply. For example, consider a simple early verb like "dancing." Is it dancing when the baby herself dances *and* when grandpa dances a hora with grandma *and* when big sister Abby dances ballet? These all look so different. Furthermore, when dancing is over, it's over, even though it is a repetitive action. That's different from using the word "truck"; the truck sits before you, visible, even though it may now be in a different location. And what part of dancing is dancing? Is it the way the legs move? The way the arms move? Or is it the whole ball of wax? No wonder verbs come into children's vocabularies more slowly than nouns.

Try This: What kinds of words are my baby's first ten words?

Is your baby starting out by using basic-level words? Go down the list for the ones that are object names and see if you can classify each word as to its level of specificity. Also, has your baby begun with predominantly object words before they acquire words of other types? Examine your child's first ten words, classifying them now as to the type of thing they name. Are they mostly object names (nouns)? Are there any action names (verbs)? Any comments on actions (adverbs)? Any properties of objects (adjectives)? And how many are proper names for people or pets (also nouns)?

Babies start out with names they hear most frequently from their parents and caregivers. Can you notice what you call something when you are teaching your baby a new word? Is the new word you offer more often than not a name at the basic level, as the research indicates? Or do you find yourself using more specific, subordinate-level names and broader, superordinate-level names just as frequently as basic-level names? Relate what you have found about your own speech to what kinds of words your baby uses most often.

How Do Meanings and Words Come Together?

Ask a person on the street how a child learns words, and the person will say, "Well, the parent points to an object and says its name." This is followed by a shrug of the shoulders as if to say, "Why are you asking me this? This is too obvious." Sorry, but there's nothing simple about the process of learning words. Linking objects, let alone actions or properties, to the words that go with them is a difficult task that we take for granted.

Some scientists agree with the person on the street. The social world paves the way for success in linking objects and words. Consider, for example, the way Nancy talked to Keith about the picture of the Dalmatian driving the car. Couldn't Keith learn the word "dog" through an interaction like that? When mothers follow their babies' focus of attention and name what the child has in mind, they have created a surefire recipe for word learning. But is this all it takes? Such a theory presupposes that all children are born into societies like our own where adults label everything for babies.

The problem of linking a word to a meaning is more complicated than it first appears. To illustrate this problem, we introduce a now famous rabbit named Gavagai. Gavagai is an invention of philosopher Willard Quine. The Gavagai problem goes something like this:

> Imagine that you are a visitor in a foreign land. A rabbit scurries by and you hear a native proclaim, "Gavagai." Just a few minutes later, a rabbit scurries by again and the native repeats, "Gavagai, Gavagai." You are determined to learn the language and record in your little notebook with some confidence that "gavagai" does indeed mean "rabbit" and you go about your day.

But how confident should the visitor be in making her bold assertion about what "gavagai" means? Why does she suppose that "gavagai" refers to the rabbit rather than to the ground upon which the rabbit scurries and the scurrying rabbit? Why assume that it refers to the whole rabbit rather than to the ears or the tail? Why assume that the native is labeling the rabbit rather than praying to it as the culture's deity? The link between language and objects—let alone between objects and actions—is hypothetically pretty daunting. We say "hypothetically" because babies like Josh don't seem to try out many different meanings for each word. So what's going on?

A number of scientists have argued that babies are not left weeding through an infinite number of possible meanings for each word they encounter because they make some fundamental assumptions about how words work. They come to these assumptions by observing how people actually use words and from their knowledge of the world. For example, children could not make much progress in word learning if they did not assume that a word represents or goes with an object. Further, a word does not stand for the concept of the object *and* the surface upon which the object rests; nor do object names stand for the name of the object *and* other objects that it is frequently seen with. Finally, the baby assumes that words they hear label the *whole* object and only the object, not the object parts. Why does the child act as though words label objects? And why does the child act as though words label the whole object? No one is really sure. Experts think the assumptions babies make about words come out of their understanding of the world. Babies don't have to see their whole bottle if it is partially hidden by the milk carton on the kitchen table to know that they are seeing their bottle. And babies don't have to see you pick up the book on their dresser to know that the book and the dresser are two different objects. Fortunately, babies seem to bring their object knowledge to the word-learning game.

Saying Your First Words: A Sobering Task

It takes a lot of energy and cognitive wherewithal to say a word, especially at the start of word learning. Consider 14-month-old Ben as he builds a block tower with Felicia, his mother:

> Felicia gets a red block and hands it to Ben. "There you go," she says. Ben takes the block, places it carefully on the tip of the tower. He then knocks the tower down. He smiles and then appears to get very serious as he looks at the tumbled blocks. "Down!" he notes with finality. Then a smile returns to his face.

Ben is coordinating his emotional expression with his newfound language ability. Notice the momentary lapse in his mirth. We can almost see him thinking as he assembles the word he is going to say. His smile drops from his face, as if he cannot both utter a word and smile at the same time.

This is in fact the case. Research shows that children at the start of word learning cannot both talk and express emotions at the same time. Dr. Lois Bloom and her students videotaped fourteen babies at play with their mothers for hour-long sessions, beginning at nine months of age and continuing until the babies produced simple sentences. The researchers then spent hours and hours coding their videotapes in minute detail looking for, among other things, the relationship between language and emotional expression. The results of this painstaking research demonstrate how much effort it takes for babies to produce their first words. The average age for the first word in this study was 13.8 months, though in many others the first word appears around 12 months of age. The researchers found that children's faces took on a sober look between two and eight seconds before they said a word. Why? Let's go back to Ben. In the time just before he said "down" triumphantly, he was working on two things: constructing the meaning he wanted to express (blocks fell down) and trying to recall and say the word that commented on the meaning (was it "up"? No, it's that other one . . . "Down!"). First words require cognitive energy. A child has to expend his energy on the emotional expression or on the word—but not on both.

This inability to express emotion and talk at the same time doesn't last long. By the time children are comfortable producing words, they say their words with much positive emotion. As if in anticipation of being able to express their ideas, babies show a steady increase in positive emotion, which peaks just around the time the word comes out. Ben at 19 months will have a totally different reaction as he knocks the tower down. He looks positively gleeful, and this look never leaves his face as he jubilantly utters, "Down!"

There is a relationship between the age when first words are spoken and children's expression of emotion. Common sense might lead one to believe that children who show lots of positive emotion talk sooner. This, however, is not the case. Babies who are more expressive—whether positive or negative—tend to say their first words later than those who have more neutral facial expressions. How come? Perhaps because a neutral face is associated with interest and thought. Those babies who are reflective by nature and who have long bouts of engagement with objects are discovering the meanings they wish to express. They are also probably working hard at storing words they hear and at retrieving them when they are needed to express their meanings. So one of the factors that may be associated with when a baby starts to talk may well have to do with the kind of temperament she has.

Try This: Does my baby express emotion when she talks?

Although we've already asked you to record lots of things associated with the production of the first words, we're going to suggest that you record one more thing in our burgeoning diary: What emotion—as expressed on the baby's face—accompanied the production of the first words? You need not categorize the emotion as happy, angry, sad, etc. Neither did the research team we've just described. All you need to do is decide if the baby's face looks positive, negative, or neutral. If you record this information around the time when these words are first emerging and then for this same set of words about six months later, you should observe big differences in the integration of emotion and language expression.

First Words Take Effort, More for Some Than Others

A Tale of Two Toddlers

All children, whether they speak orally or use sign language, reach the pinnacle of the first word. Yet for some children this milestone is reached when they are 10 months of age, and for others . . . parents seem to wait endlessly. Priscilla is the firstborn child of two English professors. At 12 months, she was the first to speak in her play group, greeting her fellow playmates as they came to her house, happily labeling some of the toys strewn around the rug. Edgar, another child in the play group, was 18 months old and had yet to speak his first real word. He was a big child, and when he grunted and motioned that he wanted a toy, both children and parents obeyed!

Adults have a tendency to think that Priscilla is smarter than Edgar, that the timing of the first word is an early clue to children's intelligence. It is true that children with identifiable syndromes, such as Down's syndrome, utter their first words later than do children of average intelligence. For those within the normal range, however, there is no relationship between when a child utters her first gem and her later IQ score. Many factors beyond intelligence can influence the timing of the first word. Michael's story illustrates this point.

Michael is Josh's younger brother. Unlike Josh, however, Mike has a history of ear infections. From 9 to 13 months he had one continuous ear infection. For the most part, Mike heard only muted sounds, filtered through the fluid in his middle ear from an ear infection. Ear infections are very common. They afflict about a third of all infants and toddlers. An ear infection generally lasts for about two to four weeks. Mike's infection, however, just kept on recurring. He was in a nursery school with other children, a virtual breeding ground for ear and upper respiratory infections. He also had two older siblings who were always bringing colds home from school. Early exposure to all of these colds will probably strengthen Mike's immune system later. At this point, however, he was hearing more noise than language. The result? His babbling was later than Josh's. He also was slower to talk. Mike spoke his first context-bound word at 17.5 months, saying "juice" for apple juice in an apple juice container. Not until 18 months of age could he generalize his new word to milk and to a bottle containing juice. Other words were slow to enter into his vocabulary.

At 17.5 months his mother decided to take him to the ear, nose, and throat doctor. Perchance Mike needed to have plastic tubes placed in his ears. If the tubes could drain the fluid, Mike might be able to hear better. As it turned out, he was saved by the upcoming spring weather. Mike's ears finally dried out. Within a month Mike added words like "Daddy" and "crack" (for cracker). His comprehension vocabulary grew by leaps and bounds, until he understood words like "go," "come," "stop," "drink," "eat," and "television" among many others.

While his comprehension was growing, his ability to speak still lagged behind, with the only consistent words being "Josh," "Daddy," "juice," "crack," "down," and "up." Even at 20 months, when brother Josh boasted a speaking vocabulary of 337 words, Mike had a mere 30 words. Not until 23 months did Mike truly start talking steadily.

Children, even within the same family and with the same parents, can have dramatically different language development profiles. If you were to meet both Josh and Mike at age five, you would never know that Josh had been on the fast track for language development and that Michael had trailed behind.

Name Callers and Social Sophisticates

Tony, 14 months old, is traveling with his family in Scotland. Like many boys his age, he is fascinated by vehicles. His parents label an airplane as it flies overhead, a train as it comes into the station, and the cars and trucks on the busy streets. Tony is overjoyed to have each new label and tries to work the new word into his vocabulary as soon as he can. "Ca, ca," he says with each passing car. There is never a quiet moment, even when he mistakenly but proudly announced the passing of each truck by loudly pronouncing the word with an *f* sound in place of the expected *tr*. Tony loves his role as a name caller.

Janet hears many of the same labels for cars, trains, and trucks. She, however, is more interested in the polite greetings that people use when they see each other. "Hi," she states with a smile when her mother comes into the room. "Tak you," she utters whenever she takes or is given food or a toy. Janet is not a name caller but rather a budding socialite who is more interested in using language for social interaction.

When researcher Katherine Nelson first noticed these different kinds of children, she was surprised. The composition of children's first 50 words differed enormously. Children like Tony, for example, had 38, or 76 percent, of their first 50 words that were names for things. Dr. Nelson dubbed this group the "referential" group. Children like Janet, on the other hand, might have only 17, or 34 percent, of their first 50 words as names for things. Janet had many social or personal words (such as "hi," " 'bye," "please"). Janet and her kind were known as more "expressive" children.

Tony and Janet represent two ends of the stylistic continuum. Most children sport a mix of words by the time they are 18 months of age, some words geared to social interaction and some toward labeling the environment. At one point researchers thought that there was some advantage to being a referential child. The latest research, however, suggests that both types of children will learn language equally well; these divergent paths represent temporary individual differences in learning. Both types are the same age when they reach their first 50 words.

Why do children adopt these different tacks for word learning? Two answers have been proposed. On the one hand, researchers argue that the environment shapes the learning process. Name callers are common among firstborn children of college-educated parents. These kinds of parents not only talk more, but tend to label more things in the environment for their children. On the other hand, the stylistic differences may be inherent in the children themselves. Maybe children harbor certain hypotheses about how language works. Name callers surmise that language is used to label objects in the environment. Socialites view language as a connection to others.

When examined from a scientific perspective, social expressions are not as easy to learn. They label *situations* and not concrete objects or even actions. Their use requires that the speaker appraise the situation and decide when they are appropriate to use. An adult saying "good-bye" before a conversation has really ended is considered rude, for example. Sometimes adults don't even realize that they are saying something in the same situation that our child is construing as a social word. For example, a mother who studies language development reported that her daughter thought that "phew" was a greeting. Each time the mother went into the child's room in the morning, she'd say "phew" in response to the smell of a diaper worn 12 hours. The baby thought "phew" was just a way to say "hi!" and included it among her social words.

"Hi" itself is deceptively simple. When is the word used? "Hi" is appropriate when you first see someone after an unspecified lag of time. You can use it to new people you're just meeting or to someone you already know. Is it okay to say "hi" when mom reappears after a short trip to the kitchen? Is it appropriate to use the word when you play by yourself for a while and then reestablish social contact? Is it okay to say "hi" in the supermarket to every stranger you meet? Learning a simple social word like "hi" can prove to be quite taxing.

Try This: Is my baby a name caller or a socialite? What kind of parent am I?

Once again, pull out the diary of your child's first five or ten words. Try to categorize them as names for objects versus social words. Are more than 50 percent one type or the other? The referential-expressive distinction is usually judged, however, not on the first ten words but on the first fifty words. If you are keeping track of these, you are in a position to figure out if your child has a referential or expressive orientation to language.

This discussion may also make you more aware of how you interact with your child. Do you find yourself teaching the names of objects all the time? Or do you emphasize social interaction words in your dialogue with the baby? And most interestingly, is there a relationship between the kinds of vocabulary items your baby uses and how you talk to the baby?

Word Comprehension Exceeds Word Production

Not only do babies differ in when they start talking, and in when they achieve their first ten and then their first fifty words, they also differ in how many words they comprehend. Most people believe that babies understand many more words than they can say. Consider what happened in Alicia's family to convince her parents of this fact:

> Alicia, an elfin blue-eyed 14-month-old, was playing in the family room adjacent to the kitchen after dinner while her mother and father enjoyed a late dinner together. The grown-ups were talking about a rug store that was having a sale. Dad asked Mom how she knew this, and she said, "I read it in the *newspaper.*" At that very moment Alicia stopped what she was doing and ran to the basket in the kitchen where the daily newspapers were kept. She dragged one of the sections out of the basket and brought it over to the kitchen table to her parents. Mom and Dad looked at each other in shock.

Occurrences like these are not at all unusual and go a long way toward convincing first-time parents that their babies know more words than come out. But exactly how many more words do babies understand than they can say?

The most comprehensive data on what babies can understand and say between eight and thirty months comes from a massive study funded by the MacArthur Foundation. These scientists developed a scale which tested for the presence of gestures, words, and phrases that are common among infants and toddlers. Mothers filled out a checklist that contained 396 words, 12 gestures (such as "bye bye" and "all gone"), and questions about babies' participation in games (like "peek-a-boo") and their pretend play. The scale included words for sound effects (like "baa baa"), food, drink, toys, vehicles, and actions, among others. Hundreds of mothers were asked to check off which of these gestures and words their children at different ages could *understand* and which they could both *understand and say*. Researchers validated the test by bringing mothers and babies into the baby lab and recording babies' talk. Mothers, it turns out, are quite good at estimating what their babies can understand and say. On the other hand, a little caution is needed since mothers are likely to give their babies the benefit of the doubt.

The results of this huge undertaking yielded a now widely used test for both research and assessment. Individual children are compared to the norms on the test to see if they are progressing at a "normal" rate. Though some argue that the norms for this test are high, given that most of the children were from affluent homes, this test is nonetheless a boon to the field of language development.

What was learned from this test about the relationship between the comprehension and production of early words? At 10 months of age, mothers reported that the average number of words babies can understand is about 40. This is pretty impressive given that six months will pass before most babies can say 40 words. So parental intuition is correct. Babies really can understand many more words than they can say.

A startling outcome was the large individual differences the researchers found at 10 months. The number of words babies could understand ranges from a low of 11 words for babies at the bottom 10 percent of the group to upward of 154 words for those at the top 10 percent. Although this is an enormous difference, the gap only gets bigger. At 16 months, the average number of words babies can understand is 169. But the difference between the top group and bottom groups widens considerably, with babies in the top 10 percent understanding 321 words and babies in the bottom 10 percent understanding only 92 words! This is a difference of 229 words. The differences between babies at 16 months for how many words they can *say* is even wider. The average number of words a baby can say at 16 months is 40. Yet the top 10 percent can say 180 words while the bottom 10 percent can say fewer than 10 words and in some cases none at all.

What does this test tell us about language development? First, there is a big difference between when babies can comprehend a word and when they can say it. Once again, an analogy can be drawn from a high school language class. Can you remember that it was easier by far to understand what the teacher was saying than to compose a response? A baby has far fewer resources than an adolescent or adult learning a second language. To say a word, the baby has to coordinate emotional expression with the difficult task of constructing a mental meaning and figuring out how to get her articulatory mechanism in just the right places for just the right lengths of time. Also, when you listen to someone else talk, you may not understand exactly what a word is but you do have to get it right when you say the word.

The second finding to be learned from this scale is that there are huge individual differences among babies starting to understand

and produce their first words. These differences are especially pronounced in saying words, probably for the reasons just discussed. Yet regardless of the big individual differences early on, the vast majority of children go on to learn language equally well. Experts are just beginning to understand the factors that make learning first words easier or harder for different babies.

Scientific Sleuthing Pays Off

Lesson 1: More baby talk = More baby's talk. The first and most pronounced lesson in the literature is that talking to baby is a good idea. A number of researchers find that children whose parents talk more to them tend to have larger vocabularies. This does not mean, however, that parents must bombard a child with language during every waking moment. Everyone needs some quiet time to play and reflect. But tailoring language for a baby is crucial for learning vocabulary items. For example, research has revealed that relatively more educated parents talk to their children more than parents from less educated families. The offspring from these educated families show a real advantage in learning words.

Lesson 2. There are big individual differences in the appearance of the first words. The ages at which children achieve language milestones vary widely. When large numbers of children are studied (as the MacArthur study did), critical insight is gained into what is "normal" and what should be checked out. An important finding is that the variation is less in word comprehension than in word production. Therefore, word comprehension is a good indicator of language delay. If children neither comprehend nor produce *any* words by 18 months of age, they are worth watching. Obviously, the first factor to check is the baby's ears. Has the child had some ear infections? Perhaps the child's ears and hearing need to be evaluated. Yet take note that children who comprehend many words but do not speak have a very different prognosis than children who do not understand any words.

Lesson 3. Picture book reading is a source of new words.

Sam is sitting on his mother's lap just before bed. They are both rocking gently in the rocking chair as they page through a worn copy of *Goodnight Moon.* " 'Goodnight kittens and goodnight mittens,' " Mother reads. Sam turns the page. " 'Goodnight clocks and goodnight socks.' Can you find the clocks? Where's the clock? Yes, that's very good, and where is your clock?" Sam looks around the room to find his clock and points. "Very good and you're right! And where are Sam's socks?" Sam looks toward the dresser and then points down at the page in the book. He turns the page. " 'Goodnight little house . . .' " his mother continues.

This common bedtime scene is rich in language stimulation and opportunity. One of the ways that parents help their children learn labels is by reading books to them. Research shows that it is never too early to reap the benefits of reading to children. The very fact that Sam knew to turn pages and to look for pictures in a book sets the stage for the reading skills to come.

Despite the powerful impact that early reading can have, it is alarming how many parents don't read to their children. Researchers report that a typical middle-class child enters first grade with 1,000 to 1,700 hours of one-on-one picture book reading while the corresponding child from a low-income family averages only 25 such hours. Fully 47 percent of public-aid parents of preschoolers had no alphabetic books in the home compared to only 3 percent without such books in professional families. While many of these studies are performed on children of three and four years of age, the findings from a massive number of studies are clear. The stage gets set for reading achievement for your child during infancy and the preschool years. What children learn about words as toddlers relates to later school performance. Reading provides another important route for vocabulary learning, a route that also gives parent and child a great deal of pleasure.

Lesson 4. When do you worry about a lack of words? Because of the wide variability in when children acquire their first words, most professionals are hesitant to raise warning flags. A child who does not utter his first word until 18 months is not necessarily off the normal path of development. This is particularly true if he seems to understand everything but has just decided not to talk. With these caveats in mind, the following are several clues that professionals use to earmark early language problems: avoids eye contact, rarely babbles, consistently does not respond to a whisper, shows little or no interest in imitating even the most basic of baby signs like bye bye, cries often without changing pitch or intensity, and shows little emotion both when trying to say words and when not producing words at all. In many cases, parents know best if there is really a reason for concern. If you do detect a number of these signs, consult a physician.

Scientists have amassed considerable data about the construction of the first words. As we look in on the developing human mind, we come to appreciate the intricate achievements that underlie children's production of even a single word. This is the time when you can best follow your child's progress, because the slow and laborious nature of word development in this period allows you to look closely and to capture each moment along the way. In just a few short months vocabulary will take wing, learning will go into fast-forward, and it will be much more difficult for you to keep a running diary of everything that your child is trying to tell you.

Chapter 5

Vocabulary Takes Wing:
Eighteen to Twenty-four Months

The Vocabulary Spurt

"I was diligently keeping a diary of Igor's growing vocabulary," writes Bertha from Dubuque, Iowa. "And just after he was able to say about 45 words, I noticed that something different was happening. Igor started learning new words at lightning speed. I could no longer keep up with him!"

Susan from Belgrade, Maine, reports that 18-month-old Jennifer picked up a "color and shapes" book when they were at play group. Jennifer flipped some pages and then excitedly pronounced, "wectangow" as she pointed at the green rectangle. "Now where did she learn that one?"

Some time after toddlers have learned about 50 words, around 19 to 21 months on average, the entire character of word learning changes. Vocabulary learning takes off in leaps and bounds. And, as our next example demonstrates, parents better watch what they are saying!

Two-year-old Hubert is with his mother, Sally, being interviewed for a space at the Bright Moments Nursery School. The school seems to be everything that Sally hoped for. The teachers are friendly and warm. There is a block corner and a dress-up area and a hamster for toddlers to watch. There are puzzles to play with and many toy cars—Hubert's favorite.

As Sally talks with the director, Mrs. Morgan, Hubert goes to play in the block corner with some of the other toddlers. "He looks like a happy and unusually polite two-year-old," Mrs. Morgan remarks. Sally beams. Hubert builds a high tower and is extremely proud of his work. Just as he is admiring it, however, another child in the group comes over to inspect the tower and to add just one more block. Crash! The tower comes tumbling down. With it, the entire room resounds with a loud swear word from Hubert, one he has heard his parents say many times in moments of frustration. Mrs. Morgan visibly recoils. Sally turns beet red.

During the last half of the second year, toddlers often experience an explosive period of vocabulary growth, including words their parents would wish they didn't have. The rate has been estimated at nine new words a day, 63 new words per week. It is at this time that parents may have to clean up their language. The adage "little pitchers have big ears" has come true.

In this chapter, we examine the "vocabulary spurt" or the "naming explosion." What are toddlers doing at this time? What kinds of words are they saying? How are they saying them? Are there differences between boys and girls or between firstborn and later-born toddlers in reaching this milestone? What is going on behind the scenes that allows the vocabulary spurt to occur? Scientists have studied this period extensively, since it represents such a dramatic change in the word-learning process. This period tells us a tremendous amount about the growing mind. Finally, the chapter concludes with a discussion of toddlers who reach the vocabulary spurt more slowly than their peers. We focus on red flags in early language learning and look at populations of toddlers who approach word learning in a less standard way.

Finding the Vocabulary Spurt

There are a number of definitions of the vocabulary spurt, but all share a common feature. The spurt occurs when toddlers suddenly change the rate of their word learning. At first word learning is slow, one word at a time, toddlers learning 8 to 11 words each month. Then it begins to explode at a rate of 22 to 37 words per month. Finally, the learning proceeds at such a quick pace that most parents stop trying to keep a diary at all. This sharp increase in the number of words seems to represent a new stage in development. It's as if the child's brain has decided to shift gears with respect to word learning. Hence, scientists call it the vocabulary spurt.

There is some controversy in the literature about when to expect this vocabulary spurt. Some scientists suggest that it occurs once toddlers have 30 words in their productive vocabularies. Others suggest that the magic number is 50, and still others contend that the word spurt occurs when toddlers have mastered between 50 and 100 words. Even given the disparity of these numbers, researchers clearly agree on the fact that there needs to be a critical mass of words in the child's head before the explosion.

Experts also debate whether all toddlers experience this dramatic explosion. Some argue that word learning is more continuous throughout development and that not all toddlers go through a word spurt at all. Others have concluded that most of the debate centers not on if there is a spurt, but on how researchers measure it. Toddlers' words are measured weekly or monthly, by scientists in a baby lab or by parents keeping records at home. In any event, to get to as many words as the four-year-old has at her command—over 5,000—there has to be a geometric increase in the number of words they produce.

Try This: Catching the torrent of words in a diary

Keeping a diary is really not as hard as it sounds, and you will be glad you have it as your toddler grows up. Jot down the date and the words that your child says. To catch the spurt, you will have to have started this diary in the last chapter. If you didn't, start now, for as a rule the spurt is just around the corner. Look at the number of words that your child produces and keep a separate section for the number of new words that are added each week. You should see the number of words increase exponentially. At the time of the spurt, some toddlers start to put two words together for the first time. Some researchers suggest that the two processes are related. Remember that different toddlers reach language hallmarks at different points in time, so please don't be alarmed if your child waits until the end of this period to demonstrate his verbal fluency.

Word Learning Is a Bear (Bare?)

As the vocabulary spurt begins, it is important to keep in mind just how hard the task of word learning really is. Even if a baby has the insight that names should go with objects, actions, and events, it still is far from clear *which* objects, actions, and events are being labeled. Parents don't always help toddlers since, given the way language works, many of the expressions that are used contain ambiguous references. This can be seen in a two-year-old's interpretation of common expressions. Jonathan, for example, decides to take a cup of juice to his mother, who is ailing on the couch. Unfortunately, Jonathan's father filled the cup almost to the brim. Regretting this, he yells to Jonathan as he makes his way down the carpeted hall, "Keep your eye on the cup." Jonathan does just that: He lowers his head and stares intently at the cup, never suspecting that his father was really telling him to "be careful."

How is a child to figure out what words mean when they sound exactly alike and mean totally different things in different contexts? Babies can't read and therefore don't notice when words that sound the same are spelled differently. If this was not bad enough, toddlers face the problem that no one provides definitions even for the words that are used in a more literal way. How is one to find a grandmother, for example? We might be able to identify the grandmother at our friend Jill's house because she is the only gray-haired lady who is bent over the stove making chicken soup. However, at a meeting of senior executives of a corporation with women on the board, there are a number of gray-haired ladies. Which of these is a grandmother—if indeed, any are?

The only real way to know a grandmother is to find out who is the mother of a mother. Defining features such as these are not readily available to the young mind who is struggling to understand kinship relations. Yet toddlers learn words like "love" and "no" that seem to defy easy definitions. Given the ambiguous information that toddlers use to figure out word meanings, learning is difficult.

What Are Toddlers Talking About?

What many parents notice first in this new stage is the emergence of the all too common phrase "What's that?" most often pronounced as a single word, "Watssat?" or "Whadat?" Parents dutifully reply with the name and often supply the same name repeatedly as the child goes back and forth around the room. In this way, toddlers get multiple opportunities to learn names for many of the things in their environment.

"What's that" clearly shows that the child using it has achieved the "naming insight," as some have called it, recognizing that all objects in the environment have a name. This may be the very breakthrough that eventually allowed Helen Keller to be a true word user, as we illustrated in the opening of chapter 4.

When she discovered "water" through finger spelling, Helen seemed to have captured the naming insight, now able to ask what most toddlers spontaneously generate when they say, "What's that?"

Early on the phrase "watssat" may be one word for the child. This is because toddlers at this stage sometimes fail to analyze the speech stream into the correct-sized units. Some children have words like "have-it" as in "have-it soda" or "want-it" as in "want-it outside." With time the child notices that each of the word "pieces" stands alone. Both "have" and "it" are used in multiple contexts and are not always used together. Thus, two new words are born from one. By and large, though, children analyze the words they produce correctly.

Toddlers also discover on their own that words name *categories* and not just an individual item. In the last chapter we described how Josh used the word "flower" to apply not just to flowers in the garden— the first place he had uttered the word—but to flowers on bedspreads, tissue boxes, and dried flowers in vases. Other than proper names (such as John or Sally), words like "window," "car," etc., name entire classes of objects. Children seem to know this even prior to the vocabulary spurt, judging from the way they name diverse members of the category of, say, "car," almost from the start.

Scientists have catalogued toddlers' early words into categories. Across a number of studies and even across varied cultures, the largest class of words used by toddlers, approximately half, are words for objects. Topping the list for types of objects are foods and drinks, animals, body parts, clothing, toys, and vehicles. Researchers have even learned what the most common words are within each of these categories. According to the norms set for the MacArthur Communicative Development Inventory—norms developed on 1,800 toddlers— toddlers are even saying many of the same words. For example, 80 percent of children between the ages of 16 to 24 months know the words "apple" and "cheese" in the food category. On the other hand, even at 23 months, toward the end of this period, only half know words like "yogurt," "potato chip" and "raisin." In the animal category, "cat," "dog," "bunny," "duck," "puppy," and "horse" come early while "wolf," "turtle," and even "teddy bear" are not learned until later. Finally, in the popular body parts category, words like "belly button," "ear," "mouth," and "nose" are early entries while "ankle" and "face" are more familiar to older toddlers.

This is just a smattering of the categories of object names. Of course, these words would not be popular if they were not spoken for toddlers by nearby adults. With the swear word in Hubert's case, we see how words parents utter in great excitement (whether positive or negative) have a better chance of being remembered than words uttered calmly.

If half of the words are words for objects, then what makes up the other word categories? One popular category includes specific names for people. Happily, Mommy, Daddy, and the names of the child's siblings are among those learned early. Even these "proper names," however, can be used in more general ways. Once a child learns that a word names a category of objects, toddlers may call many men "Daddy" and many women "Mommy." By the way, this is not as odd as it seems. In a playgroup, every mommy is called "Mommy," so the child's inference is not far off. The assumption that all words label categories can create humorous moments in the ways names are used in general.

Eighteen-month-old Michael had an unusual hypothesis. His older brother was named Josh and his middle brother, Benji. Michael decided that he didn't really need to use both names, so he chose one, Josh, to represent the category of "my brothers." Michael thought that his theory was a good one, so he applied it widely outside the home. When he met the Smiths, with brothers Ted and Alex, he decided to call each of the toddlers "Ted," and when he met the three girls in the Rosen family, he called them all "Alison," using the name of the oldest child. Michael thought that proper names worked like any other words. He implicitly decided that one name would work for the siblings in the same family in the same way that one name, say, "truck," works for all trucks.

Beyond names for objects and proper names, toddlers also say action words like "up," "sit," "see," "eat," "down," and "go," modifiers like "hot," "allgone," and "more," and a few social words such as "thank you" and the ever present "no!" In addition, toddlers understand a rich variety of words even prior to the vocabulary spurt, and once it arrives, there is an expansion in the number of words in each category, as well as an addition to the kinds of categories children can use. For example, many more adjectives and prepositions come on board, as do some adverbs like "fast."

In short, as toddlers add words, they also are doing more analysis of the words that they have. They are better able to sort these words into categories and to approximate the kinds of word categories that adults have.

Although toddlers are learning a massive number of words, they are not plucking randomly from the array of possible words that they hear. They are not learning words like "taxes" and "intuition" and "reptile." This is because parents and caregivers structure the word-learning environment of young toddlers, as is illustrated in an example from a typical book-reading session.

Yvonne, a sleepy 21-month-old, is reading with her mother just before bedtime. She sits on her mother's lap as they gently rock back and forth in the chair next to her pink crib. Yvonne has learned how to turn a page in the book so that her mother can read, and reread, and reread, the words on the page. "Bunny," she reads, then adds, "That is a happy bunny, isn't it, Yvonne? Where do you think that bunny is going? Can you touch the bunny's ear?" Yvonne complies with her mother's request and then turns to the next page, which in this book has a picture of a hamster. "It's a hamster! Yvonne, hamsters are furry little animals. See the cute hamster? Hamster. What do you think a hamster eats?" And the scene goes on . . .

This example shows in several ways the kinds of words that young toddlers learn and how they learn them. First, the mother involves Yvonne in the activity of book reading. Yvonne gets to pick the book and then to turn the pages. She is also involved in the conversation. Her mother asks her to point at the bunny's ears and asks her to produce a word for what the hamster might eat. Even if Yvonne does not respond to each initiative, she is thoroughly involved in the book reading.

What you may not be able to tell from the example is that the mother is also speaking in infant-directed speech, the slow, singsong language mentioned in chapter 3. This way of talking confers several advantages for word learning. First, it tells the child that this conversation is for her. Yvonne has mom all to herself and her mom is even using her special language. Infant-directed speech also introduces new words like "hamster" in a particular way. For one, the new word is repeated more often in infant-directed speech, giving Yvonne multiple opportunities to learn. In addition, scientists have found that new words are often put at the ends of the sentences. In one study, for example, American and Turkish mothers were asked to teach their 12-month-olds three new words, "lips," "wrist," and "lobe." Researchers tape-recorded the mothers as they taught these words to their toddlers. They found that mothers tended to put new words at the ends of sentences both in English, where such a practice yields a grammatical sentence and in Turkish, where quite often the use of a noun in the final position creates an ungrammatical sentence. In Turkish, verbs, not nouns, close a sentence. Why put the words there? At the end of a sentence a word stands out more. It is unbounded on one side and it receives heavier stress.

Yvonne's mother naturally uses infant-directed speech, but studies in our laboratory confirm the powerful effect it has. Babies between 18 and 24 months do learn new words better when they are delivered in infant-directed speech. In fact, in one of our studies, babies learned new words *only* when they were spoken in infant-directed speech. Their more sophisticated counterparts, who were all of 34 months of age, could learn the same new words whether they were spoken in infant-directed or in adult-directed speech.

There is one more lesson in the example of Yvonne's mother. When she reads a book to her child, she rarely keeps to the words on the page. Rather, she uses the words on the page as a starting point for further discussion. She expands upon the text by discussing the pictures and inviting a response from Yvonne. Yvonne's mother illustrates many of the techniques that researchers have uncovered when they tape middle-class mothers reading to their toddlers. Book reading can be prime time—not for learning to read, but for learning words.

Try This: Book reading as a classroom for word learning

You can begin to notice some of the implicit language lessons that you conduct with your child during book reading. As you read a book— just this once—try hard to stick to the words on each page without elaborating at all. You will find that it feels very awkward to read the book literally. You don't have to carry this on for too long to see how you go well beyond the pages of the book during book reading. And reading is merely one of many opportunities for conversation. Meal time, dressing time, and play time are all potentially rich moments for language learning.

You might also want to see how you introduce a new word to your child. Chapter 4 discussed how parents use basic-level words to babies, words such as "shoe," "chair," and "flower." You were asked to see what level of words your child first produced. Now see what level of words you produce and if these are related to what your child says. Take any magazine that is filled with pictures and you can see how you go about introducing a new word. Do you use words at the basic level? How do you make sense of new words for your child? Now try introducing new words by using broader, superordinate categories like "animal" and "furniture." Does that feel right? How about using highly specific, subordinate words like "limousine" or "Georgian chair"? What sounds natural to you? This will depend on two factors: whether you think your child will understand and how many words you think your child knows. In particular, if your child is firmly in possession of the basic-level name for the category (for example, "car"), introduce the more general or the more specific term.

Finally, just for fun, you can try to "teach" a new word to your baby using either adult-directed or child-directed speech. Find two unfamiliar objects around the house. Researchers prefer kitchen utensils. Most babies will believe you if you call a garlic press a "dax." After getting baby's attention, label one object several times using infant-directed speech, as in "Look at the daaaaaaxx. Wow, it's a daaaax!" Then you might label the other object in adult-directed speech, saying the exact same words, except for the name of the object—try using "modi." Later put both objects in front of the child and ask for either the "dax" or the "modi," alternating between infant-directed and adult-directed speech. Make sure that the objects are equally distant from the baby, or she will tend to pick the closer object regardless of what you say. Which word did your baby seem to learn better? Which kind of request did she respond to more readily?

Babies Overextend Themselves: Misapplying Words for All the Right Reasons

When learning their very first words, babies are cautious about how and when they should apply them. For example, "dog" is reserved for the child's dog and not for other dogs. But with their almost unquenchable thirst for new words, 18- to 24-month-old toddlers show off their new set of words in an even wider set of contexts that we would consider appropriate, as the following examples illustrate.

Jane, a 20-month-old child, uses the word "ball" to refer to balls of any color or size and also to a balloon, a marble, an apple, an egg, and a pompom on a hat. Phyllis uses her cherished word, "moon," for a full moon, a half moon, a lemon slice, a ball of spinach, a banana, and a half-eaten Cheerio.

These are examples of what researchers have called "overextensions." Compiling data from diaries kept by parents, scientists have started to make sense of what overextensions mean in the context of word learning. One point all agree on is that the period around the vocabulary spurt is also when overextensions of words show a rapid and dramatic increase.

Dr. Leslie Rescorla of Bryn Mawr College is a recognized expert in overextension. In her landmark study of early word use, she categorized the overextensions that were reported in six parents' diaries when their toddlers were between one year and 18 months of age. Though her study ends where we want to begin, she does offer some important insights. First, though it appears that toddlers are overextending all of the time, they are not. On average, toddlers overgeneralize only about a third of their words. Second, toddlers do not misapply newly learned terms, but tend to overgeneralize tried and true, familiar words. Finally, she notes that certain categories of words tend to have more generalizations than others. Letter names, for example, are overgeneralized all of the time with toddlers saying, "That's an L," for all letters. Vehicles and clothing names are overgeneralized widely, and animal names are overgeneralized about a quarter of the time.

These overextensions also tend to occur predictably around three themes. Most of the overextensions are *categorical* in nature. Toddlers might use "dada" for "mama," "truck" for "bus," or one color name for the entire range of colors. In a second area, as in the examples of Jane and Phyllis, children use words *analogically*. That is, the word "ball" is being used to refer to perceptually similar items such as an egg and an apple, which are not in the same category at all. It is as if the child is making an analogy between the original item (the ball) and any number of other items (egg, apple). A third type of overextension is called *relational* overextension. Here toddlers use words to convey some relationship between an object that is present and one that is absent. The child who says "doll" to the doll's crib even though the doll is nowhere in sight may be labeling the crib incorrectly *or* expressing the relationship between the doll and the crib.

Why do toddlers overextend words in the first place? Do they just like to hear themselves talk, or is there a more basic explanation that is related to the child's growing mind?

Jamilla is on a car ride with her parents. At 19 months, she has a sophisticated vocabulary of 120 words. As they travel through the countryside, Jamilla wants to name everything in sight. "Dog," she says repeatedly as they see the horses running in the pasture. "Dog," she repeats again as they pass the field of cows. "Dog, dog, dog," she exclaims as she sees the sheep in the meadow. Her parents are delighted by her desire to fill them in on the details of their trip. "Is that what you see? We call that a horse (cow . . . fill in the blank)," says Jamilla's mother. "There certainly are a lot of animals on the way to Grandma's!"

A number of explanations have been offered to explain Jamilla's seeming fixation on dogs. The first and perhaps most important fact about her constant "word calling" is that even with her limited vocabulary, she is desperately attempting to communicate with her parents. Jamilla is sharing what she is interested in with another human being, and her mother's responses show that Jamilla is succeeding. She is getting her mother to notice what she finds is important even if she doesn't have the right words.

Does Jamilla really think that all animals are dogs? This has been a matter of some debate. Earlier theories suggested that Jamilla was in the process of building up her storehouse of knowledge and that there were still many holes to be filled in. For example, Jamilla may know that dogs move and have four legs. She may not yet know that they have a particular shape, that they bark, or that to get a dog you have to start with puppies rather than lambs or ducklings. If Jamilla has an incomplete definition of dogs, then dogs, sheep, cats, and many other four-legged creatures would fall rightly into the category "dogs."

There is, however, another popular theory about why toddlers overextend words. According to this theory, toddlers are really searching for the right word and just don't have it in their vocabularies. Jamilla may know full well that those huge black and white bovine creatures are not dogs. She can see that. She simply doesn't know the word for "cow," so she cleverly decides to use the only close word she does know, "dog." If she engages her mother, her mother will replace her word "dog" with the proper word, "cow." In other words, it is a word-learning strategy.

A third reason why toddlers might overextend is that saying words is harder than comprehension. That is, even if the child has the word somewhere in the recesses of his mind, it might be difficult to retrieve that word just when he wants it. Thus, what comes out is the more familiar word that he has come to rely upon. You can see this yourself when you are sleep-deprived (most parents of babies are) or have the flu. Did you ever notice that the wrong word will sometimes come out of your mouth—a familiar word that is related to what you wanted to say but not exactly what you had intended? Toddlers may have the same problem. Fishing for words in the sea of their minds is difficult.

Research into toddlers' comprehension of words supports the view that children do not think all four-legged animals are dogs. In one study, for example, scientists picked four familiar words from the diaries of five toddlers' parents. These were words that the toddlers were known to overextend, "daddy," "mommy," "woof" (commonly used for dog), and "apple." They explored whether toddlers overextend as much in their understanding of these words as they did in their production of the words. They reasoned that if toddlers really thought that all four-legged animals were dogs, for example, then they should overextend the word "dog" just as often in comprehension as they do in production. On the other hand, if toddlers are using overextension to build their mental dictionaries, or because they have some problem in retrieving words, then they might overextend in their production of words, but *not* in comprehension.

To test the hypothesis, the researchers collected 42 pictures for each of the words. To examine each child's understanding of the word "mommy," for example, they used five pictures of their mother, several pictures of familiar women, and several pictures of unfamiliar women who were of different sexes, ages, facial features, and were wearing different clothes. For "woof" or "dog" there were 10 pictures of different kinds of dogs, a picture of the child's own dog, pictures of familiar animals like cats, cows, and horses, and pictures of less familiar animals like hippopotami, elephants, and buffalo. The child was shown an inappropriate picture alongside an appropriate picture and was asked, "Show me the mommy" or "Where is the mommy?" What happened? The researchers found some overextension in comprehension, but it was much less widespread than it was in production.

So toddlers do not tend to have incomplete entries in their mental dictionaries. Rather, they overextend because they often have trouble remembering the right words, and they use overextension as a way to learn the correct names for the objects, actions, and events that they want to label.

Try This: Looking for overextensions

Overextensions begin to occur quite early in word learning, although they peak just around the time of the vocabulary spurt. To recognize overextensions requires that you not only jot down in your diary the words that the baby uses, but also the contexts in which the baby applies those words. Do you see any pattern in your child's overextensions? What kind of overextensions are most prevalent? Overextensions based on shape? On category membership? On perceptual features like texture or color?

To elicit overextensions, buy an animal picture book and see what happens when you turn the tables on your baby by asking, "What's that?" as you flip through the pages. You may find that your child calls any unfamiliar animal "dog" or "cat." You may even find that they are quite adamant about their label. The following happened to one of us while flipping through an animal book and looking at a picture of a bunny rabbit:

Benj: (*while pointing at a rabbit*) Cat. Cat.
Mom: Where's the cat?
Benj: (*still pointing at the rabbit*) Cat. Cat.
Mom: Honey, that's not a cat. That's a rabbit.
Benj: (*becoming more authoritative*) Cat. Cat. Cat.
Mom: Well, it looks like a cat, but it's a rabbit. Here, let me show you the difference. (*turning pages to cat and rabbit seen side by side*) See, there's the cat. This is a rabbit.
Benj: *Cat!*
Mom: Okay, dear. If you want to call it a cat, that's just fine (*continuing in a whisper*), but it's really a rabbit.

See what happens when you try the experiment in your own home.

Does Sensitivity to Social Cues Lead to the Vocabulary Spurt?

Researchers have spent a great deal of time trying to understand why the vocabulary spurt occurs when it does. A number of theories have been proposed. Some argue that toddlers become word-learning apprentices under their parents, having learned to appreciate and then use the social cues that their parents and other adults offer them for the meanings of new words. Others hold that toddlers around the age of 18 months acquire new mental capabilities that enable the vocabulary spurt to take place. Finally, we have added our voice to the field by advocating an integrated position that argues for both increased social sensitivity and mental growth.

> Nineteen-month-old Barney is playing on the floor with some new toys. His mother is on the telephone in the background, talking about her latest computer breakdown. The exact second that Barney takes an elephant out of the bag of toys, his mother says, "The *cache dim* in my hard drive needs to be replaced. A *cache dim*. Can you imagine? I didn't even know what a *cache dim* was." She continues to chat on the phone.

Reading this scene, we know that the words "cache dim" were part of the phone conversation and not a label for Barney's new toy elephant. Does Barney know that too? After all, the toy was labeled exactly when Barney pulled the toy from the shopping bag. And his mother says the words "cache dim" repeatedly as he inspects his new toy.

Take another scene: Twenty-one-month-old Janice and her father are strolling down the block when they see a beautiful flower. Janice looks at the flower, and her dad immediately picks up on her interest. "That is called a daffodil, Janice. See the daffodil? A daffodil is a kind of flower. Would you like to smell the flower?" Her father does not notice that she has already turned her attention away from the flower to get a better view of the slug on the ground nearby. Does Janice assume that the slug is called "daffodil"? After all, her father is labeling the object while she is focused on the slug.

There are many occasions on which parents say something that has nothing to do with the objects capturing the child's interest. When Pamela's mother says, "It is time for bed" just as Pamela is playing with her toys, her words are directed at a future activity rather than at the current goings-on. How is a child to figure out if the words they are hearing map to the object they are focused on?

These three examples help to distinguish a major difference between the pre-vocabulary-spurt child and one who is ready to amass a great number of words. These children seem to know that "cache dim" is not the label for the elephant, that a slug is not a daffodil, and that neither the words "bed" nor "time" refer to the toy that Pamela is playing with. According to brilliant research conducted by Professor Dare Baldwin, these vocabulary-spurt toddlers know how to use the social cues given by adults to distinguish when a word is and is not meant for them. Barney doesn't think "cache dim" is the name of his new toy for several reasons. First, his mother is not looking at the elephant as she speaks. Second, she is not speaking in infant-directed speech, the language she uses with Barney. Finally, even her body position is not directed toward the new toy. Thus, Barney knows that the words "cache dim" have nothing to do with him. Similarly, Janice can tell that her father is describing a flower. He is pointing at the flower, looking at the flower, smelling the flower, even if Janice knows that the slug is of much greater interest. When her father finally does notice the slug, he only says, "Ooo." The word "daffodil" must refer to her father's point of interest, not to hers. Finally, Pamela has heard the routine "Time for bed" many times before. She knows that this is part of the evening ritual and has little to do with her current interest.

The socially sophisticated child knows how to use all of these visual and body cues to "read" the intent of the speaker. This ability gives the young child an enormous advantage. Adults in the world know many more words than the child does. Thus, if a child is to increase his vocabulary, judging how adults map words onto objects, actions, and events is a good start.

You might rightly argue that toddlers have been budding socialites for a long time. Younger babies can attend to eye-gaze and pointing cues too; they just don't realize that these social cues have any relevance for word learning. But there is an obstacle that saves them from mistakenly mapping words to objects. Our own research has shown that younger babies need about twice the number of repetitions of a new word coupled with the object to learn the word. In contrast, the older child need only read the social cues given by the parent to know if the word spoken is part of the labeling "game" or not. Hence, the vocabulary spurt emerges because toddlers learn both how to read adults' social cues and to recognize their relevance for word learning.

Try This: Is your child using social cues to learn new words?

You can see if your child is using social cues to expand his vocabulary. Place two unfamiliar but similarly sized objects in front of your baby when he is about 14 months of age. Sit midway between the two objects and keep your hands down. Make sure the objects are out of reach of the baby. Now get his attention by calling his name. Then glance over at one of the objects and name it in infant-directed speech: "This is a dax. See the dax?" Label the object at least ten times, alternating your glance between the baby and the object being named. What you are doing is labeling only one of the objects by using the cue of eye gaze to tell the baby which one. The question is whether or not the baby will be able to *use* the cue of eye gaze.

To see if the baby can do this, next place the two objects on a plate in front of him, now within reach, and ask, "Can Mommy have the dax? Where's the dax?" Does your child give you the correct object? Now try it again, changing the position of the objects to make sure that any result you saw was not just by chance.

At 14 months your child may not be able to select the correct object, but if you perform this experiment again after Ted has had his vocabulary spurt, and again at 24 months of age (with different sets of objects and using different nonsense words), you may be impressed with the changes you see.

The social cue of eye gaze is perhaps the most difficult one for toddlers to use because it is so subtle. If the baby can't use eye gaze to figure out which toy is being labeled when he is 14 months, try pointing at the object of choice and labeling it. If that still doesn't work, try handling the object as the baby hears you label it. You will see that toddlers become more sophisticated over time. By the time they reach the vocabulary spurt, they have mastered reading minimal social cues to learn a new word.

Do Mental Advances Lead to the Vocabulary Spurt?

Attention to social cues is important, but will not take the baby far enough. Even if she knows that her mother is giving her a label for "elephant" she needs to figure out just how to map the label onto the elephant. As noted in the last chapter, every child is faced with the dilemma of figuring out what a word is labeling. Does this label that Mom is using refer to the whole elephant? The elephant's head? The floor that the elephant is sitting on? How does this arbitrary label get "glued" to an object? A word is made up and agreed upon by a community of people who use that word to represent the object even when it is not there. What makes words so special is that they are used symbolically to "stand for" objects, actions, and events and not just to "go with" them.

It was psychologist Jean Piaget who first realized that mental advances may underlie word learning. In his view, a number of mental developments converge around 18 months of age, allowing toddlers to think about objects, actions, and events that are hidden from view. Think of the power that a child gains when he can think about and remember a scene that occurred yesterday, or can imitate what cousin Cindy did last week to make her tower stand seven blocks tall. Words are representations and symbols that free us from the confines of our current environment. Language allows us to create new worlds in our mind and to craft new ideas from old, remembered events. Thus, it is the jump into representation that forces the need for words and language. As Lois Bloom has suggested, when our mental world becomes increasingly divorced from our perceptual world, we need language to fill the gap. We need language so that we can share the contents of our minds with others.

A child evolves into a representational being, no longer locked in the here and now. However, these representations must be streamlined. The child simply cannot save every detail of every scene that he has witnessed. A child cannot remember every detail that distinguishes every object that she has touched. Rather than notice all of the details, then, human minds categorize objects, actions, and events into groups of items, and it is those categories and then their names that become the building blocks for the language of thought, the building blocks for the language we use with others. In short, one of the mental leaps that underlie the vocabulary spurt is that children can represent things that are not present. A second mental leap is that children learn to categorize things encountered in the environment and then to label those categories. There is growing evidence that representational ability and categorization reach a pinnacle at 18 or 19 months of age.

Flora, Alex, and Merry were three among the twelve participants in a classic study of categorization. The girls were 15 months at the beginning and almost 19 months at the end of the study. Every three weeks they came into the laboratory and were presented with a set of different tasks.

At age 15 months, Flora is presented with eight objects placed randomly before her on a table. Four of the objects are flat yellow rectangles, and four are bright red plastic human figures. An experimenter holds out her two hands and says, "Fix them all up" and waits to see what Flora does. The child makes the correct inference that she is supposed to give the experimenter some of the objects. The question is, which objects will she give? Flora looks at the objects and proceeds to pull out all of the human figures from the group—placing them in one of the experimenter's hands. She then starts playing with the remaining pile. Flora formed a single category (humans) and by default had been left with the other category (rectangles). But Flora did not yet realize that there were two separate categories before her.

At 16 months, Flora sees four pillboxes and four balls made of Play-doh. Compared to last time, she does something new. She handles the pillboxes one after the other, and then she touches the balls. She does not put the objects in the experimenter's hands or separate them into groups. But this is progress. Flora recognizes that there are two different groups of objects.

At 17 months of age, Flora is shown four small Raggedy Andy dolls and four red plastic cars. This time she places the four cars in the experimenter's right hand and the Raggedy Andy dolls in the left hand. She doesn't just give the experimenter one type of object or touch the objects sequentially. Now Flora notices that there are two distinct categories of objects before her and sorts the objects into these categories.

The age range for these behaviors varies. For example, Merry formed the one pile when she was 13 and a half months old and Alex did not until she was 19 months. The most difficult two-category grouping was achieved by Merry at 15 months and by Alex at 20 months. What the researchers noted, however, was that all toddlers seem to go through these different levels of categorization. More important for the discussion at hand, the vocabulary spurt comes about the same time that toddlers reach the most sophisticated stage of categorization—two-category sorting. Here is clear evidence that mental growth is strongly related to vocabulary learning. When toddlers can categorize, they see the world differently. They can find similarity among the differences in the objects and events that they witness, and they can label entire categories of objects at a time.

Try This: Categorizing objects and the vocabulary spurt

You can conduct the experiment described above. Make sure that you have eight toys, four of one type and four of another. It is critical that the toys in each group be exactly the same so that the task is easier for the child. Don't vary the color of the rectangles or the size of the cars. Put the toys on the floor in front of your baby all mixed up, hold your hands out palms up, and see what happens. Does the baby show his ability to sort things into two distinct categories just around the time of his vocabulary spurt? Or does the ability to create two distinct categories precede or follow his spurt?

Fast Mapping: Novel Names Go with Novel Categories

Forming categories is one crucial piece of the naming insight. Another mental leap is the one that Helen Keller had—that each category has a name. This insight can be pushed even further to suggest that when you hear a novel name, you hypothesize that the new name goes with a new category. To illustrate how even adults make the assumption that a new name must be labeling a category that we don't already have a name for, consider what might happen when you attend a brunch at your friend Susan's house.

As you and Susan are putting things out on the table before asking people to be seated, she says to you, "Could you please get the *caponata?*" You have no clue what *caponata* is. You do, however, want to oblige your friend. You also suspect that *caponata* is some kind of food because your friend tilts her head vaguely in the direction of the refrigerator. "Hmm," you think, "she just glanced over at the fridge, maybe I should look in there for the *caponata.*" You go over to the refrigerator, not admitting that you have no idea what *caponata* is or what it looks like. (It's a brownish, chunky spread for crackers made of eggplant.) As the door to the refrigerator opens, you are saved. Amid other familiar food items is a bowl of brownish stuff that is wholly unfamiliar. "Aha," you think, "this must be it." At the risk of being a fool you take the bowl out of the refrigerator and place it on the table. "Thanks," Susan says, to your delight. Your guess is confirmed. You found the *caponata* by searching for an item for which you didn't already have a name.

Recent research from our laboratory and others suggests that toddlers may learn unfamiliar words in exactly the same way—by a process of elimination. It's as if toddlers are saying to themselves, "I know the name of this, and I know the name of that. The new name I'm hearing must map to the one that I don't already have a name for." When do toddlers get the insight that novel names must map to unnamed categories?

This question was investigated by Drs. Carolyn Mervis and Jacqueline Bertrand. The researchers theorized that babies would be able to do this task right around the time of the vocabulary spurt. They tested toddlers between 15 and 20 months of age who varied widely in their production and comprehension abilities. Essentially what they did was a laboratory version of the *caponata* example discussed above—a test of the hypothesis that novel names (names never heard before) label novel categories.

Picture 18-month-old Sean in a Superman suit coming into the baby lab. Sean is seated with one experimenter and a pile of toys. Some of the toys are familiar ones (for example, a ball, a kitty, a truck, and a set of keys) and others are novel. Among them are kitchen utensils (a garlic press, honey dipper, and bottle holder) and some strange small tools. After Sean has had a chance to examine all the toys, the experimenter takes them away and puts them back out in sets of five, four of which are items Sean and his peers will find familiar and one that is unfamiliar. Then the researcher arranges the five brightly colored toys (a kitty, a sock, a cup, a telephone, and a red honey dipper) in a row in front of the child. "Sean," she asks, "may I have the kitty?" Sean happily obliges. "Thank you," she says, "good job!" "Sean," she continues, "may I have the lep?" "Lep" is a made-up word that Sean has never heard before. What does he do?

Sean has before him three objects for which he already has a name and a novel object—the honey dipper. He is on the cusp of the vocabulary spurt with 45 words he can speak. As it turns out, Sean is confused by the task. He hesitates and then gives the researcher one of the familiar toys. The researcher, of course, acts as pleased as punch, not letting Sean know that he gave the "wrong" answer.

Nineteen-month-old Jessica, however, who comes into the lab after Sean leaves, solves the task without effort. With 100 words she can say, and having begun the vocabulary spurt, she immediately chooses the unfamiliar object. Watch what she now does in the second part of the experiment.

The experimenter gives Jessica new objects to play with—this time three familiar objects, a new example of the honey dipper (a wooden "lep") and a novel object—a garlic press. The objects are spread before Jessica, and she is asked again, "May I have the lep?" This new version of the task has upped the ante for Jessica. Did she really attach the name "lep" to the category of honey dippers? Will she give the experimenter the new honey dipper? Or will Jessica give the experimenter the garlic press, the only object present without a name? After all, she only inferred what a lep was from hearing it once a moment ago in the first part of the experiment. Nonetheless, she immediately gives the experimenter the new honey dipper rather than the garlic press. She did indeed learn the word "lep" in one trial, and was able to generalize it to a new lep—to a new member of the category.

This behavior is called "fast mapping." For children to learn up to nine new words a day, they need some powerful word-learning strategies. Fast mapping—knowing where and when to apply a newly heard label from a single exposure to that label—is key to success. Toddlers who assume, as adults do, that a novel name goes with a category without a name can learn vocabulary items very rapidly. Fast mapping, then, underlies the vocabulary spurt.

The scientists who conducted this study found that all the children who hadn't yet had a vocabulary spurt could not fast-map. However, Sean and children like him were brought back when, from maternal report, it was ascertained that they had experienced a vocabulary spurt. The second time, Sean and his peers did map the novel names to the unnamed objects. This is compelling evidence that the ability to fast-map develops either immediately before or during the vocabulary spurt.

Try This: Fast mapping and the vocabulary spurt

This study is another that you can easily perform with your child. Again, be sure to use objects that are roughly the same size and hold similar interest for your child. If your child likes cars, then a car would not be a good familiar object to use because you can ask for a "lep," a "kitty," or a "dog," and your child will likely give you the car! Gather together two sets of ten objects so you can conduct two separate trials. Put five objects in a row in front of your child after letting her play with all the objects first. Four of these should be familiar objects that your child knows the names of; one should be unfamiliar. Ask the child on each trial you create to give you one familiar object using a known name (for example, "Can I have the kitty?") and one unfamiliar object using a novel name ("Can I have the lep?"). Half the time ask for the unfamiliar object first; half the time ask for the familiar object first.

If you try this at the beginning of the period (about 18 months) before your child has undergone the vocabulary spurt, the child will just as likely give you a known as an unknown object. If you try this again after your child has had a vocabulary spurt, however, you will probably find that your child will consistently choose the unfamiliar toy.

An Integrated View of the Vocabulary Spurt: It Takes Social Skill *and* Mental Advances

There are both social and mental advances that create the vocabulary spurt. While both undoubtedly play a role, scientists seem to religiously choose one type from among the alternatives. Some argue that it is the social arena that supplies the grist for the mill of vocabulary learning. Others hold steadfast to the view that the growing computational and representational power of the toddler's mind contributes most to the appearance of a vocabulary spurt. In our own research, we have developed a model of vocabulary development that outlines how toddlers develop different abilities at different times that feed into rapid word learning. For example, babies must start out at the beginning of word learning at around 12 months of age with some predispositions about how words work. They must know that words at least go with the objects that are being labeled. They must know that whole objects rather than object parts receive the label, and that words are not used as proper names, but rather as labels for a number of related objects, actions, and events. In the beginning, there is probably no privileged status for words per se. In fact, we suspect that music or object noises would serve the same ends. Words are treated just like the beeps of the microwave; they are simply associated with objects. At this time, babies respond to words in the same way that Fido, our dog, might respond to words. Over time, however, words become more prominent and take on symbolic significance.

In our labs we find that by 19 months of age, for example, toddlers start to use social cues as a means of attaching words to objects. Words will now take on a different significance than music or object noises. The vocabulary spurt is then born. Unlike his younger self, a child who has passed through the vocabulary spurt can say a word while emoting pleasure or pain, can pick up the nuances of a social glance, and can quickly identify a never-before-seen object as a member of a category he has just heard labeled. This child is making mental leaps and bounds. This child is only restricted by the limits that single words can impose. As we will see in the next chapter, however, lurking behind the vocabulary spurt is another gold mine. From the outside, we see a child who is producing single words. As scientists look on the inside, however, we find that toddlers are already comprehending these words in much longer sentences.

Individual Differences in Word Learning

This chapter may be giving the false impression that all toddlers go through the vocabulary spurt at the same time and that all words are learned in the same way. Differences between babies do exist. Toddlers vary widely in their ability to pronounce the words that they hear. Boys learn a bit more slowly than girls, firstborns tend to speak more than later-borns, and toddlers from poor families may lag behind those from more advantaged economic levels.

Pronunciation: Saying It My Way

The first place that you are bound to notice differences between toddlers is in their pronunciation of words. Some toddlers are more articulate than others. But never fear, all infants are at the same disadvantage when it comes to diction. All have difficulty pronouncing the full range of sounds required for the words that they know. In our opening passage, for example, Jennifer said "wectangow" without pronouncing any of the *r* or *l* sounds. To some parents, this mispronunciation is cute. To others, it becomes a cause for concern. There is no need to worry. Words like "wectangow" are quite natural because the structure of the mouth and the placement of the tongue work against the production of certain sounds (like *r*'s and *l*'s). To better understand the changes in the structure of the mouth, let's look at evolutionary changes that took place over a period of 1.5 million years.

Scientists studying the fossil remains of our ancestors developing into species Homo sapiens have noticed interesting changes in the shape and design of human mouths. The physical evidence suggests that there was significant modification. The mouth cavity and the areas involved in speech gradually changed from a structure like that of other primate species to the vocal structure that we have today.

Modern-day humans have an elongated space between the back and front of the mouth and an open air passage from the lungs that allows air to be forced past the vocal cords as it moves into and is shaped by tongue placement. In effect, creating sounds is like creating various streams of air from which different sounds emerge. As the cavity of the mouth widened and lengthened through evolution, so too did the placement of the tongue, which moved farther back and farther down in the mouth, forming a much more flexible vocal instrument. Primates can only modulate sounds between loud and soft. Humans can use placement of the tongue throughout the mouth and air flow to produce any number of different sounds. Some scientists argue that the new placement of the tongue and changes in the mouth cavity created both an advantage and a disadvantage for humans. This new architecture allows us to use language, but, unlike our primate cousins forces us to live under the constant threat that we will choke on our food because our airways are always open to intrusions.

Changes in the infant mouth mirror those seen in evolution. The good news is that infants, who have more primate-like vocal cavities, are less likely to choke on food. The bad news is that they are incapable of forming all of the sounds of language until they are a bit older. The sounds that are produced during the first two years roughly correspond to the letter sounds *p, m, h, n, w,* and *b.* Sounds like *r* and *l* don't generally sound adult-like until children are between the ages of 3 and 6. Sounds like *k, g, d,* and *t* don't emerge until between ages 2 and 4. *F* and *y* first appear between 2.5 years and 4 years and *ch, sh, z, j,* and *v* come in somewhere between 3.5 years and 8 years. Not until 8 are all of these sounds fully formed in a vocal cavity that resembles that of the adult. Interestingly, it is also up to age 8 that a child can move to another country and learn the language spoken there without developing an accent.

With all of this as backdrop, we can now understand why Aunt Martha, who moved to the United States from Poland as a child of 12, may always have a Polish accent. We can also understand why younger siblings have such a terribly difficult time pronouncing their older siblings' names when they begin with *j* (Joshua, Jennifer, Julie, Jeremy). We can predict which words will be easy and hard to say. Finally, we can see why there are enormous individual differences in the ways in which toddlers pronounce their words even if these words are spoken by twins. Sounds like *k* emerge anywhere from 2.5 to 4 years, and that is all within the normal range. One of our children, who speaks beautifully now, systematically substituted *h* wherever the sound of *s* belonged, coming up with words we still laugh about—"hoda" for "soda" and "hocks" for "socks." Another child substituted *f* for *th* for years, as in "birfday" and "wif." He too speaks beautifully now. Generally speaking, there's no need for concern about substitutions and errors of pronunciation until the child is at least 6 years old. At that point you may want to have the child evaluated by a speech therapist who can help her learn how to use her vocal instrument more effectively.

Boys and Girls: Early Sightings of Mars and Venus

There is a popular book called *Men Are from Mars, Women Are from Venus.* Small but persistent early differences between boys and girls may well be early manifestations of that phenomenon. One of the most common questions asked about early language development is whether girls really learn words faster than boys. Sarah had fraternal twins—a boy and girl—and was astonished by the difference in their language growth. By 18 months her daughter had already gone through the vocabulary spurt while her son seemed more interested in vehicles than in language. He had only forty words in his productive vocabulary, and many of them were specific names for the cars in his collection.

The latest research in this area confirms Sarah's observations. Girls do tend to talk earlier than boys and reach each of the milestones sooner than boys—but only by a little bit. The data from the most comprehensive study to date, the MacArthur survey, suggest that on average girls lead boys on every language indicator: the number of words produced, the number of words understood, the number of words used in combinations, sentence complexity, and maximum sentence length.

The explanations for these differences fall into two camps—the biologically oriented and the social. Biological theorists argue that because girls mature earlier, the part of their brains devoted to language becomes specialized sooner. It appears that our brains are quite adaptive when we are born. Language could be housed in the right or left hemispheres. For most people—especially those who are right-handed—the left hemisphere takes over many language functions as they mature. One theory holds that this plasticity in the brain gives way to specialization sooner for girls than for boys, thus giving girls a slight biological advantage.

The social theorists suggest that girls tend to elicit more conversation from those around them than boys do. In one theory, since boys are less mature than girls at birth, boys cry more than girls. Parents are quickly socialized by this behavior and learn that they simply cannot respond each time the boy cries. The result? When girls talk, parents listen and respond. When boys talk, parents listen but only sometimes respond. Girls enter into "genuine" conversation sooner than boys and hence emerge with a language advantage. This explanation seems reasonable on its face, but there is research that suggests that gender differences persist even when boys and girls receive the same amount of input from their parents.

Firstborn Versus Later-Born Toddlers

Most parents who have more than one child have noticed that their firstborn tend to talk earlier than their later-born toddlers. Several studies confirm this small but real difference. Using diary records, one researcher was able to compare the age at which older and younger siblings reached the milestone of a fifty-word vocabulary. On average, firstborns accomplished this one month before their younger brothers and sisters. Spontaneous talk collected at two times during development also suggested that firstborn toddlers tend to have more varied vocabularies. Finally, the MacArthur study examined how second-born toddlers fared against their older siblings across a range of measures and found a consistent (albeit very small) advantage for the older child.

These data should come as no surprise. Parents have many more opportunities for one-on-one conversation with an older child than with the younger. When parents have to negotiate with two rather than one, the going gets a bit rougher, as the following anecdote illustrates:

> Celia is the mother of twin boys aged 20 months. Her house is constantly strewn with toys here and there as the boys run around the house. Celia tries to have "special" time with each child, but these moments are few and far between. She knows the importance of reading to toddlers, but it seems that each time she attempts to read a book to one, the other commands her attention: A diaper needs to be changed, a child has fallen over the toy horse, the Duplo blocks won't separate the way they are supposed

to. Even when both toddlers are somewhat settled, Celia has to divide her attention so that the conversation can flow smoothly.

Researchers have observed that mothers of four-month-old twins look at objects in the environment at the same times their babies are looking at those objects only half as much as mothers of singletons. By 12 months of age, these twins also spoke only half as many words as the non-twins. Interestingly, for the single children, more shared object examination at an early age relates to more language later. For the twins, however, no such relationship was found. Looking at twins at a slightly later age, other researchers compared twins and single children at 15 and 21 months. They report that the mothers were as verbally active with both groups. From the child's point of view, however, the twins received individual language attention only half of the time because the mother's talk was, by necessity, divided between the listeners.

The research on twins sheds light on what happens with older and younger siblings. While both parents and the older child converse with the younger one, she is not getting as much speech directed to her as did her older sibling. Further, what the older child tells her may not be as linguistically rich or interactive as the speech of a parent. Adults know how to frame a conversation so that they can fill in where the child leaves off. Older brothers and sisters may not be as facile with language and may talk at the baby rather than interacting with the baby. Differences in the amount and quality of language may prompt differences in the rate of learning. Fortunately, by the time that children are three to four years old, the slight differences in language acquisition have all but disappeared.

Social Class Differences in Word Learning

Inge's mother is sitting in the living room watching television. Inge [23 months] gets her mother's keys from the couch. Her mother initiates, "Bring them keys back here. You ain't going nowhere." Inge does not answer; she sits playing with the keys. . . . Inge gets a ball and says, "Ball." Her mother says, "It's a ball." Inge says, "Ball," and her mother repeats, "Ball." When Inge throws the ball over the TV as she repeats words from a commercial, her mother responds, "You know better. Why you do that?" Inge says something incomprehensible, and her mother answers, "Don't throw it no more." Inge sits on the couch with the ball, gets down, and falls. Her mother initiates, "Now, when you hurt yourself, then what?" Inge gets back on the couch, stands, and then climbs over the back of the couch. Her mother initiates, "Hey, quit climbing over my couch." She picks up Inge and kisses her.[1]

This passage comes from one of the most extensive and troubling studies of social-class differences in language development. Professors Betty Hart and Todd Risley of the University of Kansas conducted a comprehensive study in 42 families of different social backgrounds, from professional to working-class to welfare families. Collecting data from each family for an hour every month over the course of two and a half years, the professors give the clearest view to date of how differing language environments influence language outcomes in toddlers.

The above passage offers a scene from one of the tapings made in a welfare home. Here can be seen what will become the dividing line between the social classes. Though Inge's mother is affectionate, caring, and even interested in initiating some language exchange, many differences separate her speech from that of parents from more advantaged social classes. The most notable difference is that Inge's mother, while communicative, does not engage in conversations with her child. Most of the utterances that the mother initiates are in the form of statements or directives rather than being questions that open opportunities for conversation. Even when Inge opens the dialogue by saying "ball," her mother fails to expand upon Inge's statement in a way that would encourage more talk. She might have said, "Yes, that's a ball. Let's play a game with the ball." Instead, she closes the opportunity to talk by simply repeating the word "ball." No further language is offered to the child. This example illustrates one of the main findings of the research: Welfare parents talk less to their toddlers than do either working-class parents or professional parents. In turn, working-class parents talk less than professional parents. According to the observational data, the average welfare child heard only 616 words per hour, the working-class child, 1,251 words per hour, and the professional child, 2,153 per hour. Extrapolating from these figures, over the course of a year these differences between numbers become overwhelming: 3 million words of language experience for

1. Betty Hart and Todd Risley, *Meaningful Differences in the Everyday Experience of Young American Children* (Baltimore: Brookes, 1995), 205.

the welfare child, 6 million for the working-class child, and a whopping 11 million words for the child of professionals. If more talk is a key to language ability, a finding mentioned repeatedly throughout this book, then this difference magnifies over time to create a gulf in experience and in subsequent language growth.

Not only does Inge have less opportunity for conversation in the exchange with her mother, she also hears a different style of speaking. Even in this short exchange it is easy to see that Inge's mother offers more language that embodies prohibition than encouragement. The study calculated that an average child from a professional family accumulated 32 affirmatives and 5 prohibitions per hour—a ratio of more than six to one. The working-class child accumulated 12 affirmatives and 7 prohibitions per hour, a ratio of two to one. In stark contrast to these numbers, the welfare child received 5 affirmative statements and 11 prohibitions, a ratio of more then two negative to one positive. Drs. Hart and Risley suggest that these differences in input are reflected in differences in the toddlers' productive language skill and even in their IQ scores. These differences become wider with age and may be irreversible after the age of four.

The data from this study stem from recordings of spontaneous language in the toddlers' homes. The MacArthur findings, though based on parental reports, yield the same results. Though they find a small difference between families of different means, they do report that toddlers from more advantaged families have higher reported vocabularies and better grammatical abilities. Once again, differences in the amount of language babies hear affects their language outcome.

Echoed in these comments and in the research on gender differences and birth-order differences is a now familiar theme: There is wide variation in when young toddlers achieve language milestones. Some toddlers reach the vocabulary spurt at 14 months, and others don't until they are two and a half. These extremes and all the ages in between are all considered normal.

Scientific Sleuthing Pays Off

Lesson 1. The study of normal development helps in understanding language problems. As toddlers get older, it is possible to recognize language milestones. Once we can see development, we can also see problems. Here are some of the warning signs reported by speech pathologists, along with findings that researchers have found in populations with language difficulties.

Six potential warning signs can be detected in this period of language growth. Though they are only outlined here, it is important to note that there are many reasons for any one of these signs to appear. If you are concerned, you should consult your pediatrician.

Ted is a beautiful 23-month-old child who is big for his age. He likes to run around the house and to build towers and knock them down. He also loves to line up his large collection of Beenie Babies. Barbara, Ted's mother, is very sensitive and responsive and likes to be there for her child. For some time she has been concerned about Ted's language development. When she talks to him, he always focuses on something else. She tries to establish eye contact, but *he always looks away*, as if his toys are more interesting than she is. Frankly, Barbara feels rejected. Thus, she tends to talk less with Ted than she did with Ted's older brother.

Even at bedtime Barbara notices that Ted is hardly engaged. He will sit on Barbara's lap for book reading, but he seems to be *uninterested*. She tries to engage him by reading a book, but Ted *rarely joins the conversation*. He has *difficulty pointing at the pictures that she names* in the book. He is *uninterested in talking* even when he clearly wants something. He also seems to be marching to his own drummer—constantly *tuning out other people* and their conversations. Barbara continues to try, but as Ted gets older, she is frustrated by the lack of communication.

These signs of lack of social interest and silence may result from any number of conditions. The most common cause for some of these behaviors is that the child has had recurrent ear infections. Intermittent hearing can cause a lack of interest in communication. Because the child is often isolated from the sounds around him, he might have a tendency to tune others out. Among the others tuned out are those near and dear. Because he heard so much less language than his brother, he may also not know the names of the pictures in the book, thereby creating a climate of silence. As the child hears better and hears more language, many of these conditions will turn around, producing a late talker who will be fine as he gets more language stimulation.

Of course, a number of other conditions yield some of the same warning signs. Scientists have for years studied language delay. In general, it occurs when both intelligence and hearing is normal. Some delayed toddlers understand everything that is going on around them but are just slow to talk. These toddlers will probably be indistinguishable from their early-speaking peers by the time they enter kindergarten. Other toddlers have a delay both in word production and in comprehension. For many years it was thought that this was caused by environments in which insufficient language stimulation was provided. In the example above, for instance, Barbara is trying to keep the conversation going, but Ted is not responding. As Barbara gets more frustrated, she is less likely to talk with Ted, creating a situation ripe for language delay. In the past several years, however, researchers have examined not only the parent's language to the child, but also what the child might be doing to discourage conversation.

Language delay affects from 5 to 10 percent of preschoolers. Sometimes it arises from underlying factors like fetal alcohol syndrome or neonatal hemorrhaging. In what has been dubbed Specific Language Impairment (SLI), there can also be an underlying genetic cause. In some cases, language delay arises from differences in the ability to fully process all of the sounds of language and to hold onto these sounds long enough to store words. By way of example, think of the last time that you were at a cocktail party and were introduced to a number of new people. Some people have larger sound or phonological memories that allow more words to be stored. Others have rather limited sound memories. As it turns out, toddlers with smaller memory stores in this area have more limited vocabularies and are delayed in reaching the vocabulary spurt.

Beyond language delay, warning signs appear in special populations of toddlers who are afflicted with either autism or with mental retardation. In the case of autism, lack of eye gaze can be one of the telltale signs. Autism occurs mostly in boys and can be identified from 18 to 30 months of age. For autistic toddlers, their parents suggest, language is used to talk rather than to communicate. These toddlers do not enlist other speakers and appear to be uninterested in carrying on a conversation. Researchers suggest that these toddlers do not engage in joint attention, have great difficulty in reading social cues and in interpreting others' intentions. Since these cues are central to the social aspect of word learning, autistic toddlers are delayed in reaching vocabulary milestones.

Toddlers who are mentally retarded also tend to reach language milestones later than others. Here the cause is not a decoupling of social cues and language, but of mental ability and language development. It is not unusual for a Down's syndrome child to utter his very first word at 24 months rather than 12 months. Mentally retarded toddlers do not talk because they have not yet developed the skills of representation and categorization that allow them to support a growing vocabulary. Scientists disagree about whether the language development of mentally retarded youngsters is just late or is also deviant. The prevailing view seems to be that the language of these toddlers follows the same course as in children of normal IQ and is commensurate with the child's mental age. The arguments made above for the relationship between mental growth and language would support this view.

Thus, scientific sleuthing not only helps determine what the milestones are but also what warning signs to note when something goes awry. As we learn more from scientific investigations about the factors that undergird normal development, we become better equipped to understand language problems and remediate them.

Lesson 2. More language in = More language out. There is a recurrent theme in this book: When toddlers are immersed in language, they tend to use their language earlier and more efficiently. Nowhere is this more important than the period in which the vocabulary spurt takes hold. Toddlers in this period are ripe for language learning, soaking up whatever words are presented as they quickly "fast-map" the words onto new categories.

Study after study shows that a child's vocabulary can be predicted from the number of words that the child hears. Toddlers who are exposed to many vocabulary items become children who produce many vocabulary items. The reverse is also true. With so many findings like these, we come to understand why the social-class data reported above is so disturbing. If toddlers in welfare homes are hearing only a quarter of the utterances that toddlers from professional families are hearing, they are at a significant disadvantage for language learning. Unfortunately, this disadvantage only increases with development. Early vocabulary levels, for example, have been shown to relate to later reading ability and to the ability to analyze and write stories. Perhaps this is why Professors Hart and Risley suggest:

> To ensure that an average welfare child had a weekly amount of experience equal that of the average child in a working-class family, merely in terms of hours of language experience of any kind

(words heard), 41 hours per week of out-of-home experience as rich in words addressed to the child as that in an average professional home would be required.[2]

Recent studies of children in child-care settings suggest that all toddlers benefit greatly from environments rich in language stimulation. It is in the first two years, however, that this stimulation appears to have the most potent effects. Toddlers who have had more stimulating language environments in the first two years tend to have larger vocabularies and more complex sentence structures when they are three years of age. In short, children *learn language by hearing language.* The period of the vocabulary spurt is a particularly important time to talk to toddlers and make sure their ears are clear of fluid so that they can hear.

Lesson 3. Watching TV cannot make up for real communication. All of the language-learning examples provided thus far suggest that toddlers pick up their array of new words by engaging in conversations with parents, friends, siblings, or caregivers. A child's world, however, is brimming with language-learning opportunities. There are musical tapes, stories on tape, and, of course, one of technology's greatest baby-sitters—TV. Given the richness of *Mr. Rogers' Neighborhood, Sesame Street,* and *Barney,* some learning could be expected from the language that toddlers overhear on TV. Yet researchers are somewhat divided on this issue.

Fred is a hearing child of deaf parents. His parents speak in American Sign Language and are very much a part of the deaf community. Fred will no doubt be a native speaker of sign language. His parents, however, want him to be perfectly fluent in spoken English. They have a great idea. They will place Fred in front of the TV to watch age-appropriate programs for two hours per day. As Fred overhears the language on these programs, he will build his vocabulary and learn how to talk in oral English. This will be a special type of language-immersion program.

Though a number of deaf families hoped to have their toddlers learn language by watching TV, the results of this immersion program were very disappointing. Researchers who examined the evidence concluded overwhelmingly that TV by itself is not sufficient for

2. Betty Hart and Todd Risley, *Meaningful Differences in the Everyday Experience of Young American Children* (Baltimore: Brookes, 1995), 205.

language learning. Without already knowing something about the language, it is difficult if not impossible for the hearing toddlers of deaf parents to figure out what the characters in these odd TV worlds were talking about or doing. Toddlers learn language in interactive environments in which there is conversational turn-taking. They learn in adaptive environments in which the parents talk about the things that toddlers are interested in. The TV is neither interactive nor adaptive. The program plays on even if you don't understand it. There is no time for clarification or expansion. While at first glance television may appear to provide a wonderful language-learning environment, it is far from optimal.

What about the toddlers who learn the alphabet from *Sesame Street* and *Barney* or the three-year-olds who can recite entire commercials without a pause? They must be learning something from their exposure to TV. The latest research suggests that toddlers are able to learn vocabulary from watching planned educational programming that is geared to the child's language level. In shows like *Sesame Street* and *Barney*, objects are clearly labeled for the viewers as they are handled and displayed. The effect? Toddlers who watched *Sesame Street* and other programs like it from ages two to five had higher word-comprehension levels than toddlers of matched environments who did not watch the shows. At least for learning object names, TV can provide a boost.

What should we conclude about TV viewing? Television is not all bad. Used appropriately and with caution (toddlers need not watch the news reports), it can provide a vocabulary supplement. By its very nature, however, this noninteractive medium cannot substitute for caregiver conversation and interaction. Conversation is the key to large vocabularies.

By this point the child is amassing up to nine new words a day. In the time that it took to read this chapter, your child has already learned another one or two words. The quick accumulation is an important milestone in language development. With only single words, the child cannot express even simple requests like "More juice." Around the time that they are acquiring words at lightning speed, another milestone is taking shape. On the wings of words is the emergence of grammatical knowledge.

Chapter 6

"More Juice!"—Babies Understand and Produce Simple Sentences Between Eighteen and Twenty-four Months of Age

What Toddlers Can Say

Phyllis, Gloria's mother, is an executive of a large corporation. She has arranged to take the morning off to spend time with her daughter. After taking Gloria to her Musical Tots class, Phyllis must stop at the supermarket before she drops Gloria back at the house to spend the rest of the day with the nanny. Phyllis must be back at the office by noon for an important meeting.

The morning is going flawlessly, and Phyllis is so happy that she is able to have this quality time with Gloria. Things are moving right on schedule after music class as Phyllis and Gloria head to the supermarket. With only a half hour left to buy the food, take Gloria home, and get to the office for her meeting, Phyllis becomes conscious of the clock. Her schedule, however, is about to be irreversibly disrupted.

"NO SIT!" Gloria screams at the top of her lungs as her mother tries to place her in the shopping cart. "NO SIT!" she repeats loudly, as shoppers watch closely for Phyllis's response. Phyllis plasters a nervous grin on her face, masking the anger she feels toward her fallen angel. She has never been challenged so explicitly by Gloria. In all the tumult of the scene they are making, Phyllis does not realize the significance of the event that has occurred. For the very first time, Gloria put two words together to express a complex thought. With the power of two-word speech, Gloria has become a force to be reckoned with.

Two-Word Sentences Say It All

This is the way it usually happens. Unlike the dramatic moment in the movie *E.T.* when the alien says, "Phone home," two-word speech often goes unnoticed. Children seem to reach this milestone almost effortlessly after they have mastered about fifty words. Yet combining two words is a hallmark of development, almost a defining feature of what makes us human. Combining words gives us enormous expressive power. Word combinations, for example, allow us to talk about the room we are sitting in now, and how we would like to arrange it in the future. Word combinations enable Gloria to express her desires ("want juice!") and to make imperious statements in crowded supermarkets.

In this chapter, we begin by looking at the first two-word productions. We then look within the child's mind to open for view the foundation upon which this early language knowledge is built. Young children, though limited in their speech, are nonetheless adept grammarians who are interpreting our sentences. To start, let's look at some early grammar produced by children in the last half of their second year.

Typical two-word utterances produced by Jeffrey at 20 months:

"Mommy sock"	"Allgone outside"
"More juice!"	"Car go"
"Throw chicken"	"Little dog"
"Sweater chair"	"That Susan"

By themselves, we can only guess what these two-word utterances mean. But if we were told the context in which they were produced, we could probably make good guesses as to what the baby was trying to say. This technique, called "rich interpretation," is what many middle-class parents do all the time as they interpret their babies' speech and gestures. If "Mommy sock" was said with the emphasis on "Mommy" while Jeffrey was holding up his mother's large sock, you would probably conclude that "Mommy sock" was designed to comment on a possessive relationship, as in "This is Mommy's sock." If, however, "Mommy sock" was uttered with the same heavy stress on the word "Mommy" but in the context of Aunt Matilda's trying to put on Jeffrey's sock, you might reach another interpretation. You'd probably say that here "Mommy sock" could be paraphrased as "Mommy—not you—should put on my sock!" Or take "sweater chair." If it was said in response to a question Jeff's mother asked him, you'd have no trouble interpreting it. Jeff's mother asked, without really expecting an answer, "Where's your sweater?" because they were about to go out. Jeff surprised his mother when he said "sweater chair," clearly commenting (and pointing as he did) on the fact that his sweater was on the chair in the kitchen. Knowledge of the *conversation* that precedes the child's utterance helps parents to interpret what at first may be baffling. In addition, when information is added about the *situational context* and the *intonation* with which the child's utterance was said, the mystery of how to interpret these utterances seems to vanish.

Research has shown that babies around the world talk about the same kinds of things. Here's a list of the eight cryptic two-word utterances accompanied by the probable meanings that Jeffrey was trying to express.

Two-word Utterance	*Probable meaning expressed*	*Possible gloss*
"Mommy sock"	Possessor-possessed or	"That's Mommy's sock"
	Agent (acting on) an object	"Mommy, put on my sock"
"More juice!"	Recurrence	"I want more juice"
"Allgone outside"	Disappearance or nonexistence	"The outside is allgone" (said after front door is closed)
"Throw chicken"	Action on object	"(Dad) is throwing the toy chicken"
"Car go"	Agent doing an action	"The car is going"
"Sweater chair"	Object at location	"The sweater is on the chair"
"Little dog"	Object and property	"The dog is little"
"That Susan"	Naming	"That is Susan" or "Her name is Susan"

Now that we have made headway in figuring out what these primitive sentences mean, we need to analyze why it is that they seem so primitive. What's missing from these "sentences"? For starters, they resemble the way telegrams are written omitting every inessential word. But a toddler's "telegraphic" speech is quite unlike adult telegrams. After all, Western Union levies no additional charges for including the endings on words—as in "dat*ing*" and "call*ed*." Yet young children routinely omit grammatical endings like these that convey additional information. Their omission of these endings shows two things: First, toddlers are analyzing what they hear and choosing (unconsciously, of course) to separate off these little endings and omit them. If language learning was just "dumb imitation," in the way that we can learn the words of a song in a foreign language, these endings would be included. Instead, babies are *systematic* in what they omit, and they all omit the same grammatical elements. Second, toddlers' omission of grammatical endings shows that these elements take an effort to produce. In other words, although they seem so easy for adults, these little endings are psychologically costly for toddlers to include. Babies also omit short grammatical words such as conjunctions like "and," articles (such as "the" and "a"), and prepositions (such as "with"). For example, if we sent a telegram to tell someone that we were coming on the train with Grandma, we would write something like, "Coming train with Grandma." The baby version would be "Come train Grandma." No wonder their two-word utterances can be difficult to understand!

Another way in which toddlers' telegraphic speech is different from telegrams is the absence of pronouns. When was the last time you said something like "Irving has to go to the bathroom now" or "Cynthia needs lunch"? Yet toddlers usually refer to themselves by name—perhaps because that's the way their parents often refer to them.

Although babies using two-word speech are not yet using language the way we do, consider how far they've come. Take Jeffrey. Using words now and not just nonverbal gestures and eye gaze, he has become capable of expressing about ten complex meanings. Many of these could not be expressed without words, such as "Mommy sock" (the possessive relation) or "Little dog," or "Throw chicken" among others. Babies who might have formerly had tantrums out of frustration now have a tool to express themselves. In some ways, this new capability makes it harder for parents and caregivers. As part of their new expressiveness, babies can now "argue" with their significant others, as Gloria argued with Phyllis. They can assert their desires more clearly and can do so over and over and over again. No longer can you hide behind your lack of comprehension of their signals! Now you need to confront their claims head-on.

Try This: Two-word sentences take off! But what do they mean?

Before reading this section, you may already have operated with the assumption that babies' two-word utterances mean something. Some believe, though, that babies are just linking two separate words together and are not really using language yet to comment on the world. You should be able to categorize your own child's earliest utterances using rich interpretation. In your baby's language diary, make a table using the three headings used in the table above. Then record your baby's first ten or so two-word utterances and see if you can figure out what the baby meant to say and what he would have said had he been able. (It would be additionally interesting if you could record the way the baby said each utterance. That is, "Sit wap" would be "Sit lap.") Do you have any utterances that do not fit neatly on the table among the ten meaning relations we offered? If so, add to the list. It will be wonderful when your child is older to look back with him at this chart. You will both have a good laugh about the constructions he used to first express meaning.

What Enables the Baby to Use Two-Word Speech?

Baby Monica at 19 months says "sit wap" and you are stunned. She put two words together for the first time! Where does the ability to use two-word speech come from? A number of collateral developments make this possible. First of all, most babies start to use two-word speech after they have spoken about 50 words. Before this time babies seem more concerned with building up a storehouse of words and using them in combination with nonverbal signals than in putting words together. Perhaps they need to acquire a certain amount of facility in recalling and pronouncing their words before they can put two words together in their speech.

Second, the growing complexity of a baby's thinking prompts her to put two words together. As they learn more about the world and discover more interesting relations between people and objects, they want to share these ideas with you. As Dr. Lois Bloom, the foremother of the study of language development, has written, children are motivated to learn more language when their ideas exceed what they are capable of talking about.

Consider for a moment the nature of the mental leap involved in using two-word utterances. If a baby can say something as deceptively simple as "sit lap," it means that she has created an image in her mind of a state of affairs she would like to create. She is thinking of the future, and not just in the present. The baby has also learned how to name a body part, "lap," and an action, "sit." By using two-word utterances Monica is showing that she can see objects as independent from contexts and as capable of being recombined in new ways. How do we know this? Because in the next instant she may say, "sit chair" or "Monica lap." These new combinations with the same elements demonstrate that infants can separate an event into its components and then recombine the components in new ways. This ability to mentally manipulate words to express different relations is a kind of mental might. It is what makes human language so special relative to animal communication systems. Monica, with her baby-sounding two-word sentences, has begun to tap into the tremendous *generativity* that characterizes language. As Monica's productive vocabulary increases, she will soon join us in being able to produce an infinite variety of sentences just by changing the words around.

This ability to combine and recombine is analogous to being able to create multiple relations with objects. A block can be used not just to build a tower, but also like a hammer and also like a battering ram to knock down a playmate's tower. Words in language, like objects in play, can take on many roles. Something that Monica describes at one time as the agent of the action ("*cat* jump") can later become the object of the action ("jump cat," as in "the dog jumped on the cat") or the proud possession ("my *cat*"). The ability to play with objects flexibly, in ways that go beyond what is observed and what are their usual uses, represents a first step in the ability to combine words in multiple ways to represent different meanings.

What Toddlers Can Understand

Investigating Two-Word Productions: What Children Comprehend

The appearance of two-word speech is just the tip of an iceberg. Below the surface, Monica is busy analyzing and categorizing and storing the language around her. Nowhere is this seen more dramatically than in her language comprehension. Just how much does she understand? As the following example illustrates, it is often very difficult to tease apart what we think a child understands from what a child *really* understands.

John, 18 months old, is standing in the living room. His father asks, "Do you need a dry diaper?" John feels his diapers and hurries into his bedroom, where the diapers are kept, returning with a diaper [much laughter]. His father changes him, stands him up, pats him on the seat, and says, "There! Now you have a dry diaper." John feels his diapers and hurries into his bedroom, returning with two diapers.

How much of the sentence "Do you need a dry diaper?" does John understand? We have to go beneath the surface and investigate what young children know about the meaning of sentences.

Clearly, at this tender age, babies are starting to put the pieces together to make sense of the language addressed to them. What are the pieces John put together in this example? Think of the cues John drew upon. First, he seems to understand the word "diaper." But even here he probably had some help. In all likelihood, when John's father asked if he needed a dry diaper, Daddy gestured and looked in the direction of his diaper. So John had nonverbal cues about what his father meant. Second, John had a lot of prior experience to draw upon. He knew his diapers were kept in the bedroom. So when he heard the word "diaper," he made a beeline to the source.

Even though John's comprehension was less than perfect (the second set of diapers is a dead giveaway), he is due some credit. John is capable of putting together several pieces of the puzzle that he could not handle just a few months ago. He is starting to use the same puzzle pieces that we as adults use to understand what someone is saying to us.

Try This: What are the cues my baby relies on to understand sentences?

Babies are very good at using people's nonverbal cues as well as the context to figure out sentence meaning. If you wish to observe this in your baby, it is difficult both to talk to the baby and to attend to the cues you are inadvertently offering. It is easier to look for these cues in someone else's conversations with baby—say, your spouse or the baby's caregiver. Watch how the person speaking to your child acts as they talk. Do they use gesture and eye gaze? Do they use these cues differently (perhaps exaggerated?) than they might if interacting with an adult? Do they orient their body in a way that tips off the baby to what they are talking about? Do they put emphasis on key words in the sentence, more than they would if addressing an adult? Is the context one that might give away the meaning of the sentence? For example, is the speaker holding out the thing he wants the baby to do something with? And finally, does the speaker repeat parts of the original sentence, unconsciously breaking it up into smaller units to make it easier for the baby to understand?

If you observe these sorts of behaviors in yourself or in adults who talk to your baby, you might conclude that your baby doesn't quite understand as much language as you had thought. On the other hand, you will have a fresh appreciation for how clever your baby has become in using bits and pieces of the situational context and the speaker's nonverbal cues as aids to interpreting sentences. The fact that parents provide these sorts of cues to language-learning babies is not a bad thing at all. By offering a benevolent world where there are multiple, overlapping cues for sentence interpretation, they help the baby discern what sentences mean. Eventually, babies will not require this extra support to understand sentences.

What Does It Mean to Understand Sentences?

Language is more than merely connected words. True, words are essential. But words need to be shaped by grammar if they are to be understood by others. Anyone who has traveled to a foreign land with a pocket dictionary can attest to the limitations of words without grammar. For adults, learning grammar in a foreign language is hard and demanding. Toddlers, however, work out the grammar of their native language without any explicit tutelage.

To appreciate the task at hand, let's look at what seems like a simple example. How do you form a question in English? We use questions every day. We never really think about how to formulate them. Yet there are very clear rules about how to make a statement into a question. By way of illustration, how does the sentence "John will come" change into the question "Will John come?" "Easy," you might say, "you need only move the second word in the sentence ('will') up to the front." As a general rule, however, this would generate ungrammatical sentences. "John's sister will come" would turn into "Sister John's will come?" So, words can't just move depending on the particular position they happen to occupy in the sentence. Perhaps we can formulate a rule that depends on the type of word that gets moved. "To make a question," you now suggest, "we must move 'will' [a helping verb] to the front of the sentence." Again, we quickly run into trouble: "The man who will come is John" would become "Will the man who come is John?"

The solution? Categories like main and relative clauses, subject of the sentence and object of the sentence—all of those terms that harken back to eighth-grade English class—are the stuff from which grammatical rules are made. What counts is not the position of the word, but the grammatical function that the word is playing in the sentence. Rules of question formation have to be put in terms of the grammatical structure of the sentence. Complicated? You bet! That's why it is so impressive that babies learn these rules, and why mothers and fathers can't teach these rules to their babies. Indeed, even if you bothered to think about it, you would be pressed to think of a way in which you could teach such a rule to a two-year-old. Imagine saying, "Listen, Irving, when you want to make a question, move the helping verb from the main clause, not the subordinate clause, up to the front of the sentence."

If parents don't teach babies grammatical rules, then how do babies learn them? The field of language development has been in hot pursuit of this question for years. Regardless of the specific theory, there are three major underpinnings of language babies have to learn before they can speak and understand their native language. They must:

- Find the words, phrases, and clauses in the language they hear.
- Realize that the words in a sentence describe the events in the world.
- Recognize that different arrangements of the units in sentences changes sentence meaning.

Next we explore each of these feats in turn.

Babies find the units in the language stream. Where are the words? The phrases? The clauses? Although babies have to find these, this doesn't mean that they have to be able to *name* these units. In fact, they can't. Nor can adults in preliterate cultures where grammar is not taught at all. At some unconscious level, however, babies need to be aware of these grammatical units if they are to learn to produce grammatical sentences.

We've seen that babies at 18–24 months are becoming expert at finding words in the language stream and are building up large vocabularies. Surely words, the basic building blocks of all the world's languages, are the easiest language units to find. But in language development nothing is as simple as it first appears. Words are composed differently in different languages. For example, in languages such as Chinese and English, words don't carry much grammatical information. Each word serves a separate function. In a sentence such as "You saw me," each word conveys a different idea. To say the same thing in a language such as Imbaburra Quechua (spoken by the Indians of Peru), it takes only a *single word.*

        riku - wa   - rka - nki
        see - first person object - past - second person subject

Thus, in Imbaburra Quechua a single word can be composed of a rich combination of small grammatical particles. Someone might argue that languages containing separate word-like units should be easier for children to learn than languages which "paste" together different grammatical elements, but this is not true. For children, no language is harder to learn than any other. The milestones of acquisition occur at around the same time in children around the world.

Not only do words come in different shapes and sizes, but they are so deeply embedded in the speech stream that they are often hard to extract. As noted in chapter 3, words in speech are not surrounded by blank spaces, commas, or pauses. Finding the words and other grammatical units might prove difficult indeed. Yet by the age of eight months, babies are already working on this problem. They use their statistical knowledge about the kinds of sounds that occur at the beginnings and ends of words. By nine months of age, they already are listening to the sounds of language that we unconsciously use to end sentences and phrases. Rising pitch at the end of English questions, elongated vowels in the last words of sentences, all become familiar cues that allow babies to find the units of speech long before they will need them. Taken together, these cues provide a rich foundation onto which the first grammatical categories will be built. With these building blocks in the first year of life, our babies are prepared to learn grammar in the second year of life.

Babies realize that words in sentences describe events in the world. Finding the words, phrases, and clauses in the language stream is not enough. After all, sentences tell a "story." Babies have to become aware of the fact that a bunch of words strung together in a sentence are *more* than just a bunch of words. A sentence describes a particular event taking place in the world. The words in a sentence hang together to create meaning that is more than the sum of its parts. The way the words in sentences form "packages," or specific meanings, is parallel to the associative principle in arithmetic. Where parentheses are put in a mathematical expression makes a world of difference: $(4 + 3) \times 5$ is not the same as $4 + (3 \times 5)$. In the same way, "Dog bites man" describes a particular relationship where the (dog bites) the (man). If the sentence was the reverse, (man bites) (dog), we'd have a newsworthy event!

When do babies know that a sentence like "She's eating the cookie" describes a relationship between a person doing something to a cookie and not just a person (she), an object (the cookie), and a particular action (eating)? When do babies integrate the words they recognize in sentences to form "packages of meaning"? When do they go beyond understanding that words label objects and actions and learn that words can work together to describe events in their world? And how could we ever find out?

One research team, the authors of this book, decided to accept the challenge of probing babies' sentence knowledge. After five years we hit upon a methodological solution. We called it the "Intermodal Preferential Looking Paradigm," a mouthful now referred to as the IPLP. The method is "intermodal" because it uses two sensory modalities—the auditory (presenting language) and the visual (presenting pictures). Babies watch scenes on two televisions, only one of which matches the language they are hearing. Like the Head-turn Preference Procedure, the IPLP calculates how long babies look (preferential looking) to determine what they understand. Using the IPLP, we learned that a full five months before this period begins, babies already know that words in sentences work together to refer to particular events in the world.

Gertrude and her baby Bertha come into the baby laboratory. Gertrude tells us that Bertha, at 13 months, says only one word, "Dada," and understands thirty words. To be tested in the IPLP, however, the baby doesn't have to say a thing. We know Bertha understands the names of the objects she's about to see on the televisions because we asked Gertrude when we set up the appointment.

After acquainting themselves with our cheerful space and friendly testers, Gertrude and Bertha are escorted into the television room. There, Bertha sits cozily on Gertrude's lap facing two televisions. Gertrude's chair is carefully placed two feet back from the middle of the two televisions, which are themselves about a foot apart. Bertha will have to turn her head slightly to see what is on each television. Her mother wears wraparound sunglasses with the lenses painted black so that she cannot inadvertently influence her daughter.

To see if Bertha and her peers recognize that sentences map to unique events in the world, we show Bertha two different but very similar scenes. On one screen, Bertha sees a woman kissing some keys while dangling a ball. On the other screen, she sees the woman kissing the ball while dangling the keys in the foreground. On both televisions Bertha sees the same woman, ball, and keys. What is different is the *relationship* between the objects. Then she hears a centrally placed voice saying, "Where's she kissing the keys? Look, she's kissing the keys!" Remember the analogy between the associative principle in math and the way sentences create packages? Will Bertha create a package from these words and look at the scene in which the woman is kissing the keys? If Bertha is only paying attention to individual words, she will watch both screens equally. After all, the same woman is on both screens, the same objects, and the same action (kissing) is taking place.

Bertha, and her contemporaries between the ages of 13 and 15 months, watched the television screen that matched the language they were hearing. These results suggest that even babies who are just uttering their first words already know that sentences map to relations in the world. Babies are already integrating the words in a sentence to find the relationships the words describe. Plus, they are able to perform this integration on relationships that they have probably never seen before, such as kissing keys and kissing a ball.

Try This: Can my baby understand
that language maps to unique events?

Try this when your baby has some object names he comprehends but can't yet say. Assemble some objects randomly on the floor. Your baby should know their names, even though it is not necessary that he can say them. You also want to write down the names of the actions (verbs) you think your baby understands, for example, kiss, tickle, hug, or push. Before you begin, you will need to write down some sentences that create new relations, ones your baby has not created or heard about before.

When he is not holding any specific object and you have his attention, tell him to "Give the truck a kiss," for example. Can he carry out this novel command? Does he instead pick up an object (say, a stuffed animal) that is more likely to be kissed than a truck and kiss that? If your baby can carry out novel commands, it will turn out to be a fun exercise, another game you can play together. If your baby doesn't do this for you, don't be at all concerned. We created the IPLP because toddlers (as any parent can tell you) don't often do as they are asked.

Different arrangements of the units in sentences change sentence meaning. It is impressive that 13-month-old babies who can't say anything are sensitive to the fact that sentences describe relations in the world. This, however, is not enough to be credited with real language. The third thing babies have to do is recognize that different *arrangements* of the units that compose sentences make a difference in meaning.

Poor Alice, of Lewis Carroll's *Alice's Adventures in Wonderland,* was caught in a conversation with the Mad Hatter and the March Hare when she received her unwanted lesson: Changing the order of words in a sentence can change a sentence's meaning.

> "Then you should say what you mean," the March Hare went on. "I do," Alice hastily replied; "at least—I mean what I say—that's the same thing, you know." "Not the same thing a bit!" said the Hatter. "Why, you might just as well say that, 'I see what I eat' is the same thing as 'I eat what I see!' " "You might just as well say," added the March Hare, "that 'I like what I get' is the same thing as 'I get what I like!' "

English is very dependent on word order. Thus, in English (but not in Serbo-Croatian, Hungarian, or Walpiri, among other languages), the order of the words often determines the meaning of the sentence. John Kennedy used English's reliance on word order to coin the unforgettable sentence, "Ask not what your country can do for you, but what you can do for your country." When do toddlers know that differences in word order signal differences in meaning? Do babies even recognize that the order of the words in a sentence has been changed?

The answer to the first of these questions is startling. Using the Headturn Preference Procedure, researchers discovered that babies as young as two months of age can detect a difference in word order. In the experiment, babies listened to the sentence, "Cats would jump benches" over and over again. After they seemed bored, they were presented with the sentence "Cats jump wood benches." The babies perked up again and paid renewed attention, indicating that they had indeed heard the difference. That babies can detect this change in patterns is probably not a surprise given babies' early statistical prowess. What they cannot do at two months, however, is assign any meaning to this change. Children do not know that differences in word order signal differences in *meaning* until the second year of life, when they have amassed at least some words they can understand.

Once again we used the IPLP to test when toddlers can tell that "Cookie Monster is tickling Big Bird" means something different from "Big Bird is tickling Cookie Monster." Some of the children tested had only two words in their productive vocabularies. Let's follow Bertha and her mother, Gertrude, through this experiment again.

For these videos we used the brightly colored Sesame Street characters Big Bird and Cookie Monster (overheated graduate students dressed up in costumes). Bertha knew who Big Bird and Cookie Monster were and knew their names. If Bertha didn't, she would not have been in any position to reveal her ability to comprehend sentences based on the order of their words.

On one television, Bertha sees Cookie Monster tickling Big Bird. Both are facing sideways in the same direction. As Cookie Monster tickles Big Bird's waist from behind, Big Bird is shaking a big box of toys as if in response to the tickling. On the other television, the roles are reversed: It is Big Bird who is tickling Cookie Monster while Cookie Monster holds the box of toys. Both scenes are equally attractive and action-packed. Now a female voice using infant-directed speech emanates from the central speaker between the televisions and says, "Where's Big Bird tickling Cookie Monster? Find Big Bird tickling Cookie Monster." Bertha can't find the matching scene just by looking for the scene where the first-named character is moving. The characters are moving on both screens. To indicate that she understands that word order makes a difference, Bertha has to watch the television that matches what she is hearing. If Bertha looks more at the television that the sentence requests, it tells us that Bertha does have the ability to use word order to find the correct event.

Even children who could say only one or two words paid attention to the order of the words in sentences like these. They watched the event where Big Bird was tickling Cookie Monster when they heard the sentence that described it ("Big Bird is tickling Cookie Mon-

ster"). But when they heard "Cookie Monster is tickling Big Bird," they watched the other screen. Toddlers between the ages of 16 and 18 months of age, who can say at most a few single words, can understand five- and six-word sentences.

This word-order test is harder than the prior test we described. In that experiment when Bertha was asked, "Where's she kissing the keys?" Bertha didn't have to pay attention to the order of the words; the sentence could be interpreted only one way since the keys could not kiss the lady! So Bertha could rely on her knowledge of the world, in addition to her knowledge that words in sentences create packages, to look at the correct event. In the study on word order, however, Bertha had to listen closely to figure out which of two possible relations was being described. Sentences like "Big Bird is tickling Cookie Monster" are called "reversible" sentences because either character can perform the action. She had to pay close attention to the order of the words to figure out which of the two, virtually identical events taking place before her was being described.

The ability to use word order to find differences in meaning is no small accomplishment. At the same time that toddlers are amassing a large number of words in their second year, they are also listening to the structure of the language around them. They have already figured out that the order of the words in a sentence makes a difference for the meaning of that sentence. Plus, babies who had small vocabularies did just as well as those who could already put two-word sentences together. Their comprehension lays the groundwork for the rudimentary language that will emerge during this period.

Try This: Does my baby know that differences in word order signal differences in meaning?

Investigating this question at home is not at all difficult. One way to test for word-order comprehension is to do what Professor Steven Roberts did. Write down a few reversible sentences using what the baby calls you. For example, if you are a mommy, write down some sentences with actions for which the baby knows the names, such as "mommy tickle" and "tickle mommy" or "mommy kiss" and "kiss mommy." When you have your baby's attention, say them one at a time to your baby, and wait and see what happens. You have to be patient and not rush the baby's response. You may also need to ask the question a couple of times and then be very still waiting to see what the baby does. When "mommy" is first in the sentence, the clear implication is that Mommy is going to do the action. When "Mommy" is named after the action (as in "tickle Mommy"), however, the implication is that the baby will do the action to you. Does the baby look to you to perform the action when you say sentences like "Mommy tickle"? Does the baby perform the action when you use sentences like "Tickle Mommy"? If you get different responses with the two kinds of sentences, your baby is indeed becoming sensitive to how word-order differences signal differences in meaning.

Another way to test for word-order comprehension is to find two props of similar size (two different small plastic animals or two different vehicles). See if the baby can *act out* reversible sentences. You have to be sure that the baby knows the names of the objects you have selected and understands the verbs you're going to use. Otherwise, you won't have created a fair test. Clear the area of toys. Take a cow and a dog, and place them side by side and equidistant from the child. The baby should not be handling either object. Make sure you have your child's attention and then say, "Show me the cow kisses the dog." Repeat the sentence a few times if your child doesn't respond. What does the baby do? Does the baby create the relation you've described? Or does the baby create the reverse relation, having the dog kiss the cow? Then say "Show me the dog pushes the cow." It doesn't matter much which actions you use as long as you know they are reversible and your baby understands them. If your child enjoys playing at this, you've created a new game. And if your child shows you different responses depending on the order of the words in the sentence, you have succeeded in getting your child to reveal his or her burgeoning grammatical knowledge.

Beyond Word Order: Children Attend to Grammatical Elements

Even at the one-word stage of language production children are attending to five- and six-word sentences. As they advance to two-word speech, their underlying grammatical capabilities, not yet revealed in their speech, are even more advanced. Let's return to Monica, who was just beginning to say two words together. She routinely left out the little words like "a," "the," and "with," along with endings such as -*ing* and -*ed.* Does she really fail to notice these grammatical elements in the language that she hears? When do babies become sensitive to these grammatical elements? Think of what Monica would gain if she were aware of these elements even though she doesn't yet say them. These little words and elements give important clues to what kinds of words we are hearing. That is, they are essential for helping to *categorize* what part of speech words belong to. ("If it has an *-ing* on the end, it must be a verb" or "If it is preceded by 'a' or 'the,' it is probably a noun.")

To test whether babies like Monica, not yet saying grammatical elements like "the" and *-ing*, are sensitive to them and expect them to be present, several toddlers were brought into the baby lab and shown a picture book with four pictures on each page. The pictures were of things for which Monica already has names: dog, chair, book, and truck. The friendly researcher who tests Monica allows her to look through the picture book first. Then she starts asking Monica to point at things in the book, just as Monica's parents do. She gives Monica one of four kinds of requests. For example, if she wanted Monica to point at the dog, she would say either:

1. "Find the dog for me."
2. "Find gub dog for me."
3. "Find was dog for me."
4. "Find dog for me."

How do these sentences differ? The first is obviously normal, the kind of sentence Monica hears all the time. So the first sentence provides a baseline against which responses to the other types of sentences can be compared. The second sentence substitutes a nonsense word ("gub") for "the," a word that Monica has never heard before and which she might be expected to ignore if she's just paying attention to the content words she knows anyway. The third sentence substitutes a real word, "was," that Monica hears all the time in place of "the." If the slot before the word "dog" has a familiar word in it—even though it doesn't belong there—perhaps Monica won't care. The last sentence omits the article altogether, sounding like what Monica herself might say. The question is whether Monica will respond differently when asked these different kinds of questions. Will her ability to point at objects and animals whose names she knows be disrupted when she hears a nonsense word or a grammatical word that is misplaced instead of the expected "the"? If Monica's ability to point at the pictures declines when she hears the strange commands, we will be able to argue that Monica is aware of the article "the" in some way even though it is missing thus far in her own speech. What did Monica do?

Not surprisingly, Monica and her peers were able to point to the requested picture with the greatest success when they were asked with the normal sentence (#1). They were correct 86 percent of the time with that question, and this is about as good as it gets with toddlers. They achieved their next greatest success (75 percent correct) with the sentence in which "the" was omitted altogether (#4). So they seem to have noticed that the obligatory "the" was omitted, but it didn't seem to bother them much. What did bother them, however, and seriously disrupted their ability to point at the correct picture were sentences containing a misplaced but perfectly legal word of English— "was" (#3)—as well as the presence of a nonsense word (#2) where "the" belonged. To those questions, they were able to get only 56 percent and 39 percent correct, respectively.

These are intriguing findings. They suggest that although Monica is not yet saying articles, she expects them to be there. She notices when they are missing, and she notices when a word she's heard many times before ("was") is used inappropriately. She is really thrown when a nonsense syllable takes the slot reserved for "the." Once again, using the route of comprehension, we have evidence that Monica is far more sensitive to language and its nuances than what she shows us in her own speech.

Perhaps sensitivity to "the" is to be expected, though, because it is so common in speech. Perhaps if toddlers were tested for other grammatical elements—especially ones tacked onto words—babies wouldn't notice.

The ending -ing (as in "dancing," "pushing") tells us that an action is taking place. This suffix is never heard alone and never begins a sentence in English the way that "the" does. It should be harder, then, for babies to notice. But if babies did notice -ing, despite the fact that it is arguably harder to detect, they could use it the way they may use "the." While "the" tells us that what follows is a *noun*, the particle -ing tacked onto the end of a word tells us that what we are hearing is a *verb*. The ending -ing may also help segment the language stream, since it is an excellent bet that what follows -ing is a new word. Other than long adverbs like "swimmingly" and "blindingly" that babies are not likely to hear addressed to them, -ing does not often occur "inside" words.

The particle -ing is one of the first grammatical elements that babies incorporate into their talk. Usually, around 24 months of age, babies include -ing on the ends of their verbs when it is appropriate (as in "doggie running"). (The past tense ending -ed will not follow for a while.) It makes sense to think that even before babies include

-ing reliably in their own speech, they have been analyzing the speech they hear, computing the frequency of *-ing*, and noticing the kind of word (action words) in which it appears.

Twenty-month-old Curtis, not saying much at all yet—let alone adding *-ing* on the ends of his verbs—comes for a visit to the baby lab. Curtis and his peers between 18 and 20 months of age are presented with two simultaneous video events in the IPLP. The same woman is seen doing a different action on each television screen. A woman is dancing happily on one screen and waving to the baby on the other screen. Curtis hears the female voice emanating from between the televisions ask, "Which one is dancing?" If Curtis and the others couldn't find the correct action when they were asked for "dancing," it wouldn't make sense to go on with the experiment. But they have no difficulty finding the woman dancing or waving.

As a next step, the *endings* that babies heard on the verbs were changed. One group of babies heard, "Where's dance*ly*?" The ending *ly* is perfectly acceptable in English; it just doesn't happen to be found on verbs. Another group heard, "Where's dance*lu*?", a distinctly strange ending for a two-syllable word in English.

The results were fascinating. When babies heard *-ly* at the end of the verbs, they were at first confused and could not find the matching verb. But halfway through the four sets of verbs on the videotapes, they began to watch the requested action (say, dancing) when the voice asked for "dancely." It was as if babies said to themselves, "Maybe *-ly can* end verbs in English. What do I know? I'm pretty new at this language stuff." The fact that they could eventually find dancing when they heard "dancely" implies that they recognized that *-ly* was a possible English word ending. This is pretty interesting since babies won't be using adverbs like "quickly" or "happily" for at least a year.

Babies had an entirely different reaction when they heard "dancelu"—a nonsense ending. These babies *never* found the matching verb. That is, they watched both screens (dancing and its mate waving) about the same amount of time, moving back and forth between them. Babies could have ignored the *-lu* or the *-ly* and watched the correct action based on the main part of the verb, "dance." But they didn't. They tried to make sense of the endings. When they heard *-lu*, it really threw them.

Babies are indeed sensitive to the fact that *-ing* and not just any frequently heard syllable in English belongs at the end of a verb. This result shows the fact, yet again, that babies know more about language than they show in their own speech. But perhaps this isn't so surprising. After all, by the age of nine months babies have already computed what sounds and sound sequences are possible in their native language. Given another nine or so months of language experience, and a number of verbs in their comprehension (if not production) vocabularies, and why shouldn't babies notice the frequency of different kinds of endings for words?

Try This: Is my baby sensitive to grammatical elements?

Would your baby respond incredulously when you use bizarre words or word endings? First try the experiment on articles. As you are reading a story book with your baby, and you are sure you have your baby's attention, throw in a zinger every now and then. Ask your baby to "Find the doggie" in the typical way, waiting for the baby to point at a picture and reinforcing their brilliant choice as you probably do anyway with a "Wow! Good job!" But also ask of another picture "Find gub kitty" and of another, "Find was car." Try this as you move through the book, varying the order of the different kinds of questions. Be sure your baby knows the names of the things you are asking her to identify. That way, if you get a response to the bizarre substitutes for "the," you'll know that these substitutions do indeed have an impact. What does your baby do? Does she do a double-take or look puzzled? Or does she go right ahead and point at the requested object, apparently ignoring the anomalous words? Try this experiment first at the beginning (around 18 months) of this period and then again at the end (around 24 months). By the end of the period, you should get a response from the baby even if you didn't at the beginning.

Play another game using verbs to see if your baby can show you that she is already sensitive to verb endings. If you make it fun for the baby to carry out a requested command, you can probably make this one work. Use only actions your baby knows the names of and can carry out. Start out by saying, "Can you jump? Show me jumping." If the baby jumps, clap and cheer. If the baby doesn't jump, *you* jump and clap and cheer. Then try asking the baby again. If this works and you have the game going, do a few more normal ones and then start throwing in bizarre ones every now and then. "Irving, listen closely. Show me dancelu!" Or, "Irving, show me wavely." How does your baby respond to the strange endings? Can you see any hint that the baby thinks these commands are a bit weird? We used the IPLP to reveal this sensitivity and don't know if babies will show you different sorts of responses in their actions when asked in this way. But if it works, you've revealed language capabilities that are grand indeed.

"With"—A Grammatical Element in Action

Babies' attention to small, unstressed grammatical elements represents a finer, more sophisticated analysis of language than merely attending to the order of the words. One further study shows how by the end of this period—although not at the beginning—babies can use grammatical elements to *override* word order in their sentence interpretation. The grammatical element they discover is the preposition "with."

One of the ways in which babies learn about sentence meaning is by paying attention to how the words in the sentence are arranged. If someone says "Sally blixed John. She blixed him but good," we have a sense that Sally did something to John (and it probably wasn't particularly pleasant). But someone says, "Sally and John blixed yesterday" or "Sally blixed with John," we assume that Sally didn't do something to John but that they did something together. Now, in each of the sentences "Sally" is the first name mentioned and "John" is the second. So, if babies paid attention only to the order in which a name was mentioned *and* if they ignored the grammatical elements, they would falsely conclude that Sally was always doing something to John. Unstressed grammatical elements, although they are small and pronounced with little stress, serve as the glue for the sentence and make all the difference in interpreting the correct meaning. When do children attend to this rather subtle information?

Once again the IPLP was used to test this question. Fraternal twins, 23-month-old Judith and Phillip, come to the baby lab with their mother, Kiki. On one screen, Judith sees Big Bird holding Cookie Monster's shoulders and gently pushing him down to bend from the waist. On the other screen, both Big Bird and Cookie Monster, standing side by side, are bending from the waist at the same time. Judith hears, "Where's Big Bird bending with Cookie Monster?" Judith and the other girls were able to zero in on the screen where the characters were bending *together*. This means that by 23 months of age, girls recognize that "with" is telling them that the characters are doing the action together even though Judith and her peers are saying only two- and three-word sentences.

Then Phillip is tested. His response to the same videos and language is most interesting. He and the other boys tested consistently watch the screen where Big Bird is making Cookie Monster bend, as if the sentence they are hearing is "Big Bird is bending Cookie Monster." Thus, Phillip and other 23-month-old boys are ignoring the "with." By 28 months both the boys and girls have no problem interpreting the "with" sentences correctly. Consonant with earlier information, boys lag a bit behind girls in their sensitivity to the way grammatical words like "with" can affect sentence meaning. Yet even the boys are analyzing the grammatical structure of the sentences. That is, they are figuring out which character is the subject of the sentence and which is the object of the sentence.

Comprehension Far Outpaces Production, but Why?

These examples lead to a single, stunning conclusion: babies know a lot more than they can tell us. At a time when they are using mostly single-word speech, they are understanding fundamental properties of grammar. This finding accords well with the experience in high school foreign language classes. Students often find that they can understand their teachers even though they feel incompetent when asked to form their own questions and make their own conversations. What is it that limits them in production? Why would nature "build" a baby whose comprehension greatly exceeded her production of language? Psychologists have pondered this question for years, and language specialists now seem to have some reasonable explanations.

First, the comprehension-production distinction can be likened to the difference in recognition and recall in memory. Many people can recognize that they have seen a person before but have great difficulty remembering his name. Or, people tend to prefer multiple-choice types of questions to essay exams because it is easier to choose among possible alternatives than to devise an answer. These examples parallel the differences between language comprehension and production. In comprehension, we need only recognize a word or sentence and not assemble it ourselves. With an increasing number of words filling our mental dictionaries, it is easier to reply passively than to construct a sentence.

Second, and related to the first explanation, the information a person receives in a sentence is already organized by the speaker. She has put the words in a particular order, added the grammatical nuances, and put stress on the relevant words. It is so much easier than searching for the words and putting them together. There are so many places where you can go wrong in the latter case. It is also easier to understand an organized sentence because you don't need to make sense of all of the elements to get some idea of what is going on. For example, children of this age generally assume that the first living thing mentioned in a sentence is the actor and that the second is the object of the action (as in "The dog chased the cat"). This is a viable comprehension strategy and one that is generally, though not always correct ("The cat was bitten by the mouse"). In production, the child must be the organizer—the grand conductor who puts all of the language pieces together. This job requires that the child know the full score for all of the language parts and know how each of these parts fits in. This is a most difficult job.

Finally, children live in a world in which people speak about things that are generally in the immediate context. Thus, the child has the here-and-now advantage in comprehension. If part of a sentence is unclear, the child need only turn to the surrounding context to glean the meaning. This is exactly what happened in the diaper example earlier in this chapter. The child did not really need to understand what was said to solve the problem of obtaining the diaper. He needed only to hear the word "diaper" and look at his father's gestures. In saying words, a child must create the match between context and language and generate the meaning from scratch.

So it is not surprising that production is a more difficult task than comprehension. For this reason comprehension might be a better gauge of a child's language progress at this age than production. Yet despite these findings in the literature, most tests of language are more heavily weighted toward production. When you visit the doctor's office, you are asked what your child says, not what she understands. When you go to Aunt Matilda's for a family function, people rave about what the child says, not what she seems to know. And, depending on the day, Junior might not say anything. Indeed, when asked to perform for aunts and uncles, children find a way of becoming shy and silent. Production is an important clue to language development, but much more is going on in the child's growing mind. On the surface, children are just putting two-word sentences together. In their minds, a grammatical garden is starting to blossom.

Scientific Sleuthing Pays Off

Lesson 1. Engage in rich interpretation but don't bother to correct. Perhaps we've convinced you (or you already knew) that you should be having conversations with your toddler. But how? They say things like "sweater chair" and "have it soup." What kind of conversation is that? It's the kind that babies use to express themselves to us. They know it's not perfect—in fact, if you listen closely, you may catch babies engaging in spontaneous repairs of what they have just said. So what's a parent to do? Build on what you think your child is trying to say. There are several steps involved when we analyze what parents do. First, they listen closely to what their baby is saying. This can already be a tremendous challenge. When their pronunciation is less than ideal, sometimes you can struggle through several back-and-forth conversational turns before you get it. Consider the following anecdote,

> At 22 months, Jason stood in front of a large bay window and said "bi winow" while pointing. What was he pointing at in the street? He said "bi winow" three more times before any of the four adults present understood what he was trying to say. Finally, his mother said, "Oh, big window!" and Jason seemed content.

Second, once parents decipher what syllables the child is uttering, they appraise what the child is saying in relation to the situational context, the child's intonation, and the prior conversation. This is just what Jason's mother finally achieved: Jason was trying to share information. The bay window was one big window. Without the context of the bay window, however, it is very doubtful that Jason's mother would have figured out what he was struggling to say.

Third, parents often try to translate what the child has said into a complete sentence. Don't worry that you're putting words into the child's mouth. As in the negotiation of failed-messages episodes described in chapter 4, babies will tell you in no uncertain terms if you got it wrong. When you reformulate what the child is trying to say, think of the language material you are providing for him to work on. You are implicitly teaching the child that there are many ways to express this idea. You are also showing him that he left out a lot of material that expresses his ideas more clearly. So what you are doing is providing a model for how to express these ideas. Also, babies whose parents take their communicative attempts seriously are often calmer than those whose parents ignore them. Ignored babies go to great lengths to get their parents' attention.

Along these lines, perhaps you are wondering if correcting the way babies say things helps them to improve their grammar. Consider the following anecdote, courtesy of the late language researcher Martin Braine:

Child: Want other one spoon, Daddy.
Father: You mean, you want the other spoon.
Child: Yes, I want other one spoon, please, Daddy.
Father: Can you say "the other spoon"?
Child: Other . . . one . . . spoon.
Father: Say "other."
Child: Other.
Father: Spoon.
Child: Spoon.
Father: Other . . . spoon
Child: Other . . . spoon. Now give me the other one spoon.

This is not unusual. Babies do not seem to learn from correction. First of all, they are often not certain exactly which part of their utterance is being corrected. Second, as in other parts of their lives, they are resistant to correction. This is not necessarily because they are obstinate but more likely because they are not yet ready to alter their internal grammar to suit the model that parents are providing. Such errors fall by the wayside when the child is ready to abandon them and move on.

Babies react much better with hearing the right way to say something after they have said it wrong or incompletely. For example, if 21-month-old Robert says, "Mommy work," his father might say, "Yes, Mommy went to work." What he did here is called "expansion." His utterance extends what Robert said by adding the grammatical information Robert left out. In this way the parent reiterated and confirmed the child's communicative intention *and* provided a model for a more complete way to say it. Although the research literature is divided on whether expansions like this make a difference for children's grammatical development, parents actually expand their two-year-olds' utterances about 20 percent of the time. Furthermore, there are studies showing that children who hear sequences that are partially repetitive (as in "Put the cat in the cradle. That's it. In the cradle") have more rapid grammatical development than their peers. Expanding on children's utterances by providing the material they left out can at a minimum make children feel understood and eager to share more of their thoughts through language.

Lesson 2. Your baby's caregiver is your ally. By the time a child is between 18 and 24 months of age, approximately half of all mothers have reentered the work force. In these cases a caregiver becomes the first line of defense. This person spends many waking hours with her charges. It is crucial to use a caregiver as an ally in a child's language (and total) development.

As noted earlier, "silence is golden" is not a rule that a potential caregiver should embrace. If you select a caregiver, pick someone or some environment where babies are talked with a lot and engaged with language. This is really important to reinforce and encourage in your caregiver, and you can only do this if you see your caregiver as your ally in your child's development. You want to see your caregiver talking to your baby and taking his immature attempts seriously and not ignoring them. It's easier to ignore them, especially if there are other children around. But that is not the best language-learning environment for a baby.

If you treat your caregiver as a partner in your toddler's development, you will be greatly rewarded. Ask your caregiver questions and share your concerns. Your caregiver can fill you in on things that Isaac said or did. You want to know what Isaac is interested in so you can capitalize on this when you read and talk with him. Building on what he likes can only help to maintain his attention. You also want to know because it's fun to know what he did while you were away. And if you are keeping a diary, you will want to enter the things he says.

Nonetheless, remember that the Kaluli don't talk to their children until they hear the words "breast" and "mother," and their babies turn out just fine. As mothers, we have been through the child care search ourselves and know that things are never perfect. Sometimes sacrifices are made in one area because of pluses in another. However, finding someone or someplace that honors your toddler's primitive language attempts and stimulates her through language is essential to your child's development.

Chapter 7

The Language Sophisticate at Twenty-four to Thirty-six Months: Why? Why? Why?

The Emergence of Grammatical Capability

Josh is 31 months old now. He is playing with a banana peel at the kitchen table as his mother feeds baby brother Benj. Excitedly pointing at his new arrangement of the banana peel, he exclaims: "Mom, look, I made a moon. Will you pick me up so that I can put it in the sky?"

"Oh, Josh, that's beautiful. You made a crescent moon."

"Yes. Will you pick me up?"

"In a minute. I am feeding Benjamin."

"Oh, okay, first you'll feed Benjamin, and then you'll pick me up so I can put this in the sky."

Enter the next phase of language learning. Josh, once restricted to a single word like "flower," is now a full conversational partner. He uses complex grammar when he asks questions that begin with the word "will," when he uses contractions like "you'll" for "you will," and when he can create a 20-word sentence that strings three separate thoughts together with an "and" and a "so." This is a child with a plan and with the language to carry it out.

Children make enormous leaps in grammatical development between the ages of two and three. Not all children make these leaps at the same time, but they are all unconsciously working toward the same goal: the ability to use language so fluently that they can take the building blocks of language—words—and create an infinite number of grammatical sentences. During this period toddlers quickly move from telegraphic speech to torrent-like speech. The very child who you thought would never say a word is now talking endlessly. It is said that some children talk so much throughout the day that they end up falling asleep in the middle of a sentence.

This chapter sketches some of the developments in language acquisition that occur between ages two and three. This is when children add the "ifs," "ands," and "buts" to their speech. Children also learn to ask "why," and "why," and "why"—and then "why" some more. We will explore the new language terrain and ask what could possibly be going on in the mind of a child that enables such sophistication to occur. Are children simply imitating what they hear? This is unlikely, since they say things that we would never say, such as "My feets hurts!" and "Do you are sad?" Do parents correct their speech so that they come out with proper English? No, parents don't give children explicit language lessons. Could it be a biologically driven system informed by hearing our language? Are children really destined to learn language in the same way that spiders are destined to spin webs? We'll show you what scientists know about the contribution of mind and environment during this particularly sensitive period. The discussion begins, however, with a look at the new milestones that take place after the child starts to combine words into sentences.

Adding Glue to the Sentence: Function Words and Particles

'Twas brillig and the slithy toves
  Did gyre and gimble in the wabe;
All mimsy were the borrogoves,
  And the mome raths outgrabe.
     —Lewis Carroll, *Jabberwocky*

You have no trouble identifying this piece as written in English, and in some weird sense, you feel as if you understand Carroll's poem even though most of it is gibberish. Although most of the content words are nonsensical, the important little words like "and" and "the" provide the "glue" that holds these sentences together. It is this glue, the so-called "function" words and particles, that establish, for example, which words are adjectives and nouns. Words like "the" signal that a noun is coming; endings like *y* and *s* mark adjectives and plurals. They let you know that there are multiple "toves," and that in the setting of this poem, the "toves" (whatever they are) are "slithy."

Children's first sentences are noticeably void of function words like "the" and "and" and of markers like *-ing*, *-s*, and *-ed*. Though 18-month-olds and two-year-olds are aware that these markers exist, their first sentences are constructed out of content words—words packed with powerful, concrete images that can be yoked together to get meaning across, "sentences" such as "Mommy sock" or "sweater chair." Yet these little, often undefinable words (can you define what "the" means?) and the particles like *-ing* on verbs are the stuff that holds our sentences together. To master a language, children have to include them in their speech.

Much of what is known about the development of function words and particles comes from one of the most comprehensive studies in developmental psychology. Professor Roger Brown, one of the founding fathers of child-language research, conducted an extensive observational study of three children whom he affectionately named, Adam, Eve, and Sarah. Eve was the daughter of a graduate student at Harvard, Adam was the son of a minister, and Sarah was the daughter of a man who worked as a clerk outside the Boston area. The study began in 1962, when Eve was 18 months old and when Adam and Sarah were 27 months. Professor Brown and his students continued to observe the children's language growth until they were 50 months old.

Researchers examined their speech to see when they started using grammatical "glue." In particular, they focused on 14 of these function words and particles. They determined that these started to enter children's speech just when they began to use three-word sentences. They also found that the three children acquired the 14 function words and particles in the same *order*, even though the children progressed at very different rates. Thus, Eve, the most precocious of the children, developed these first while Adam and Sarah followed the same order of acquisition at a later age. Several other studies have since confirmed these results.

What is the progression? The first particle children include in their speech has to do with indicating a continuing action. In English, the ending *-ing* indicates that an action is ongoing, happening now. Children sound much more sophisticated when they say, "Daddy running" (still omitting the helping verb "is") rather than just "Daddy run." Next, children include the prepositions "on" and "in." An utterance like "sweater chair," which required some interpretation by a parent, now becomes "sweater *on* chair." The ability to use the plural marker *-s* comes next. At first children use the correct form of irregular plurals too, saying "feet" and "men." Once they figure out, however, that most plurals are indicated with *s*, you may start to hear "mens" and "foots." Not to worry—this phase will pass too.

Next, children become able to indicate that an action has taken place in the past by using the past tense of irregular verbs (as in "went" and "came") as well as the regular past tense, as in "walked" and "kissed." The possessive *-s* (as in "Mommy's book" and "Nathan's rabbit") then makes its appearance. Notice that the *-s* ending for the possessive is the same as the *s* used to signal a plural. The *-s* ending is also used for the third-person singular, as in "she walks." No wonder it takes children so long to learn these endings and sort them out. The same ending serves three different purposes.

Articles like "the" and "a" come next. Consider their usefulness. They can make clear to a listener whether the object being described is one of a class (as in "*A* dog has four legs") or a particular item being singled out (as in "*The* dog has four legs"). With several other additions in between, the list culminates with the ability to use contractions like "I'm" and "you'll."

Try This: Finding grammatical function words and particles in your child's speech

The best way to detect grammatical glue is to sit down with the list of function words and particles and to write the date that your child first says them. Watch carefully after your child has just begun to produce two- and three-word speech. All of a sudden you will hear your child expand his speech in ways that sound more like adult language.

A second way to look at your child's burgeoning knowledge of these function words and particles is to borrow from a simple test developed by Professor Jean Berko Gleason, one of Roger Brown's students. She developed this test for use with four- and five-year-olds, but you might want to try a home-spun version on your three-year-old just to see what happens. The test was designed to examine development of the plural, the present progressive (*-ing*), and the possessive ending *-s*, among others. It's really quite simple. First you need to draw two pictures of a novel (and very simple) creature on two different pieces of paper. Present only one of these pictures to the child and say, "This is a wug." You might want to repeat this a few times and maybe say something about where the wug lives. Just be careful *not* to use the plural form "wugs"—because this is what you are going to test for. After you show the child another wug, present the two pictures of the wugs side by side and say, "Now there are two _____," giving the child the opportunity to fill in the blank. If the child doesn't, you might say something like, "What do you see now?" giving the child the opportunity to say "two wugs" or just "wugs."

The plural test is the easiest to perform. You can be adventurous and try the present progressive by acting out a scene with some Duplo creatures. Make the Duplo figure jump up and down and ask, "Space man or (name) is _____." Will your child fill in the blank by adding a verb with *-ing* on the end of it?

Eliciting some of these responses from children at home is very difficult, but it is exciting if you can get your children to show you the new language rules that they have learned.

Overgeneralizations: It Breaked!

The best way to observe a child's emerging sophistication with grammatical function words and particles is to watch for times when she overgeneralizes her new knowledge. Sometimes children glue things where they do not belong. Perhaps the most celebrated case of overgeneralization is with the past-tense marker *-ed*, as shown in the following example.

> Baby Bertha at 26 months: "I went bed. No tired!"
> Baby Bertha at 32 months: "I goed to bed. Not tired!"

What happened? Is it possible that children *unlearn* the correct grammar and wildly glue *-ed* to all verbs as they grow older? Researchers suggest that such overgeneralization occurs precisely because children are learning grammatical rules. At two years and before, children might memorize some of the words that they heard. They then use these words appropriately in a sentence. But, as seen from earlier discussions, children are exceptional pattern analyzers. As they exponentially increase the number of words that they hear and use, they come to notice dominant and regular patterns in the ways that adults speak. Most of the time when we express past tense, we simply add *-ed* to the verb that we are using. Not surprisingly, the young statisticians who overhear us create a general rule, "For past tense, add an *-ed* to the end of the verb." The only problem is that children become overzealous in their use of the rule and apply it not only to "look," "talk" and "kiss," but also to "go," "break," and "fall." Children have induced a general rule from the patterns of language that they hear. This is a major mental leap.

When we first hear overgeneralizations, we think that they are a dominant feature of children's language from two to three. They seem to stick out of the language stream like a sore thumb. Recent evidence suggests, however, that overgeneralizations are not as frequent as they appear. One researcher analyzed 11,521 irregular past-tense verb forms used by 83 children and found that there were many fewer overgeneralizations than correct usages of the past tense. In fact, overgeneralization occurred in only 2.5 percent of the cases for past tense and in 8.3 percent of the plural cases (as in "foots" and "tooths"). This research suggests that children do have it largely right. They have memorized the irregular forms of "went," "broke," and "foot" but occasionally fail to retrieve the right form of the word. When the right word does not come to mind, they invoke their newly learned rule and overgeneralize. Overgeneralization persists for quite a while in child language at a low but consistent rate throughout the preschool years. In fact, just the other day one of our children (age eight years) said, "I *seed* the books before I bought them."

Asking Questions

Simultaneously, children are learning to ask questions so that they become not only respondents in conversations but also inquisitors. Two types of questions enter into the dialogue: yes/no questions and *wh-* questions.

Bill in a game of Twenty Questions:
   Okay, I'm thinking of a person.
Crowd at party:
   Is the person a male?   Yes
   Is he dead?   No
   Is he in politics?   Yes

and the game goes on.

In this game each of the questions must be posed as a yes/no question. Adults have no trouble molding questions into such a form. But how do they sculpt their speech to meet the requirements of the game? Scientists suggest that people start by unconsciously forming a statement like "The person is a male" or "He is dead." They then shift the statement to a question by moving the helping verb into the front of the sentence to create "Is the person a male?" or "Is he dead?"

Yet the task has some hidden hurdles:

Did he used to be a governor?   Yes

Where did the "did" come from? The base sentence was "He used to be a governor," not "He did used to be a governor." Yet we implicitly know that the "did" must surface if we want to make a yes/no question and when there is no helping verb on call.

Yes/no questions are the easier of the two types of questions, but children don't start to use them until they are using three or more words in their sentences and until they have acquired a bounty of helping verbs. Even with these verbs, however, the first yes/no questions are signaled by intonation rather than by inverted word orders. Parents are likely to hear the following progression:

Phase 1. Mommy apple?
Phase 2. Mommy want apple?
Phase 3. Does Mommy want apple?

What determines how fast children progress through these phases? In part, the language that children hear is a determining factor. Research suggests that parents who ask more yes/no questions are modeling helping verbs for their children. Notice that as they ask these questions, they are also putting the helping verbs in the front of the sentence, making them more prominent. The result? Parents who ask more questions have children who ask more questions. Keeping the conversational engine going, and inviting children to respond, leads them to ask more questions too.

What's Up, Doc? Wh- Questions

The second type of question to examine is called the wh- question, affectionately named for the *wh-* that begins most of (though not all) of the wh- forms. A journalist is well acquainted with the wh- format:

Who was that masked man?
What was the man's name?
Where did you last see him?
When did he give you the package?

Why did he choose you? and
How did you get it?

The first wh- form in children's speech occurs when they are about 18 months old and ask, "What's that?" This first appearance, however, is somewhat deceiving, for it is not clear whether this oft-used phrase is really composed of two separate words or is really one word used to mean "Give me the name for that." Real wh- questions appear in between two and three years of age and are often yoked to the appearance of helping verbs. In wh- questions, children quickly learn that the wh- part goes in the front of the sentence. What they don't know at first is what to do with the rest of the question. Thus, in the initial phase wh- questions seem to be stuck onto the front of an entire sentence. They come out sounding like this:

Phase 1. Who that? What she make? Where Daddy is? Why Mommy
go store?

In the next phase of acquisition, children begin to include the helping verb but fail to move it to its proper place. This leaves the child producing rather odd sentences that sound like this:

Phase 2. Where the other boy will go?
What she did say?
When Daddy will come?

Finally, the child seems to get everything in its proper order:

Phase 3. What did you doed?
When will Daddy come home?
Why is Mommy at tennis?

As with the yes/no questions, children have a lot to learn, and much of what they do during this period of development is to listen carefully to what they hear and constantly adjust their own speech until they get it right.

Why? Why? Why?

Wh- questions come in different forms and in different levels of difficulty. By far the hardest to learn and understand are *why* and *how.* To answer a "what" question you need only name an object. For example, if Mom asks two-year-old Sarah, "*What's* that?" all Sarah has to do to answer is supply a single word: "Truck." To answer a "where" question (as in "*Where* is your truck?"), Sarah need only state a location ("Under chair"). For a "when" question, again a short answer will suffice. When Mom asks Sarah, "*When* do you want lunch?" all Sarah has to do is state an approximate time, "After *Sesame Street.*"

Answering a "why" or "how" question is a bit more complicated. This is why children often rely on that all-purpose word "because." "Why did you hit your brother?" Mom asks almost three-year-old Jessica. "Because I want to" is the infuriating reply. On the converse side, parents often unwittingly provide far more information than they meant to in response to the continuing barrage of their children's "why's." Take this conversation with 30-month-old Kate:

Dad: Good-bye, Kate, I'm off to work.
Kate: Why?
Dad: Because I have a meeting.
Kate: Why?
Dad: Because a client is coming in from Florida.
Kate: Why?
Dad: Because he wants to hire me to do his financial planning.
Kate: Why?
Dad: Because that's how I make money.
Kate: Why?
Dad: Because we need money to eat and buy good things.
Kate: Why?
Dad: Because that is how the capitalist economy of the United States of America is organized, and now that we are part of a global economy . . . arrgghhh!

Dad didn't mean to deliver a dissertation on the economy, but many a parent has been trapped in similar cycles. We sometimes take our children's questions at face value and give them answers that are far above their current level of understanding. By the time Dad has described the meaning of capitalism, the child generally is bored and moves on. Indeed, some researchers suggest that you needn't give detailed answers to inquisitions. Short, simple explanations will suffice. Children may not really want to know the answers to the questions. Rather, they are trying to figure out how the words "why" and "how" work. As they practice using these words, they come to realize just what a word can do. It can keep my parent engaged—with me controlling the discourse by my questions—for a long time. Children like this feeling of power. In addition, since "why" and "how" questions, unlike the other wh- words, tend to yield long answers, children get to hear a lot of useful language from which to construct their next grammatical achievements.

Ifs, Ands, and Buts: The Grammatical Spurt

From two to three there is a dramatic change in children's ability to use grammar—to express many of their ideas and intentions through the powerful tool of language. By the time children reach the age of three, they are virtually fluent in all of the rules of their native tongue. Just as the period between 19 and 21 months is called the "vocabulary spurt," this period could be called the "grammatical spurt." At two years of age, children are putting their first words together. At 27 to 30 months, they are up to three- and four-word speech—with the accoutrements of function words and particles and wh- words. By the time children are approximately 30 to 36 months of age, their average sentence can be as long as five or six words as they add even more complex forms to their talk. When children use six-word sentences, you begin to see what are called "embedded sentences."

The first of these new forms to enter the child's language include sentences like "I see you sit down" or "Watch me bake a cake" or "I think he's bad." In each of these the object of the sentence is a sentence in itself. For example, "I see" is one sentence and what is seen ("you sit down") is another, and the object of the verb "see." Children are learning ways to combine two sentences into one. This is a big step for a toddler because it means that he can generate longer sentences that contain more than one idea.

After you hear embedded sentences, like "Can I have ice cream when we get home?" or "When we get to the store, can I have a cookie?" be on the lookout for the "ands" and "buts" that often pull two sentences together. "He said I took it, *but* I didn't" or "I want the truck, *and* he has it!" Shortly after they can coordinate sentences, "because" and "if" make their debuts as children continue to master causality on the grammatical level. "I hit him because he did not give me the toy," or "Can I have dessert if I eat two more bites?" These last sentences are the most difficult, for they not only require the coordination of two sentences, but also some relationship or contingency between the two sentences. That is, the child seems to know that the first sentence (getting dessert) will not be satisfied if she does not comply with the second sentence (eating two more bites).

By the time that children are using coordinated sentences, they are full-fledged members of the language community. They no longer require parents to be their interpreters because they can make their feelings and intents known. While there are still some refinements to be added, the job of putting words together to form grammatical sentences is largely complete.

Is It Really Grammar?

Children between the ages of two and three are operating with a real grammar, with nouns and verbs, adjectives and adverbs, with categories like subject of the sentence, object of the sentence, etc. Of course, until children take grammar in middle school they don't know the names of the categories that they so deftly manipulate. Indeed, in preliterate cultures where children do not attend school, they still learn a human language with the same ease. For this reason some researchers have argued that we are analyzing children's speech through adult eyes and giving them too much credit for sophisticated structures that they simply do not have.

After debate in the field of early child language research, most experts have decided that even the very first sentences uttered by children do indeed reflect the use of categories such as nouns and verbs. The very stuff learned in grammar classes is possessed by the two-year-old human mind. There are three types of evidence to support the claim that young children possess grammatical categories of various types even though they are not conscious of it. The first type can be seen in the following conversation with twenty-nine-month-old Stacy and her mother as they lie on Stacy's bed prepared to read bedtime stories.

Mom: Should we read the animal book with the lamb on the cover?

Stacy: Lamb on there.

Mom: Yup, do you want to bring me the book?

Stacy: Stacy get lamb book. Put lamb on here. (*indicating the bed*)

Why is this interchange—which resembles many others like it—significant? If all Stacy was doing in her speech was using a word in a particular slot in the sentence with no cognizance of its grammatical functions, she would use the word "lamb" only one way. Instead, Stacy uses "lamb" in a variety of grammatical roles—as a subject of a sentence ("lamb on here"), as an adjective ("lamb book"), and as a sentence object ("[I] put lamb on here"). Stacy's grammatical knowledge enables her to use "lamb" in a variety of grammatical roles in her sentences. She has grammatical sensitivity that is belied by her unsophisticated-sounding speech.

Sensitivity to part of speech is also revealed by 33-month-old Allison when she is pretending to read a *Curious George* book that had been read to her many times before. The list of words (written on a blackboard) are "bag," "cage," "bed," and "feed." When Allison pretends to read them, she spontaneously changes the verb "feed" to the noun "food," making it conform to the part of speech of the other words on the list (all nouns). With this change Allison shows how, at some implicit level, she recognizes the part of speech of the words in the list.

A second type of evidence that young children are using grammar comes from an interesting observation about what children do and do not say. For example, in English we can say, "Big dogs" and "Dogs are big." We can't say somewhat parallel structures like "Big Fred" or "Big he" even though we can say, "Fred is big," and "He is big." Why can't we say "big Fred" and "big he"? Nouns can be modified by adjectives unless they are proper nouns like "Fred," or "Beth," or pronouns like "he," "she," "I," "me," and "it." Do children who are but two years old really know that they can't just use an adjective indiscriminately, with any type of noun?

Researcher Paul Bloom found that young children do indeed respect grammatical rules involving different types of nouns. Examining utterances from the speech of 13 children between the ages of 18 and 34 months, Bloom found mistakes like "Big Fred" in only 5 percent of the cases. Children act as if they are aware of grammatical categories in their speech and tend not to violate these categories. Children are aware of the rules that govern how different types of nouns work with adjectives.

A final compelling piece of evidence comes from languages that use articles to indicate gender. Languages such as French assign a gender (male = *le*; female = *la*) article to all nouns. Yet the articles are not based on the true gender of an item. For example, one hypothesis would be that children start out using *"le"* (the masculine article) for all nouns relating to men, and *"la"* (the feminine article) to all nouns relating to women. However, right from the start French children respect the abstract grammar and have no trouble assigning the feminine marker *"la"* to both a man's shirt and a necktie and *"le"* to a woman's shawl. These children are learning grammar not based on meaning but based on far more abstract categories.

The Source of Grammatical Capability in the Human Species

Where Does the Grammar Come From?

How do children learn to put grammatical function words and particles in their sentences and to move the words around in sentences to create questions from statements? Perhaps the most straightforward answer comes again from Grandma's folk psychology. If you want children to learn language, you have to talk to them a lot and then they will imitate what you say. Yet if imitation was the whole story, children would never make the kinds of mistakes they do, saying things we as adults do not. They would never generate sentences like "I goed to the store," or "I hurt my foots." Yet children say the darnedest things, as in the following example:

> Thirty-four-month-old Jill is eating a dinner of chicken and rice. She is lifting a spoonful of rice toward her mouth when. . . . Achoo! she sneezes. The rice flies off the spoon and onto the table and floor. "What happened?" her mother says. Jill replies, "I bless you-ed the rice off the spoon."

Instances like this one show that children are, at least partially, finding their own way in language learning. They are taking what we say and interpreting it through their own internal language-learning "machine."

Grandma's view of grammatical learning is also challenged in a classic study that examined how well children could imitate sentences. Professor Roger Brown and his colleagues asked children, 25 to 31 months of age, to imitate a series of sentences like "I showed you the book," and "I am drawing a dog." What did they find? Eve (25 months) responded, "I show book," and "Drawing dog." Another child, Ian (31.5 months) imitated the sentences by saying, "I show you the book," and "Dog." The children imitated what the researchers said in a systematic way. But the system that they used was not imitation—they filtered what they heard through their own language system. That is, the children left out the structures in the adult sentences that they had not yet mastered in their own speech. This suggests that children are not learning language just by imitating what adults tell them. They are reinterpreting the language that they hear through their own less mature language knowledge.

Grandma would probably also say that parents teach their children language, correcting them when they make a mistake. But she would be surprised to learn that study after study has shown that parents and caregivers tend *not* to correct children when they make a mistake. Surely if we were teaching our children to talk, we would correct them when they made a grammatical error. But when parents are faced with scenes like that which transpired with Billy below, it is hard to imagine that grammatical corrections occur with any frequency.

> Billy comes running inside, looking for his mother. He is out of breath and breathing loudly. With his brow furrowed, he grabs his mother's hand and says, "I hitted Barry. He breaked my truck."

Perhaps the occasional mother would finish this scene by saying, "Honey, the word is 'hit,' not 'hitted' and 'broke,' not 'breaked.' " More likely, however, Billy's shocked mother would take his hand and make a beeline outside to assess the carnage.

Numerous studies have examined whether parents correct their young children's language attempts, and they have come to a similar conclusion. Parents do not draw attention to the error and then ask the child to correct it. At age two, parents do tend to repeat sentences or phrases more often if they are said incorrectly than if they are said correctly. Yet the evidence suggests that even this more subtle kind of correction does not occur often enough to make a dent in a child's learning. Indeed, in a study that one of us conducted, we found that mothers offered a grammatical rendition of an ungrammatical phrase in only a fifth of the cases. Teachers who correct their students only one in five times are not going to be effective.

We are left therefore in a bit of a quandary. If children don't say what we say, if they cannot imitate us faithfully, and if we don't correct them when they say things that are wrong, how do they learn the rules of grammar? How can they possibly master the function words and particles, the questions, the word order, and all the rest of what makes up language knowledge, if we do not teach it to them?

A Language Instinct?

Some answer this question by suggesting that while hearing parents talk is important, children also come to language learning well prepared for the task at hand. Just as spiders spin webs, rabbits dig burrows, and bats emit sound waves to avoid hitting obstacles as they fly, humans are designed to learn language.

A fascinating natural experiment with deaf speakers makes this point. For this example, we go to Nicaragua in the year 1979. In her report Ann Senghas writes:

> Only 16 years ago, public schools for special education were first established in Nicaragua. These schools advocated an oral approach to deaf education; that is, they focused on teaching spoken Spanish and lipreading. Nevertheless, the establishment of these schools led directly to the formation of a new *signed* language. Children who previously had no contact were suddenly brought together to form a community, and they immediately began signing to each other. The first children to arrive at these schools ranged from four to fourteen. They all entered with separate means of communicating that they had used with their families. Some had a lot of miming and gesturing skills, some had home sign systems that were slightly more elaborate, but none entered with a developed sign language.[1]

To speak with one another, these children were placed in the awkward position of having to develop a language from scratch. There were no adults around using sign language for these children to watch. The language that was to emerge was constructed jointly by innate forces for grammar development and the need for rapid and effective communication among its users. Researchers like Dr. Senghas observed how the Nicaraguan sign language was developed by its very first users and how it came to change over time as new children entered the school and became members of the deaf community.

1. Ann Senghas, "Conventionalization in the First Generation: A Community Acquires a Language." *Journal of Contemporary Legal Issues*, 1995, 503.

What Ann Senghas found is that the children quickly developed a sign language, choosing from the vast array of available signs they had brought with them. Amazingly, the children created signs that used a consistent gesture order and that made clear distinctions between who was doing what to whom. The key point is that children created grammatical aspects of this new sign language on their own. *Children enriched and expanded the new sign language without any tutelage from adults.* Each child joins the human species primed to learn a human language and often more than one language.

The Critical Period: Time Is Running Out

Could it be that humans are predisposed to learn language, but if the process does not take place within a given time, we lose the ability to learn a language with a high degree of proficiency? Is there a "critical period" of development in which to become a fluent speaker of a language? A critical period is a time when the development or learning of a specific skill takes place most easily. After the critical period ends, learning that same skill is difficult and in some cases impossible. Several natural experiments, some going well beyond the bounds of ethical behavior, help address these questions.

On November 17, 1970, a headline in the *Los Angeles Times* read, "Girl, 13, Prisoner Since Infancy, Deputies Charge; Parents Jailed." The authorities might never have found out about the girl had her blind mother not come into a welfare office seeking help for herself. Social workers, however, found her little girl, with an olive-shaped face, undernourished body, and autistic-like gaze. Though she weighed only 59 pounds and was 54 inches tall, investigators found that she was a teenager. Her story shocked the world. Genie, as she has come to be called, had spent her entire childhood strapped to a potty chair in the back bedroom of her house. At the time she was discovered, she could not cry or make any noises. Apparently, her father had only allowed her mother to bark at her like a dog, and she was punished if she made any noise. She could not focus her eyes beyond 12 feet.

In a beautifully written account, Russ Rymer narrated the child's life story and her remarkable ascent from the dungeon of her childhood. Scientists rushed to help Genie recover from her isolation. Among them were scientists who observed Genie's condition to see if it was possible to help her learn language. Genie was beyond the presumed critical period for language learning since she was past puberty. Being isolated, she had learned virtually nothing of her native tongue.

As you might imagine, Genie did not talk when she first escaped her imprisonment. After four years of intervention, however, she had learned enough vocabulary to resemble a five-year-old child. While her vocabulary advanced, her grammar did not. Conspicuously absent from her speech were the grammatical function words that hold language together and that permit people to talk more specifically about the relationships between objects and actions. Her grammar was not unlike that of patients who have had the left side of their brains removed due to tumor or injury. Her utterances sounded like this: "Mama wash hair in sink," and "I want Curtis play piano." Not only was her grammatical development forever impaired, but so was her conversational ability. Researchers noted that Genie never seemed to initiate a conversation. She would respond if asked—but only if asked repeatedly. When she did respond, she often simply mimicked what had just been said.

Genie was not exposed to language until after the critical period for language learning. While she was able to learn some language, it did not include the grammatical elements that children many years younger learn.

What Genie's case demonstrates is that exposure to language is necessary for learning a language. Further, this exposure has to occur before the critical period for language learning ends at around puberty. This finding has enormous implications for second-language learning as well as for first-language learning. It suggests that second-language learning must begin during the critical period as well.

Together, the research on critical periods and on language in the deaf indicate that there is a biological basis for language learning. Humans are preprogrammed to learn a language. What this means is that it is a rare child who does not develop language. The ability to learn a human language comes for free along with species membership.

Scientific Sleuthing Pays Off

The study of early grammatical development in toddlers provides a number of practical lessons. When should we worry about children's grammatical development? What can we do to enhance children's development? When should we introduce children to a second language?

Lesson 1. When should you worry? The point at which children achieve language milestones varies widely. The period from two to three years of age lays the groundwork for a child learning to talk. However, this time period is also important because it is the first time that language problems can be identified. For example, children with hearing problems are not always identified until they fail to form grammatical sentences. Only then do parents learn that their children were not having the crucial language exposure they needed. Because the grammatical spurt is such a fertile period for language growth, lack of development in this period tends to flag a language-learning problem.

What are the warning signs? Speech therapists say that one of the key signs is a lack of eye contact. If children are not engaged in conversation and do not show any desire to communicate, there may be either a hearing or a learning problem. Children should also be putting words together during this period. Indeed, many children reach this milestone between the ages of 18 and 24 months.

There are two reasons why certain children do not put two words together during this period. Some simply don't want to talk, even though they are very good at comprehending what is said. The child who comprehends everything will probably develop normally. Many parents report that by age three these children decide to talk at last. The second reason for language delay is that children do not comprehend the language used around them. These children may need language therapy, and they should be assessed immediately by a professional so that intervention, if it is needed, can begin.

Children between two and three often have learned a few nursery rhymes or songs. If they go to a preschool, they might know the "clean-up song" or the "snack song." If your child has trouble learning these simple repetitive patterns, it might be a clue to deeper problems. The memorization of nursery rhymes and songs demonstrates the ability to remember sequences of sounds which are crucial to language growth. A child who cannot name the most common of household objects, body parts, foods, etc., by this age may also have language-learning difficulties. Well into the period at which children should be soaking up words, children who stumble in vocabulary growth should receive professional attention.

Another cause for concern is the inability, especially of three-year-

olds, to attend to a book or a movie. Though two- and three-year-olds are not known for their long attention spans, it should be possible at this time to engage them at least for a short period of time. Children who are constantly jumpy and on the move, children who *cannot* be engaged, should be watched carefully. Again, a history of ear infections is sometimes the cause, and parents would do well to try to structure some down time in which language is a focus. For example, these children would benefit from a nightly bedtime story and from conversations over dinner. A child who continues to resist these attempts might have an attention or hearing problem and should be seen by a professional.

Finally, by the age of three, children should be understandable. As noted in chapter 5, it takes a long time to master all of the sounds used in language. Nonetheless, by this age, children should be able to speak clearly enough to be understood by most people. If a child is very difficult to understand or if the parent and immediate caregiver are the only people who can make sense out of the child's talk, then professional help should be sought.

Lesson 2. What should we do or not do to promote language growth? Although children are prewired to learn grammar, becoming a fluent speaker requires language exposure. In order to add the glue of language such as the 14 grammatical function words and particles and the wh- questions, children must hear how these grammatical elements are used in the speech of their parents and caregivers. We provide the grist for their language-learning mills by producing sentences that serve as models of what a fuller sentence looks like. Further, by using more questions in speech to children, we offer examples of how certain forms like wh- questions and helping verbs work.

Asking questions not only allows parents to model the missing grammatical pieces for children that they leave out of their own speech, but provides a forum for learning to use language. It is through questions that we keep conversations going and that we acknowledge the child's contribution to the dialogue. Research suggests that children whose parents elicit conversation talk more and talk earlier. These parents also use fewer commands in their speech to their children, and they tend to stay on the child's topic longer without shifting the direction of the conversation. Children who learn language earlier may have better social skills than those who learn later. Children who have better language skills can get what they want more easily and need not resort to more aggressive behavior.

Techniques that correct children are not as helpful. Children spend a lot of their time trying to be understood, and parents and caregivers must try to understand them and not constantly correct their communicative attempts. Don't worry, children will eventually figure it all out on their own.

Lesson 3. It's never too early to start learning a second language. The LeBlanc family has just moved from Paris to a suburb outside San Diego. Though the LeBlanc adults have long awaited the move, the children are not as enthralled. Three-year-old Jean Paul really doesn't understand much of what is happening. Seven-year-old Pierre and his older sister, 12-year-old Fabrienne, had many friends and a good school in France. They see the move as devastating. Worse yet, though Mr. LeBlanc speaks English, the children barely do. In school, they will not be able to understand a word that anyone is saying.

How will these children fare? If there really is a critical period for language development, the 3- and 7-year-old should become fluent within the year while Fabrienne and her mother lag behind. What does research have to report about learning a second language?

In one study, adult Italian immigrants who had arrived in the United States between the ages of 6 and 20 read a short paragraph into a tape recorder. Judges were then recruited to determine if they could detect an accent. As might be expected, those who had arrived before age 12 had little or no accent while those who had arrived later did. Interestingly, the number of years lived in the United States had little to do with the results. The only factor that counted was the age of arrival in the country. For the LeBlanc family this means that Fabrienne and mother will speak English with a French accent while the younger children will sound more like native English speakers.

The same pattern emerges in the acquisition of grammar. What matters is the age at which a person first starts learning a new language. The number of years spent speaking the language is less of a factor. In one experiment, Professors Jacqueline Johnson and Elissa Newport studied Chinese and Korean adults who spoke English as a second language. They divided the adults into two groups: those who learned English between 3 and 15 years of age and those who did between 17 and 39 years of age. The groups had the same number of years of exposure to English.

The adults were asked to judge whether sentences of English were grammatical or ungrammatical. The sentences were constructed to reflect many of the grammatical nuances of English; half were correct and half were not. One example was: "Yesterday the hunter shoots a deer."

Despite the fact that these two groups had equal length of exposure to English, the 3-to-15-year group consistently outperformed the second group. Further, within the younger group, the study found that the younger the exposure to English, the higher the grammatical proficiency. In other words, those who had learned English between 3 and 7 years of age did better than those between 8 and 10 years of age; these latter adults did better than those who had been immersed between 11 and 15 years of age. Native-like fluency in English was evidenced only in the group that arrived between ages 3 and 7. For the LeBlanc family, this means that 3-year-old Jean Paul and 7-year-old Pierre will have a distinct advantage over their 12-year-old sister and mother.

This research on second-language learning reaffirms that there appears to be an optimal time to learn language. Though the facility for learning does not close down totally after puberty, factors like the entrenchment of the first language and a diminished language faculty make learning a second language much more arduous. Given such compelling evidence for a critical period in language learning, we might question why second-language learning in schools is introduced only after the critical period has ended. In multilingual countries such as Belgium and Switzerland, language learning is central to the curriculum and begins early in primary school. Americans, on the other hand, wait until children are in middle school to expose children to a foreign language. Americans make foreign language learning difficult by design!

One of the reasons that schools wait so long is a wide-ranging belief that young children can cope with only one language at a time, that children who are forced to learn more than one language will suffer from smaller vocabularies and from poorer grammar. Anecdotal reports suggest that children learning two languages talk later and might even mix words from both languages in their speech— failing to distinguish between the two languages. Since over half the world is bilingual, it is time to reexamine these claims.

Chesney is a two-and-a-half-year-old from Philadelphia. Her parents are both lawyers, working long hours from eight in the morning until six at night. Though Chesney is enrolled in the Bright Start

Nursery, she spends the bulk of her day with her caregiver, Felicia, a Puerto Rican woman of 30 who recently moved to the United States. Felicia is a kind and gentle caregiver who was a teacher before moving to the States. Felicia speaks Spanish and very little English. Her command of English includes but a few broken words. Although Chesney's parents were concerned that Chesney would have trouble with English since she hears Spanish most of the day, they discovered that Chesney is fully in command of her different languages. When addressing her mother and father, she uses impeccable English. When she turns to Felicia, Chesney speaks in Spanish.

Chesney's ability to switch back and forth between the two languages shows that children can keep two languages apart. In the first months of life, young children recognize that they are hearing the sounds of two (or more) different languages. From the beginning, children learn words in both languages for the same concept. They learn "milk" in English and *"lait"* in French, clearly building two separate systems. Two (or more) languages are as easy to learn as one. Being bilingual is a gift.

Scientific research indicates not only that learning a second language is not bad, but also that it might confer some real advantages on a young child. Findings from French-English bilinguals in Canada suggest that bilinguals performed better than monolinguals on a host of cognitive tasks designed to assess thinking and reasoning. For example, when asked to arrange a set of nine different-sized cylinders in a three-by-three matrix and then to explain the pattern that they made, bilinguals were better at generating the explanation and at explaining the rules that they had used. It is as if learning two languages had better prepared them not only to talk in two languages, but to be better rule seekers. In light of earlier discussions in this book of how infants and young children are pattern seekers, perhaps we should not be surprised that giving children the opportunity to look for patterns in more than one language hones their pattern-inducing skills.

Yet there are better and worse strategies for promoting bilingualism. In Chesney's case, for example, she hears English from her parents and the dominant culture, but Spanish exclusively from her caregiver. This division of language source creates a perfect climate for learning. When one parent speaks in one language and the other in another language, similar results are found. In each of these cases, children are exposed to two languages under the same roof—and there is no confusion about who speaks which language.

Languages are not only separated by their source, but also by the location for learning. The LeBlancs, for example, continued to speak French in the home after their move. The school language, however, was English. Thus, the children had a clear demarcation of which language was appropriate where. The result was bilingual learning that was maximally successful.

We must keep in mind that it is not only exposure per se but amount of exposure that influences learning. The only Spanish that Chesney hears is from her caregiver and even that is for a limited time when compared to the exposure to English that she gets from home, nursery school, and friends. In keeping with the adage "more talk to the child equals more talk from the child," we should expect that Chesney will learn Spanish, but not as well as she learns English. The LeBlanc children, on the other hand, are getting large doses of English that should enable them to master their new language quickly.

Many practical lessons can be taken from scientific investigations of first- and second-language learning. As we investigate the ways in which young children learn complex grammar, we can better understand what children bring to the task of language learning, and what we can do to assist them in their quest. The study of how children put words together into sentences also offers another advantage. It gives us a window into the human mind. As we watch children learn the complex rules of language, we witness firsthand how children abstract rules that parallel the complexity of learning chess. Children generalize from our examples on the road to language proficiency. Now that they know the basic rules, they need only figure out how to use them in real social settings. As we see, this task also requires complicated rule learning, which is investigated in the next chapter.

Chapter 8

"Please" and "Thank You": Using Language to Get Things Done Between Twenty-four and Thirty-six Months

Mastering the Uses of Language

Art Linkletter: (*speaking to a three-year-old*) And who is in your family, Scott?

Scott: My mommy, and my daddy, and my brother Harry. Oh, and when Daddy goes away on business trips, Uncle John comes and stays with Mommy.

In the 1950s Art Linkletter had a television show on which he interviewed young children. For many people this segment was the highlight of the show and the only part they remember. The segment couldn't have worked as well as it did if children used language the way adults do, keeping personal family details close to the vest. But children don't use language as adults do, and that is what this chapter is about.

With the inclusion of grammatical morphemes like *-ing* and *-ed* on their verbs, and with the ability to produce complex sentences like "I want the big one and you have the little one and Daddy has the one with the point," children between the ages of 24 and 36 months are sounding increasingly like adults. We must not be fooled, however, into thinking they have nothing more to learn about language. Toddlers must obtain the social veneer that makes them acceptable to their culture. This is because language is first and foremost a social behavior.

How children learn to use language to get things done in social situations is a fascinating achievement that rivals their acquisition of grammar. With language we can get things accomplished far more easily than we could without it. Consider, for example, trying to tell your hotelier in Russia (you don't speak Russian and he doesn't speak English) that you want an extra pillow or that you're waiting for a phone call. This would not be easy, even with the use of props. Language provides a systematic way of interacting with the social world. It is a vehicle for creating shared attention, altering our own and others' behaviors, and even creating new realities (such as company reorganizations, or personal reorganizations like marriage and divorce) that we then adhere to as much as we adhere to the facts of nature. But children must *learn* to use language to accomplish their goals.

They need to learn, among other things, how to formulate their requests, how to say no in a socially acceptable way, how to tell a story, and how to carry on a meaningful conversation. All these tasks involve considerable knowledge about people and what can be expected from them, about the typical course of events, and about the social categories that influence how we talk to people. For example, you talk differently to your best friend than to your employer; and you talk differently to your best friend around other good friends than around other acquaintances. Without realizing it, we are constantly making decisions about how to address people we encounter from varied walks of life. Yet, as the famous sociologist Erving Goffman pointed out, we become aware of the crucial role that language plays in social interactions only when something goes wrong. When we make a faux pas, the thing we should have said, it haunts us. Only after we have erred do we notice the social rule that we violated or the lightning-speed decision-making process we go through in deciding how to address someone.

Up to now the baby has not shown tremendous social sensitivity in either the comprehension or production of language. Remember that in the first year of life the child relied on attention to the cadences in the sound stream to make sense of speech. After a bad night when the baby was up every hour teething, we could have said, "I hate you" in a loving tone to the baby and the baby could have been thrilled. Finally, the baby started to pay attention to how words go together in sentences to make meanings, meanings that are different from the meanings that individual words can convey. With sentences in their quiver, toddlers now had the opportunity to say things that we had to apologize for. When two-and-a-half-year-old Allison blurted out, "You have big teeth!" to a future sister-in-law or when two-year-old Oren told his nursery school teacher, "You smell bad," we wondered if language development was a good thing after all.

At two years of age, children are capable of understanding and producing lots of sentences, but still have a long way to go. What are they missing? What does it take for a toddler to be able to use language as a tool to communicate without giving offense? Clearly, knowing a human language entails more than just producing sentences. It requires knowing how to use the rules of language to express ideas. But it encompasses even more than this. Just expressing ideas whenever and to whomever is at hand may not be appropriate (remember that woman on the supermarket checkout line who told you all about her divorce in excruciating detail?). Knowing a language is knowing *what* to say and knowing *when, where,* and to *whom* to say it.

Not surprisingly, years of practice are needed to become a successful communicator who takes the age, status, role, and knowledge of the listener into consideration when speaking. Everyone knows individuals who never seem to extricate their feet from their mouths, making presumptions that they shouldn't, and saying things out loud that should only be thought. Richard Nixon made an error at a news conference during Watergate that people still remember. He said, "I am not a crook," thereby presupposing that the country thought he was a crook.

The last chapter covered children's considerable facility with grammar. This chapter discusses how children struggle to master the pragmatic aspects of language. Being pragmatic involves mastering the social conventions for how to get things done with language. To be pragmatic in general means to be practical and sensible and utilitarian. A pragmatist is a person who can maneuver through sticky situations with skill, can forge compromises, and is often therefore considered a person with wisdom. That some people learn these things only poorly is what keeps Dale Carnegie in business.

In this period children begin to acquire the social conventions or politeness rules of society. They begin to acquire the social polish that will get them what they want when interacting with adults who control lots of goodies. The most obvious social conventions that make children impossible to resist are the magic words "please" and "thank you." In one clever study, researchers followed families around at Halloween. With all the greetings at the doors, all those compliments on costumes, followed by the candy giving, researchers figured correctly that Halloween would be a bonanza for observing which social conventions parents thought important for their children. The study found that even infants who can neither walk nor talk are schooled to say "please" and "thank you." When children who can talk are reluctant, parents do all kinds of things to get these key words out of them. They coerce and cajole and finally even speak on the child's behalf. Clearly, middle-class parents believe that it is never too early to teach those magic words "please" and "thank you."

Learning a Language Is Learning a Culture

The scientific research on language development shows how children strive to uncover how language works. From acting like little statisticians in the first year of life to uncovering the grammatical rules of their native language in the second year, children are working pretty much on their own from the language data provided for them in the way adults talk. In this chapter, however, the parental hand becomes more visible. All cultures have beliefs about what is appropriate to say and not to say; when it is appropriate to ask for something and when it is not; and how one should greet people of higher status and age than oneself. While children certainly pick up much of this information from watching what others do, many cultures, including our own, explicitly train children in how to do these things with language. Consider the following dialogue between a young child and her mother:

Child:	Mommy, I want more milk.
Mother:	Is that the way to ask?
Child:	Please.
Mother:	Please what?
Child:	Please gimme milky.
Mother:	No.
Child:	Please gimme milk.
Mother:	No.
Child:	Please . . .
Mother:	Please, may I have more milk?
Child:	Please, may I have more milk?

Sound familiar? Once children can talk—and even before they can utter a word—parents begin training them in how to use language. There is a right way and a wrong way, for example, to ask for things in every culture. In our society parents often model for their children what they wish them to say, as in the example above. Among the Kaluli of Papua, New Guinea, parents have a specific word that tells children to repeat the parent's last utterance. The word is *"elema,"* roughly translated as "say like that." Dr. Bambi Scheiffelin, who studies how children learn language among the Kaluli, recorded the following interaction between 25-month-old Abi and his mother, which occurred as Abi watched his mother prepare some pandanus, a tropical vegetable. Remember that the word *elema* means that the mother is asking the child to repeat what she has just said:

Mother:	Mother, I want pandanus, *elema*. Abi!
Abi:	Huh?
Mother:	Pandanus, I want pandanus. Abi!
Abi:	Huh?
Mother:	I want pandanus, *elema*. Mother, I want pandanus, *elema*. Yes, Abi.
Abi:	Huh?
Mother:	(*trying to get* some *response from Abi*) I want the knife, *elema*. Abi. (*There is no knife in sight.*)
Abi:	I want the knife.
Mother:	Give it to me.
Abi:	Give it to me.
Mother:	The knife, I want the knife, *elema*.

Assertions of ownership and possession are considered the polite way to make requests among the Kaluli. Kaluli parents, like American parents, do not believe in waiting for their children to figure out how to ask for things; children are taught how to do it. We may not have a word like *elema*, but we elicit speech from our children in social routines in the same way. The two examples above are remarkable for their similarity, given that they come from very different cultures on opposite sides of the globe.

What is considered polite in one culture is considered impolite in another, and these rules are taught to children through language. For example, in our culture it is considered impolite to sit with one's back to someone. We teach our children to either turn around or apologize for showing their back. Among the Samoans studied first by the famous anthropologist Margaret Mead and then by Elinor Ochs, it is considered impolite to show the bottom of one's feet.

Children from 18 months on are continually reminded to keep their legs folded ("Cross your legs" said in Samoan) to avoid showing people the bottom of their feet.

In American society it is considered inappropriate for adults and especially for small children to curse. Yet among Samoans "shit," a contraction of the phrase "Eat shit," is considered to be the child's first word! In Samoan society, children are considered mischievous, bold, and cheeky in the same way that we talk of the terrible two's. Cursing is just part of how children express what Samoans consider to be human nature and part of what the Samoans expect from their children. In fact, from very early in their language development, Samoan children use the curse appropriately during conversation to reject something, disagree, or stop some action. Shocked? Consider this vignette recorded between two American siblings:

Two-year-old: (*to his five-year-old brother*) Hi, stupid butthead!
Five-year-old: You're a poopy butthead.
Two-year-old: We don't talk like that.

The most interesting part of this vignette is when the two-year-old tells the five-year-old the social rule they have probably both heard their parents recite many times before: "We don't talk like that."

Parents teach children what *not* to say all the time. It is "not nice," for example, to talk about bodily functions at the dinner table or to tell Grandma that she is fat. Although unwritten rules for what is appropriate or inappropriate vary by culture, all cultures instruct children in these social uses of language, teaching children how to fit into the society in which they were born.

What Are You *Really* Asking? How Toddlers Understand Requests

Without realizing it, many informal conversations adults have are made up of incomplete and ambiguous utterances. This is easily seen by looking at transcripts of actual conversations. They are a mess, and even the most polite people interrupt each other's speech all the time. Conversations are filled with places where people mumble and start the same sentence more than once and switch topics without warning. Yet somehow we manage to understand what our conversational partners are saying. Why are we so good at overlooking incomplete, ambiguous, and interrupted utterances? One reason is that we are constantly making inferences about what people really mean. Just think for a moment about how adults use their inferential abilities to interpret requests. In our culture, when speaking to someone we are not intimate with, it is not considered polite to ask outright for what we want. We often ask for things indirectly, not even mentioning what it is we really want. The sentence "Gee, it's hot in here," uttered by the company president, can make junior executives rush to open windows as if by royal command. Most requests are like this. They have a literal meaning (as in "the temperature is high in here") and an indirect meaning (as in "make it cooler").

Psychologist Herb Clark demonstrated the two-layered nature of requests by having his students place calls to pharmacies in the area around Stanford University, where Clark teaches. Would the individuals answering the phone recognize that they were being asked what time the store closed (the indirect meaning) or would they just respond to the literal question (if the pharmacy closed before a certain time)? The question could have been answered with a simple yes or no if it was interpreted literally. However, if the merchant was sensitive to what was really being asked, a different kind of answer was supplied.

Merchant: Green's Pharmacy.
Caller: Hi. Do you close before seven tonight?
Merchant: Uh, no. [This is the answer to the literal question.] We're open until nine o'clock. [This is the answer to the indirect question.]

Most pharmacies did answer the indirect question in addition to answering the literal question.

Toddlers are another story, however. An abundance of research studies show that children are pretty poor at understanding what people are really asking. They seem only to tune into the literal meaning of the question, ignoring the indirect meaning completely. Since they don't make conversational inferences as adults do, they require nearly everything to be spelled out for them.

Have you ever called a home, only to get the resident two- or three-year-old on the telephone instead of the parent? You say, "Hello, Jessica, what are you doing?" Jessica answers, "Talking on the phone." She is answering the literal question, as if you were asking, "what are you doing now?" She fails to understand the indirect question,

"What were you doing before you answered the phone?" But wait, it only gets worse. You then ask, "Is your mommy home?" Jessica says, "Yes," and then there is dead silence. An adult would know that the speaker is really asking the indirect question "Could you please get your mother to the telephone for me?" and not the literal question about whether or not she is home. Not so for the two- or three-year-old literalist. Although you may think that the dead silence means that Jessica has gone to find her mother, you discover from her breathing that she is still there, holding the line. Jessica is waiting for you to speak next. After all, she took her turn when she answered your question with yes. And of course, your next question is: "Will you please go get your mother for me?" Imagine if we, as adults, responded similarly:

Stranger: Excuse me, do you have the time?
Reply: Yes. (*and keep walking*)
   or
Stranger: Can you pass the salt?
Reply: Yes. (*sit there without moving*)

The strangers who encountered us would think our social skills very poor indeed! And yet these are exactly the sorts of mistakes young children make. With such answers they reveal that they have not yet mastered the subtexts of their language. The child is not born knowing that the speaker is really asking the listener to do something and not merely to indicate having the time or ability to pass the salt. The speaker wants action.

How do children learn these social conventions? Parents don't explain these things to them just as they don't teach children the rules of grammar. It probably starts with the way we talk to children when we want them to do something. To illustrate how we model the way requests are made in our culture and how we may indirectly teach children to respond to them, consider the predicament two-and-a-half-year-old Courtney and her mother, Heather, find themselves in. They have been playing with blocks when Heather gets a call that Great-aunt Shirley is coming over for a surprise visit. The blocks must get put away now because Aunt Shirley doesn't see so well and could trip. Besides, the place is a mess. How to get Courtney to clear up the blocks so Heather can pick up the other toys? Consider what Heather might say to Courtney:

1. You put the rest of those blocks away.
2. Put the rest of the blocks away?
3. Can you put the rest of those blocks away?
4. The rest of those bocks must be put away.
5. My, it's messy on the floor!

Sentence #1 is the most explicit of all and the one that contains an imperative. It mentions who is to do the clearing up ("you"—the child) and exactly what is to be done (put the blocks away). There is no arguing with the command in that sentence! Sentence #2 is a bit weaker and might get some disagreement from a child because it ends in a question and doesn't mention the child explicitly. Sentence #3 is an even more polite way to get the child mobilized. While it is pretty explicit and mentions who is to do the clearing up and what is to be done, it is in the form of a question. There is a literal meaning ("Can you . . . ?"), but Heather is in no mood to hear yes followed by no action and certainly doesn't want to hear no. What Heather is really saying is the indirect meaning ("Put away the blocks"). Sentence #4 is a command to no one in particular, but the action that is desired is clearly mentioned. Courtney must infer that she is the one to do the job. Finally, sentence #5 is the least explicit of all, mentioning neither the action desired nor who is to carry it out. Therefore, #5 requires that Courtney infer that her mother is trying to get clean-up going. All of these examples are called "directives"— although some are more indirect than others—because they are designed to get the listener to do something.

Research has shown that the younger children are, the more directives of all types mothers use in their speech to them. Psychologist David Bellinger observed 40 mother-child pairs in a playroom at Cornell University and counted the number and type of directives mothers produced to their children of different ages. When children are about a year old, fully half of the sentences mothers address to their babies tell them what to do. By the time children are about Courtney's age (two and a half), only about a fifth of mothers' sentences are directives. Why the decline? By that time toddlers have learned many behavioral and language routines. After all, parents and caregivers have had over two years teaching their children such things as we clean up after we play. Therefore, mothers probably experience less need to give children explicit marching orders.

What is most interesting about this study, however, is how the *type* of directive changes as the child gets older. The first type—the straightforward imperatives that say essentially "do this" and leave little to chance—dominate when the child is around a year of age. By Courtney's age only about half of Heather's directive sentences are of this type. The rest of Heather's directives are type 3—complete questions—and type 4—statements of the desired action without mentioning who is to do it. According to Bellinger, not until children reached the age of five did their mothers use the kinds of indirect directives that required their children to infer both the action they wanted to see performed and who was to carry it out. Even at age five, type 5 was only observed 11 percent of the time.

What is also interesting is how mother's directives move in the direction of becoming increasingly explicit if the child fails to respond. Consider the following examples that Bellinger recorded:

Mother: Why don't you lay the board down? [Type #3]
Child: (*doesn't comply*)
Mother: Lay the board down. [Type #1]

Mother: You're going to hurt someone. [Type #5]
Child: (*continues to wave scissors in the air*)
Mother: Put that down. [Type #1]

When children don't comply, mothers make their requests more explicitly directive and more complete. Whether from lack of patience or from deciding that they are being too subtle, mothers move their requests up the list above, getting more and more clear about what they expect. This is exactly what happened with Courtney and Heather:

Heather: Aunt Shirley is coming, Courtney. We need to clean up. [Type #5]
Courtney: (*continues playing with the blocks*)
Heather: The blocks have to go back in their box. [Type #4]
Courtney: (*keeps playing*)
Heather: Can you put the blocks away? [Type #3]
Courtney: (*shakes her head no*)
Heather: Courtney! You put the blocks in their box *now!* [Type #1]

Did Courtney comply when faced with an explicit imperative? Of course not. Courtney was ready for her nap and not in a mood to comply, regardless of the wonderful language lessons Heather was providing by making her directives more and more explicit. But consider what Courtney is learning from the way her mother talks to her. She is learning that there are multiple ways to say the same thing. She is even learning that sometimes people don't explicitly state what it is they want her to do. She is also learning that if she fails to carry out the requested action, Mom will get angry. This is an important life lesson as well!

When children are not too tired to respond, they often respond to indirect questions with action. For example, if you say to a two-year-old, "Can you jump?" they are likely to respond with a jump rather than saying yes. Although it appears as if the child is responding to the indirect and not to the literal meaning, psychologist Marilyn Shatz has another explanation for this behavior. She has found that children often respond to adults' indirect questions as though they were requests for action. It's as if children have evolved the following strategy: If a grown-up asks me a question, they want me to do what they ask. Questions are not analyzed for their literal and indirect meaning during this period; children simply respond to them by carrying out the action mentioned in the question, whether or not an action was really requested.

Try This: How do I ask questions? Does my child make conversational inferences?

This "Try This" has two separate parts. The first involves observing how you make requests to your child. Do you use more indirect requests or commands? Are you likely to use more indirect requests when you have time and more commands when you are stressed out? Do you find yourself running through the sequence above from bottom to top? From top to bottom? It is easier to observe this with someone else (your spouse or caregiver) rather than judging your own speech. After all, you have a concrete goal to accomplish, and focusing on your speech may be difficult when you are trying to get something done.

The next part focuses on your child. Does he seem to understand both the literal and indirect meaning of questions and requests? Not until children are well into their third year do they begin to pull out the indirect meaning, what is really being asked. You might even try setting up a situation just like the one Courtney and Heather experienced. After an enjoyable play session, try starting with a version of directive type #5, slowly moving up the list until your child responds. When is your child capable of responding to the more indirect versions of the request? Your child's responses may show more capability than you thought the child had. Part of this apparent sophistication may be due to the fact that the baby recognizes some routines now. That is, playtime is followed by clean-up time.

Try a version of the Shatz experiment. Make a list of things you might ask your child to do that you know he can do. Then make it into a game. Turn some into imperatives, as in "Jump!" Turn some into questions, as in "Can you jump?" that require only yes or no answers. Intersperse these and see how your child responds. At the beginning of this period (around 24 months), babies will interpret both imperatives and questions in the same way: by carrying out the action. By the end of this period (around 36 months), they will be better but not perfect at distinguishing between questions and commands.

How to Ask: Getting What We Want

We've discussed how toddlers *understand* requests that adults make to them, but not yet how toddlers formulate their own requests. In chapter 4 we described how preverbal children formulate nonverbal requests. With such limited means at their disposal, the success of such requests depends upon the willingness of the adult present to decode what is wanted. By the time children have acquired some language, they can ask a variety of questions (especially the maddening "why?"). But how effective are toddlers in making requests? Can they recruit the adults (and peers) around them to get their desires met?

Think about what is involved in making a request. When an adult makes a request of someone, she is really doing two things at once. She is carrying out a communicative act (requesting), and she is indirectly conveying how she perceives the social status of the listener and her relationship to the listener. In other words, a request is not just a request. She will frame a request differently if she is talking to her best friend than if she is talking to her boss. Without thinking about it, the way we request something of someone is a litmus test of how we perceive their status relative to our own. Consider the following examples:

Student 1:   (*to another student*) Gimme that ruler.
Student 2:   Yeah, when I'm done.

Student 1:   (*to teacher*) Gimme that ruler.
Teacher: I beg your pardon?
Student 1:   Sorry. Can I have the ruler, please?

Notice how differently Student 1 framed her request to her fellow student and to the teacher (true, the teacher needed to give the child a reminder). What's different about these situations? It can't be the goal. Regardless of who is being addressed, the goal of obtaining the ruler is identical. So why were the student's requests so different? Because in our culture a person asks things more formally and politely of people who are of higher status than himself, older than himself (by a considerable amount), and more distant from him. This is why we say that the way we make requests of someone indirectly reveals relative social status.

When do toddlers take these factors into consideration when they make requests? Even at the age of two, children who are already talking seem to be able to differentiate between listeners of different ages and roles. One child, Sarah, studied intensively by a psychologist, used simple imperatives to her peers at school, such as "Give me apple," but to adults at school she stated her desire for something as "I want an apple" or asked a question (sometimes permission) as in "Can I have an apple?" Sarah's behavior is evidence that already by the age of two children are capable of tailoring the language they use to the person they are addressing. This surprising social sensitivity from such a young child undoubtedly is still fragile. That is, in the same way that adults sometimes say things in a less polished way when they are upset, children at this age are best at tailoring their speech to their listener when they are not desperate to have something immediately.

Sarah made additional social distinctions in how she made requests when at home. She treated her mother much differently—and more familiarly—than her father. To her mother she said things like, "Mommy, I want milk" while to her father, she rarely made direct requests. Instead, she often beat about the bush, and used lots of polite forms over and over again. "Is that milk, Daddy? Please, some milk, Daddy. Milk, please, Daddy, please, please." Whether Sarah's different treatment of her mother and father was a function of familiarity because Mom was at home with her more or Sarah perceived her father to be of higher status than her mother is something we can't tell.

At nursery school, Sarah also differentiated between her listeners by *age*. While "give me apple," an imperative, was used with her two-year-old peers, she gave no commands at all to the big four-year-olds, saying things like, "Can have an apple, Nora, please?" To the three-year-olds she did use a few commands, but she added softening words like "please" or "okay" to the ends of her requests, as in "Give me apple, okay?" Even with relatively limited language resources, Sarah reveals social sensitivity. She and her two-year-old peers, after only a year of speaking, and a far shorter time producing sentences, are already using some of the social factors associated with how adults make requests.

These results are bolstered by an experiment Dr. Elizabeth Bates conducted with Italian children to see if they could control their ability to make different kinds of requests: A gray-haired, elderly puppet named Mrs. Rossi who had "lots of candy" was introduced to children between two and five years of age. Picture Marcello, almost three years old, to whom Bates says that Mrs. Rossi will be glad to give him a piece of candy if he asks for one. Marcello makes his first request of the puppet, "Want a candy?" said in a charming way. The puppet, however, does not immediately comply but "confers" with Bates. She then tells Marcello, "Mrs. Rossi said that she will surely give you a candy. But, you know, she's a bit old, and she likes it when children are very, very nice. Ask her again even more nicely for the candy."

Marcello rises to the occasion and frames another request that is more polite than the first one he made. He and his peers show their capability to manipulate the form of the request to be more polite. Marcello may not have the range of request forms that the older children tested in the study have, but even he is capable of making his second request less direct and even more respectful. "Please, Mrs. Rossi, can I have one?" Incidentally, regardless of what Marcello would have said on his second try, Dr. Bates had Mrs. Rossi give him the candy.

Even in their second year, these children knew what it meant to ask "more nicely." This means that even toddlers have learned the social rules for requesting and can "soften" their requests in a number of ways. This is pretty impressive from a child who cannot yet tie his shoes, make a phone call, or reach a light switch. Through parents' and caregivers' explicit instruction, as well as from their own astute powers of observation, two-year-olds have learned how to get what they want with polite requests. As children become more effective in accomplishing their goals through language, they will be able to be less insistent and even more polite.

Try This: Can my child consciously use polite speech?

Find a puppet—any puppet. It doesn't have to be an old woman. Play the same game that Bates played with the Italian children. Be sure to give your child a candy (or treat) in the end, though, regardless of how she frames her second request. Do you notice any difference between her first and second requests? Is the second request more indirect and more polite? Around 24 months, unless your child has lots of language, you may not see much of a difference. When you try this again at the end of the period at around 36 months, however, you should see a noticeable difference.

You can also watch how your child makes requests of your spouse or caregiver as opposed to other children. You can prompt your child by saying something like, "Ask Aunt Martha to give you a toy." For comparison purposes, use the same sentence, "Ask Pam to give you a toy" in roughly the same context (plenty of toys visible). Compare these requests. Does your child seem to take the listener's age and status into account in the ways she frames her request? Is she more polite with the older person, for example? If you see these differences, your child is using the social tools of language.

Learning Social Routines

More evidence for young children's early sensitivity to social conventions comes from children's use of little scripts in social situations. Consider how Louis shows his eagerness to conform to middle-class social customs.

Louis is having his third birthday party, and he's very excited. He opens the door himself for the first guest, and it turns out to be a cousin of his he has never met and her mother. "Hi," he says. "it's so nice to see you again!" But this is the first time Louis has met these people!

Why does Louis say, "It's nice to see you *again*" if he'd never met these relatives before? He has learned a sort of "script," or routine, for how one greets visitors who come to the house. However, he fires it off whether he knows the people or not. He has heard his mother say this many times when guests arrive. Louis's inappropriate use of this script may seem mindless, but it's not. It requires that Louis recognize that visitors have arrived—he wouldn't say this to Daddy or to his big sister or to his friend Sammy—and that Louis remember the greeting given to adult guests. Louis has come a long way in being able to rattle off this sentence, even in an inappropriate context.

Consider what it would be like for us, as adults, to be transplanted into a culture that had different routines for how to greet people and specific rules for how to talk with people who were older or of higher status. We might be reluctant to say much under these circumstances, too, just as toddlers sometimes hide behind their parents when meeting new people. As adults, we would want to avoid giving offense. This is definitely not the two-year-old's motivation. More likely, children are unclear about what exactly is the right thing to say. Parents are sometimes annoyed when their children do not greet or take leave of individuals as the parent sees fit. But looking at this behavior from the perspective of an adult learning the ways of a new culture puts this apparent shyness into a new perspective. It is a daunting task to encounter strangers when you don't know the social routines. Some children, of course, sail right into every social situation. These children may differ temperamentally as well from the ones who literally hide behind their mothers' skirts. But even children who are outgoing need to learn the routines used for greeting people, for taking leave, for receiving gifts, for declining offers, and on and on.

Even common holidays have specific scripts associated with them that children need to learn. Consider the following dialogue between a daughter and her mother about Christmas.

Daughter: Maybe somebody, we are gonna coming in say "trick or treat"?
Mother: No. They're not going to say "trick or treat" on Christmas. . . .
Daughter: What say, then?
Mother: Say "Merry Christmas."

Each time a child learns what is expected, her anxiety about how to act in a certain situation is reduced—just as an adult's would be in a foreign culture. Learning what to say and when to say it makes children feel good as well, because knowing these things allows children to act like the adults around them, confident that they too know the social drill.

Conversations with Two-year-olds?

Parents have conversations with their babies from the get-go. Observe the following conversation between a mother and her 32-month-old son:

Eric: I jus' go that zoo once. I jus' go that zoo once bu' I did, Mommy.
Mother: Yes, you did.
Eric: Yeah.
Mother: Who else went?
Eric: Um-no-not-nobody.
Mother: You went all alone?
Eric: Yea. You and Tommy and me and Daddy.
Mother: Mm. Anybody else?
Eric: Don—nobody else jus' Mommy n' you an' Daddy.
Mother: Mm, and what did you see at the zoo?
Eric: Jus' see the e'phants, Mommy.

Eric shows in this example some of the things he has figured out about how to use language. First, to be involved in a conversation means that you take turns. Actually, he figured this out very early in the first year of life, even before he could talk, but now he carries it over into his conversations. Think about the people you have interacted with who constantly interrupt. You certainly find it annoying and may come away from the conversation wondering why these individuals have such trouble sharing the floor. Didn't their parents ever teach them about taking turns? Second, having a conversation requires observing the *principle of cooperation*, as enunciated by the linguist Paul Grice. The conversation has some general purpose and direction, and each participant is expected to help it along.

More specifically, the principle of cooperation in conversation can be broken down into four "conversational rules." These are principles that adults usually, although not always, observe in their conversations. When one or more of these rules are not observed, they jump out at us and we can often state what the violation is. Depending on how egregious the violation, we may avoid future conversations with these individuals.

Eric continues to discuss the zoo with his mother, a topic he has initiated and wishes to pursue. In doing so, he observes the *principle of relevance*: Keep your conversation on the topic at hand and warn your listener in advance if what you are about to say will not be relevant. Adults do this all the time, as when they say things like, "Not to change the topic but . . ." and proceed to a new topic, after all. Although the example doesn't follow Eric's conversation further than a few turns, the research literature overall shows that he, like all children his age, may well change the topic in future turns in a way that leaves his mother guessing as to what he is talking about. Why would Eric do that? He is unsure of what his listener has in mind. It's as if he thinks, "I have X in mind so my mother must have X in mind too."

The principle of relevance is pretty fragile and may be sacrificed in the face of excitement and wanting to get in on the action. While at home, Mom and Dad are willing to listen to toddlers if they change topics in midstream. But when children enter a group situation, like nursery school, where many children are competing for the teacher's attention, they have to learn how to answer the specific question that was asked. Plenty of children raise their hands wildly as their peers do and then, when called upon, launch into a monologue about who hit who yesterday. The question, however, was about the day of the week!

The *principle of quantity* is observed when Eric answers each question crisply and provides no more (or less) information than is requested. For adults, quantity violations—either when people say too little or too much—can be a serious deterrent to future conversations. The person who answers in monosyllables and makes having a conversation feel like pulling teeth is just as bad as the one who tells every unnecessary detail of their gallbladder operation. Children may vacillate between the two extremes depending on the circumstances.

The *principle of quality* is one which Eric does not observe. His failure to accurately recount the fact that other people went to the zoo with him leads him to err. Furthermore, when given a chance to correct himself when his mother asks if he went alone, his apparent failure to understand the meaning of the word "alone" leads him to compound the error. Despite initially denying that he had companions, Eric then goes on to tell his mother who else went to the zoo. Quality involves saying what is true, adding to the conversation by offering new and useful information that the speaker is fairly sure about. Certain adults routinely stretch the truth in conversations. Sometimes this is because they like to use hyperbole, and sometimes it is because they are basically dishonest. Regardless of the cause, if people violate the maxim of quality, we are likely to consider it very serious indeed and to avoid conversations with them. Like Eric, children may fail to observe the principle of quality for a variety of reasons. This sometimes leads parents to think that their young children are lying, but children do not understand what it means to lie until they are at least four years of age. When they embellish or make up stories, they are not consciously twisting the truth. Rather, they cannot yet tell the difference reliably between what did and did not happen. Or, they could see the event in a different way than an adult would, focusing on different aspects and making unusual interpretations. Sometimes, the failure stems from a lack of understanding of what is being asked. Finally, quality can suffer when children forget what really happened and attempt to fill in the blanks with incorrect details.

To maintain a cooperative conversation the speakers must try to observe the *principle of manner*. Manner involves being clear and unambiguous. One way in which Eric observed manner was by answering the question of what did you see ("just the e'phants") without using ambiguous pronouns. He could have said "saw them" if he couldn't remember the word "elephant," making his contribution very ambiguous indeed.

The foremother of the modern-day study of child language, Dr. Lois Bloom, conducted an extensive study on how the nature of children's conversations change over the second year of life. Conversations of the same four children at three ages were studied, first when the children were 21 months old and still using predominantly single-word speech, next at 25 months, when they were using mostly two-word speech, and finally at 36 months, when they were talking in three- and four-word sentences. When are children capable of building on other people's utterances and keeping the topic of the conversation going? In other words, when do children observe the principle of relevance? Interestingly, even in the single-word period, children already produce more utterances that continue the topic than change it. In this early period, children use imitation of what a parent has said about 20 percent of the time, as if this is the best they can offer. So the mother says, "Take your pants off" and the child says, "Pants off." By the second and third periods, imitation as a conversational strategy drops out, probably in proportion to the child's increasing language capabilities. After all, when you have a limited vocabulary and you're using mostly single words, there's not too much you can add to the conversation. In addition to the decline of imitation, two complementary changes occur in children's conversation that make them seem far more skilled than they were in the single-word period. The proportion of children's utterances that build on—are relevant to—the prior conversation increases dramatically, going from about 20 percent to 30 percent at 25 months to 45 percent by the time the child is using three- and four-word sentences.

An example of a conversation in which the child maintains the adult's topic and adds to what the adult said is the following: The mother says, "There's a doggie." The child responds, "There doggie and kitty." Not surprisingly, as relevant conversation goes up, irrelevant conversation declines. An example of an irrelevant contribution is when the mother says "There's a doggie" and the child says, "Want cookie." The percent of irrelevant utterances goes from about 30 percent to about 20 percent by the third period.

A finding that again shows the importance of talking to children is that children responded better to parents' questions than to parents' statements. Parents provide what the famous Russian psychologist Lev Vygotsky called a *scaffold* for children's utterances by asking them questions, and indirectly supporting and nurturing children's ability to produce relevant answers. Other researchers have also found that mothers' speech serves this function for young children. When mothers respond to their children's prior utterance and request a further response, children's conversations tend to sound more advanced. In other words, when mothers continue topics initiated by their children—topics children are likely to have an investment in—and try to elicit more language, children find it easier to participate in the conversation at a higher level.

Think of conversation as a game of catch, as the linguist Charles Fillmore argued. Conversation works when a speaker throws a ball into the air and a listener catches it. Each participant in the conversation has their own basket of balls and knows that only one ball can be in the air at a time. That is, conversationalists must take turns. Tossing a ball into the air to the other speaker is like contributing to the conversation. Examining children's conversations shows that children start out playing one game of catch and gradually change the game. In the first two periods (21 and 25 months), about half the time children wait for the ball thrown by the other speaker to fall to the ground. Then they throw one of their own balls rather than catching the ball that the speaker threw and throwing it back. This game of catch leads to disjointed conversations in which the speaker and child don't always share topics. By the last period, at 36 months, the game of catch children play involves catching the other speaker's ball and throwing it back instead of throwing one of their own. Most of the time the child adds new information to what the adult has said and an interactive, quality conversation takes place.

Try This: Can my child observe conversational rules?

If you listen carefully when your child talks to you or your spouse or care-giver, you will notice occasions when he violates conversational rules. Now that you are explicitly aware of these rules you will also notice when adults in your daily life violate these rules. When your child does something in conversation that gives you pause, it is probably because he has violated one of the rules. Can you figure out which one? These would be great conversations to record in a language diary because they are often very funny.

As you will see when you observe your own child, while the Gricean rules are easy for most adults to follow, toddlers have to work at making their conversations conform to these principles.

Beyond Conversation: Telling the Stories of Our Lives Through Narratives

Up to now we haven't talked much about the *contents* of children's conversations. Until this period (24 to 36 months), children's talk is very much about the here-and-now, tied directly to the context in which it is spoken. Even at the start, though, children can talk about things that are not present in the immediate context, as when they say "all gone," commenting on the cereal they just finished or "more milk" when their cup is empty. But it will take more language and more understanding of events in the world for children to talk about events that took place in the past, events for which there are no local props (no cereal bowl or empty cup) to help them out. One of the wonderful things language affords us is the ability to model reality. Using language, we can tell people about an event that they did not witness. Using language, we can re-create for our listener the stories of our lives. Narrative is used in every culture, and some scientists think it is one of the main reasons why language evolved: so that we could gossip and tell tales about our neighbors! The ultimate tool that embodies past experiences in the absence of even a speaker is written symbols. When we learn to read, we are treating language as an object, a kind of external symbolic memory for past events. But before children can learn to deal with the abstractness of written symbols, they must take an intermediate step. They must learn to use language to represent reality beyond the immediate context. They must learn to create *narratives.*

Narratives, like conversations, are a series of sentences that present an orderly and interconnected sequence of events. Here's a narrative produced by Emily at 33 months of age:

> We bought a baby. 'Cause, the, well, because, when she, well, we thought it was for Christmas, but when we went to the store we didn't have our jacket on, but I saw some dolly, and I yelled at my mother and said I want one of those dolly. So after we finished with the store, we went over to the dolly and she bought me one. So I have one.

Elegant? Not quite yet, but it's clearly a story. However, unlike a conversation, in which the two participants share the responsibility for keeping it going, the responsibility in a narrative falls solely on the teller of the tale. Just as there are rules that underlie conversations, there are rules for constructing narratives. The main one is that narratives must be temporally organized: What happened first comes before what happened last. They must also be causally organized, or else the link between events will be unclear. Narratives must also set the scene. If you rush up to someone and say, "It happened! The day it was supposed to!" the listener would be clueless. What does the "it" refer to? This violates the conversational maxim of manner, making a totally ambiguous comment on some event. Good narratives also take the perspective of the different actors involved.

How do young children learn to tell stories about their lives? First of all, they hear their parents tell stories. From a very young age, a child hears all kinds of personal narratives, stories of things that happened to parents that they share with other adults. Sometimes these stories are about the children who are listening, undoubtedly heightening their attention and comprehension. Another influence on children's ability to tell narratives is parental involvement. Adults often collaborate with children in constructing narratives, initially coaxing children to fill in the blanks, as it were. Consider the conversation between Eric and his mother earlier. Although he initiated the conversation about having gone to the zoo, the mother then provides opportunities for Eric to elaborate by asking him questions. Without realizing it, his mother is teaching Eric about narrative structure and the kinds of things one might include in a story.

Try This: Does my child tell coherent narratives?

Record some of the stories your child tells of events that happened to her. If your child is loquacious, this will not be easy! In fact, you may opt for audio or video recording these narrative gems rather than attempting to capture them in writing. Such tapes become priceless treasures once children are grown. Catching your child telling a story on videotape is like capturing the child's construction of her self.

Eavesdrop on your child before nap time or bedtime using audio or videotape. Researchers have long noted that children often practice conversations and stories right before falling asleep, as if recalling the events of the day. Sometimes children do little monologues, going on and on, using their gestures wildly and inappropriately, as they attempt to recount in garbled detail some exciting event that occurred to them. Very often, research shows, children describe unpleasant events in which they experienced negative emotions. However, before you get out the Prozac, consider that the child is probably struggling to understand events that violated her expectations and were disappointing. The following is 21-month-old Emily's pre-sleep monologue as recorded by Professor Katherine Nelson:

> The broke, car broke, the . . . Emmy can't go in the car. Go in green car. No. Emmy go in the car. Broken. Broken. Their car broken, so Mommy Daddy go in their car, Emmy Daddy go in the car, Emmy Daddy Mommy go in the car, broke, Da . . . da, the car . . . their, their, car broken.

Clearly, the fact that the car broke down was a major event for Emily. Also, the difference between these pre-sleep monologues at the beginning of this period, around 24 months, and at the end, around 36 months, are fascinating. Differences in the quality of the organization and clarity of the monologue will just jump out at you.

Using Language for Fun: Jokes and Pretense

"Daddy's proud of you; Grandma's proud of you; Uncle David's proud of you; hamburger not proud of you, ha ha!"

As this string of statements suggests, toddlers can make jokes! In the first year of life, babies tend to laugh at physical humor, such as tickling or being thrown up the air or hiding and reemerging suddenly. Then babies start creating situations that they know are violations of what actually takes place to make "jokes." Babies also find it wildly amusing to have adults perform acts that are violations of typical routines.

Once language comes on the scene, young children can actually tell jokes. They're not necessarily ones that would amuse an adult, but who can resist when a two-year-old is hysterically laughing at some attempt at verbal play?

At 24 months of age, Bambi and her father, Ted, had evolved a little word game where they would identify the gender of all the people in the family. Ted would say, "Bambi is a _____" and wait for Bambi to fill in the blank. At first Bambi would give the expected answer "girl," but one day she surprised her father by saying "boy," accompanied by raucous laughter. When they got to "Mommy is a _____" and Bambi said "dog," Ted and Bambi had a good laugh. Mother did not find this one as amusing.

Think about the capability that this kind of verbal play reveals. Bambi now recognizes several things. First, words can be used to represent reality. She can use language to talk about people's gender (already a somewhat abstract concept). Second, through language she can violate what is really true about someone's gender (or species) and create humorous episodes that she can share. She can—for the moment, and for fun—invent a new reality. Language has become a tool for the toddler for describing reality and for creating new realities. Making jokes shows how language is becoming "decontextualized," a fancy way of saying "no longer tied to the context." As early as two years of age, toddlers realize the flexibility language affords in allowing them to alter their own ideas and the ideas of people around them. And consider what else toddler humor tells us. When a child says something outrageous and counter to reality, accompanied by gales of laughter, he is implicitly showing that he believes in the conversational rule of quality. He grasps the assumption that what a speaker says should reflect the speaker's beliefs. Violating that assumption turns the ordinary, communicative function of language on its head.

Toddlers also enjoy games when they give objects the wrong names. The fact that these games are played more with people the toddler knows well rather than those she doesn't demonstrates a further capability. It suggests that using the wrong name requires that the person she is playing with is aware of the fact that she really does know the correct name. Verbal humor can work only if your listener holds the same assumptions you do, otherwise, you haven't made a joke. The toddler knows that she knows the correct name but doesn't know if a stranger knows that she does. Thinking about another's thoughts is pretty sophisticated stuff.

Although not necessarily humorous, pretend play is another way in which toddlers show how they decontextualize language and use it to represent make-believe relations. In pretend play, objects can stand for other objects, just as people can take on roles that they don't ordinarily play in real life. Children spend a vast amount of time in play of all kinds. Some of this play is verbal and reveals children's sensitivity to the roles that people in their lives play and how those people talk. Researchers have found that toddlers can duplicate the way adults talk to babies and the way babies talk to adults. When toddlers play the role of mother, they increase the pitch of their voices and talk in shorter sentences. They also ask the "baby" many questions about their physical needs. Finally, toddlers talk much more when they are playing the mommy role than the baby role. When toddlers play the role of "baby," on the other hand, they talk in little squeaky voices, substitute sounds in their speech that they can already say quite well, and, by and large, use short, simple utterances. Toddlers clearly are aware of how mommy and baby act and talk in everyday life.

Children's pretend play is often the origin of their earliest narratives. When adults play with children, they model how to tell a story about the objects involved in the play. Further, parents' talk during play provides a structure for the child's actions. That structure helps the child to set up the pretend reality, showing him how useful language can be for transforming situations. In addition, parents tend to use more talk about motivations and beliefs than children do in their pretend play, giving children insight into how language can be used to talk about others' thoughts and feelings. For example, two-year-old Maria was playing with a doll, blanket, and a baby carriage as her mother helped out. When Maria covered the doll with a blanket, she described her action by saying, "Blanket on." When her mother covered the doll a little later, she said, "Oh, look, the baby's tired!" Once again, interacting verbally with adults raises the level of the interaction and provides important models for the child. Pretend play using language is another way in which language comes to be separated from the immediate context and used to describe situations that exist only in the mind.

Try This: Does my toddler make jokes?

Capturing jokes and verbal play is a rewarding experience. It reveals a sophistication in your child that you will find quite surprising. Use a diary to re-create the situation and what the child said.

Eavesdropping on your child's play times is also interesting. See how your child uses language during play to transform reality. Toward the end of this period your child will start to attribute motives and feelings to the dolls and stuffed animals he uses during his pretend play.

Scientific Sleuthing Pays Off

Lesson 1. Constructing life stories with your child promotes narrative development. In this period children are just learning to construct narratives. Parents play an important role modeling how this is done. Research indicates that mothers work with their children in different ways to create narratives about past events. Mothers whom researchers have called "repetitive" tend to talk about practical matters with their children, focusing on getting children to answer "who" and "what" questions when they build narratives. They did not seem to focus on "where," "when," "how," and "why," questions that often require more complex answers and more thought on the part of the child. An example of a narrative constructed by a repetitive mother and 30-month-old Arnold shows the mother's determination to elicit only the right answer about their recent trip to Florida.

Mother: Where did we eat breakfast? Where did we go for breakfast?

Arnold: What?

Mother: Where did we go for breakfast? Remember we went out, Daddy, you and I? What restaurant did we go to?

Arnold: Gasoline.

Mother: Gasoline? No, what restaurant did we go have breakfast at?

Arnold: Ummm . . .

Mother: Do you remember? It was Burger . . . ?

Arnold: King!

The mother is intent on getting a single bit of information out of Arnold. Because she is so focused on this, she loses opportunities to follow up on his contributions ("gasoline") and to fill him in on details of their trip that he may have forgotten. The result is more a Q and A session than a true narrative.

Contrast this style with an "elaborative" mother. This mother makes up stories of the experiences she shares with her child, but she isn't confined to the facts. She invites the child to join her in creating a story, and as they proceed she shows the child how to go about it. Even though the child might not add much at first, eventually the child will participate more fully, having been guided repeatedly through this story game. Here is a discussion about fish seen at the aquarium:

Mother: Did we see any big fishes? What kind of big fishes?

Alyse: Big, big, big.

Mother: And what's their names?

Alyse: I don't know.

Mother: You remember the names of the fishes. What we called them. Michael's favorite kind of fish. Big mean ugly fish.

Alyse: Ugly fish. (*a few more turns*)

Mother: Remember the sharks?

Alyse: Yeah, big sharks. Scary fish. Sharks bite.

Mother: Do they? What else did we see in the big tank in the aquarium?

Alyse: Divers feeding the fish.

Mother: Yes, you're right, the divers were there in the tank. And remember when we first came in, remember when we first came in the aquarium? And we looked down and there were a whole bunch of birdies in the water? Remember the names of the birdies?

The difference between the mothers emerges after Alyse's mother does not continue trying to elicit the names of the fish. Instead, she moves on, supplying Alyse with the requested names and attempting to get Alyse to recount more memories about their visit to the aquarium. When Alyse does not remember, her mother does not belabor the point but constructs a basis for her child to re-create a specific event.

While all parents act repetitive at some times and elaborative at others, it turns out that researchers have found long-term effects of these different parental styles. Children with repetitive parents do not produce narratives that are as rich in complexity as children whose parents use an elaborative style. Based on the style mothers used with their offspring at age two, researchers were able to predict which children would produce better, more richly structured narratives a full year later.

This result impacts language development in three significant ways. First, elaborative mothers *model* how to organize memories into coherent wholes. Second, they provide a *scaffold* for their children's retrieval of memories, helping them to dig out details that they might not have remembered on their own. Third, by asking more complex questions of their children during the course of story construction, they require more complex answers, thereby getting their children to talk more.

At first in developing narratives, it is clearly the parent's or caregiver's burden to make it work. The child doesn't have the linguistic or conceptual resources necessary to tell a whole story. A two-year-old can tell a simple story such as "The dolly cried. The daddy put it to bed." But they can't yet put together a well-structured tale. By the time they are three, though, many children are telling fairly coherent stories and on the way to developing autobiographical memories. Implicitly, and without offering any more reward than the joy of participating in a conversation where their children have their full attention, elaborative mothers help their children learn to sequence events and hold them in mind fixed with causal and temporal glue. Events hang together better when there is a frame to contain them.

Lesson 2. There's more to storybooks than meets the eye. Thirty-month-old Perry is in his pajamas, ready for his bedtime stories. His mother brings the usual armload of books to his bedside.

Mother: Okay, Perry, what stories would you like to hear tonight?
Perry: *Runaway Bunny, Runaway Bunny!*
Mother: (*stifling a grimace*) But we read that every night and sometimes before your nap. Wouldn't you like to hear some of our new books? These look so good."
Perry: (*eagerly thrusting* Runaway Bunny *into his mother's face*) *Runaway Bunny, Runaway Bunny!*

You may have found yourself in a similar situation. No matter what the range of the books available, children often select the tried and true—the story that they have heard over and over again. Why? The old-time favorites are comfortable and familiar. They have become part of the social routine of bedtime. Just as children feel good when they learn the right thing to say, they feel good being able to predict what will happen next in the story they are hearing. You will also notice that children resist mightily when you attempt to change a *single* word in that familiar story or (being exhausted yourself) try to skip ahead.

Although it's important to satisfy your child and read and reread the same stories, you should try to introduce new stories. This will allow you to use the storybook as an instrument to build on the child's language development and budding narrative skills. New books allow parents to go beyond the words in print and to talk about the pictures on the page. Books provide the fodder for conversations with children. How does the story relate to the child's life? How might the child change the story to make it better? Parents and caregivers can ask questions like, "What do you think the little boy will do next?" or "How do you think he feels?" Questions like these help the child learn to think ahead, to take the perspective of the characters, and to think about why things happen. Conversations about books can be very important vehicles for expanding on children's world knowledge and concepts. All kinds of new things and new ideas are introduced in books, and children and parents can explore these without being restricted to what is in print.

In addition, an understanding of the structure of narratives, how stories start with a problem, pose solutions, and then are resolved is a crucial by-product of early book reading. Researchers show that the narrative skills that are born of early storybook reading form the basis for later reading and writing ability and serve children well in their school years.

Epilogue

Tying It Up: Language Development from Birth to Age Three

How Far Have Children Come?

Approximately 120,000 years ago our ancestors developed language. One reason why children are such masters at language learning while they are still so small and before they can do much else on their own is wonderfully illustrated by the biologist George Williams:

> We might imagine that Hans and Fritz Faustkeil are told on Monday, "Don't go near the water," and that both go wading and are spanked for it. On Tuesday they are told, "Don't play near the fire," and again they disobey and are spanked. On Wednesday they are told, "Don't tease the saber-tooth." This time Hans understands the message, and he bears firmly in mind the consequences of disobedience. He prudently avoids the saber-tooth and escapes the spanking.[1]

Fritz escapes the spanking too, but for a very different reason. The ability to represent experiences through the use of verbal symbols must have been an awesome advantage to our ancestors. As Steven Pinker speculates, "Perhaps it is no coincidence that the vocabulary

1. George Williams, *Adaptation and Natural Selection: A Critique of Some Current Evolutionary Thought* (Princeton, NJ: Princeton University Press, 1966).

spurt and the beginnings of grammar follow closely on the heels of the baby, quite literally—the ability to walk unaccompanied appears around 15 months." All members of the human species, barring those with the most serious retardation, come to be in possession of human language by the age of three. Consider for a moment how far the child has come.

The opening chapter began with a baby who couldn't do much more than eat, sleep, and eliminate. Nonetheless, this baby entered into the world—empowered by thousands of years of evolution—prepared to learn a human language. The results of clever research studies showed over and over again that even before birth, the baby was attuned to human language in a number of ways. She could even discriminate between her own and foreign languages shortly after emerging from the womb. She could have "conversations," empty of content but looking deep into her parents' eyes and connecting with them in a profound way. Little by little the milestones of language emerged, and this baby, like babies all over the world, slowly continued the inevitable march to mastery of a human language. Although humans share a good deal of DNA with our closest biological cousins, the primates, and although we share fully 95 percent of our genetic material with the chimpanzee, no species has a communication system that approaches the complexity of human language. Having language as a tool has allowed us to create complex cultures and artifacts to serve us.

By the end of this book the child is on the doorstep of a range of accomplishments unknown elsewhere in the animal kingdom. The magnificent human feat that is language enables us to declare love, enmity, or indifference. The feat that is language enables us to have an argument without killing each other and to report mild illness instead of attending that boring cocktail party. No other species has this capability, and no other species can communicate the range of emotion and ideas that we can.

Humans are specially designed to perceive the sounds of language, and there is no other auditory stimulus that we perceive with the same degree of accuracy in the same unit of time. More specifically, we can identify individual speech sounds at the rate of 20 to 30 per *second.* It is impossible to achieve this rate with nonspeech sounds. When nonspeech sounds (cows mooing, car noises, and taps, for example) are strung together, research has shown that once we exceed 15 sounds per second, the individual sounds merge into a buzz. Humans' ability to identify and produce a large number of speech sounds in very short units of time is undoubtedly a product of our evolutionary history. It's certainly where the baby begins to break into language.

The next step to language ascendancy is meaning. Once babies find the sounds that strung together make up words in their language, they learn to attach meaning to those sounds. In these pages babies were sometimes compared to Fido, that precocious pet who seems able to read our thoughts. But Fido's ability to make sense of the language addressed to him bears no resemblance to the numbers of words (around 100) that babies begin to accumulate in their comprehension vocabulary by one year of life. By the end of the second year, many babies have speaking vocabularies of several hundred words. Babies are experts in acquiring symbols. Fido and his ilk can learn the association between only a few words and the people or places these stand for. To learn even these few words, Fido must hear the words paired with objects and actions many, many times.

The grammatical portion then comes to the fore. None of the previously dominant factors loses sway; they simply come to serve a higher master. Babies learn to comprehend and then produce strings of words to make sentences. Finally, the pragmatic or social uses of language moves into ascendance. According to some researchers, social interactions form the cornerstone of language. In the end, the manipulation of social relations through language and the three systems (sound, meaning, and syntax) that make it up are what language is all about. Undoubtedly, language gives humans enormous advantages over other species—even those with complex social groups like ants and primates—in social exchange. With language we can share information, teach our progeny, tell the stories of our lives, and create new realities. However, as cases of children who have learned language but fail to use it effectively in social exchange show, the social and formal aspects of language can be separate. That is, these children can learn about the sound system, the meaning system, and the grammatical system of language, produce clear and grammatical sentences, and still be unable to use language for effective social purposes. In normal language development, though, all the factions covered in this book come together in service to all kinds of expression and communication by the beginning of the third year of life.

The child goes on to use language in a variety of ways to enhance both thought and social interaction. By age three language has shaped the child's worldview in many important ways. The culture in which the child is raised uses language as the medium to convey messages about how the society works. Someone once said, "To know a language is to know a culture." By learning our native language (or languages), we gain a perspective on how the world operates. And, as bilingual individuals who have learned different languages can tell you, each language has concepts that the other language cannot express.

Where Is the Child Going?

All cultures greatly value language prowess. If this were not true, we would not put such stock in the IQ test, which has a large verbal component. Some researchers have even argued that emphasis on verbal prowess comes at the expense of expertise in social relations and in the arts. By the age of three children are well on their way to dealing with virtually any sentence thrown at them. Within the next two or three years they are able to understand sentences that express causal and temporal relations such as "Because he hated spinach, he fed it to the dog." They also begin to understand the difference between the verbs "promise" and "tell," as in "John promised Mary to walk the dog" versus "John told Mary to walk the dog." They also come to recognize sarcasm in others' speech. No longer are they fooled into thinking an older peer is praising them when the peer says, "Big deal."

By the time children enter kindergarten, they have approximately 14,000 words in their vocabularies. The language that children have learned plays an important role in their school achievement, and especially in their ability in learning to read. If they have been exposed to lots of written materials, they are able to tell the difference between letters and numbers, even though they can't correctly identify them all, by the age of three. If they have heard and constructed many narratives with adults, they likely are ready to accept that printed pages carry exciting new meanings.

At age three a child still can't tie her shoes or be left alone in the house. But the child is a proficient social member of the human race. Professor Mabel Rice at the University of Kansas shared an anecdote about her daughter that reveals the paradoxical nature of young children's social understandings. On the one hand, two- and three-year-olds sometimes seem communicatively incompetent, failing to make inferences about information that is being indirectly requested and saying more than needs to be said. On the other hand, they occasionally do things that suggest that they are in possession of pockets of rather remarkable social knowledge, as the following vignette indicates:

> When Mindy was three, an acquaintance of mine babysat with her for a few hours one evening. After I had gone, Mindy, a very verbal little girl, proceeded to lace her comments with profanities, demonstrating a remarkable knowledge of when and where to insert these obscene expletives. Because the babysitter was not familiar with how I handled such matters (and Mindy's facility seemed to indicate considerable practice), she chose to ignore the obscenities. Near the time when I was to return, Mindy produced another string of swear words, and then looked up at the babysitter and said, "My mommy doesn't let me say those words." Obviously, Mindy had mastered several rules. She knew where and how to use swear words, and knew that her use of those words was not condoned by her mother, and knew that she had taken advantage of her babysitter's uncertainty as to how to respond, and I also believe that she knew that her reporting of the household rules served as a means of informing the babysitter that she had been taken advantage of by a three-year-old.[2]

You have this to look forward to and more. Children's language development endows them with great power, a power that they will come to harness even more effectively in the coming preschool years.

As this book has demonstrated, language *is* the crowning achievement of the human species. In the years to come, children will indeed learn to swear (despite parental admonitions). More critically, however, they will use their growing language skills in learning to read, in making jokes, in chatting endlessly on the phone, and even in engaging in heated debate over why they should get dessert without eating their dinner. Children's language development endows them with great power.

In the last two decades, teams of scientists have uncovered the story of language development. Who would have guessed that language learning begins in the womb? Or that children are such expert grammarians by the end of their third year of life? With this

2. Mabel Rice, "Cognitive Aspects of Communicative Development," in *The Acquisition of Communicative Competence: Language Intervention Series* (Baltimore: University Park Press, 1984), 157.

knowledge at their fingertips, parents and caregivers can now fully appreciate the amazing capabilities that are present in every child. They can better recognize when something goes awry and, most important, can create a stimulating and enriching environment in which language development can flourish.

References

Introduction: Setting the Stage

Chomsky, N. *Syntactic Structures*. The Hague: Mouton, 1957.
———. *Aspects of a Theory of Syntax*. Cambridge, MA: MIT Press, 1965.
———. *Lectures in Government and Binding*. Dordrecht: Forris, 1981.
Eimas, P., E. R. Siqueland, P. Jusczyk, and J. Vigorito. "Speech Perception in Infants." *Science*, 171: 303–06, 1971
Pinker, S. *The Language Instinct: How the Mind Creates Language*. New York: William Morrow, 1994.

Chapter 1: Watch Your Language!

Adamson, L. *Communication Development During Infancy*. Madison, WI: Brown & Benchmark, 1995.
Bertoncini, J., C. Floccia, T. Nazzi, and J. Mehler. "Morae and Syllables: Rhythmical Basis of Speech Representation in Neonates." *Language and Speech*, 38: 311–29, 1995.
Bushnell, I. W. R., F. Sai, and J. T. Mullin. "Neonatal Recognition of the Mother's Face." *British Journal of Developmental Psychology*, 7: 3–15, 1989.
DeCasper, A., and W. P. Fifer. "On Human Bonding: Newborns Prefer Their Mothers' Voices." *Science*, 208: 1174–76, 1980.
DeCasper, A., J. P. Lecanuet, M. C. Bushnell, and C. Granier-Deferre.

"Fetal Reactions to Recurrent Maternal Speech." *Infant Behavior and Development,* 17: 159–64, 1994.

Dodd, B. "Lip Reading in Infants: Attention to Speech Presented in and out of Synchrony." *Cognitive Psychology,* 11: 17–27, 1979.

Eimas, P., E. R. Siqueland, P. Jusczyk, and J. Vigorito. "Speech Perception in Infants." *Science,* 171: 303–06, 1971.

Fernald, A., and P. Kuhl. "Acoustic Determinants of Infant Preference for Motherese Speech." *Infant Behavior and Development,* 10: 279–93, 1987.

Fifer, W., and C. Moon. "Early Voice Discrimination." In *The Neurobiology of Early Infant Behavior,* edited by C. V. Euler, H. Fossberg, and H. Lagercrantz. New York: Stockton, 1988.

———. "The Effects of Fetal Experience with Sound." In *Fetal Development: A Psychobiological Perspective,* edited by J. Lecanuet, W. P. Fifer, N. Krasnegor, and W. P. Smotherman. Hillsdale, NJ: Erlbaum, 1995.

Goren, C. C., M. Sarty, and P. Y. K. Wu. "Visual Following and Pattern Discrimination of Face-Like Stimuli by Newborn Infants." *Pediatrics,* 56: 544–49, 1975.

Gottlieb, G. "Development of Species Identification in Ducklings: IV. Changes in Species-Specific Perception Caused by Auditory Deprivation." *Journal of Comparative and Physiological Psychology,* 92: 375–87, 1978.

Gustafson, G. E., and K. L. Harris. "Women's Responses to Young Infants' Cries." *Developmental Psychology,* 26: 144–52, 1990.

Harris, M. *Language Experience and Early Language Development: From Input to Uptake.* London: Erlbaum, 1992.

Hepper, P. "An Examination of Fetal Learning Before and After Birth." *Irish Journal of Psychology,* 12: 95–107, 1991.

Hong, T. "Experimental Study on the Affection of Fetal Music on the Fetus." *Acta-Psychologica-Sinica,* 26: 51–8, 1994.

Johnson, M. H., and J. Morton. *Biology and Cognitive Development: The Case of Face Recognition.* Cambridge, MA: Blackwell, 1981.

Kuhl, P. K., J. E. Andruski, I. A. Christovich, L. A. Christovich, E. V. Kozhevnikova, V. L. Ryskina, E. I. Stolyarova, U. Sundberg, and F. Lacerda. "Cross Language Analysis of Phonetic Units in Language Addressed to Infants." *Science,* 277: 684–86, 1997.

Lecanuet, J. P., C. Granier-Deferre, and M. C. Bushnell. "Differential Fetal Auditory Reactiveness as a Function of Stimulus Characteristics and State." *Seminars in Perinatology,* 13: 421–29, 1989.

Locke, J. *The Child's Path to Spoken Language.* Cambridge, MA: Harvard University Press, 1995.

Mehler, J., P. Jusczyk, G. Lambertz, N. Halsted, J. Bertoncini, and

C. Amiel-Tison. "A Precursor of Language Acquisition in Young Infants." *Cognition*, 29: 143–78, 1988.

Meltzoff, A. "Imitation, Intermodal Representation and the Origins of Mind." In *Precursors of Early Speech*, edited by B. Lindblom and R. Zetterstrom. New York: Stockton Press, 1986.

Meltzoff, A., and M. K. Moore. "Imitation of Facial and Manual Gestures by Human Neonates." *Science*, 198: 75–8, 1977.

Menyuk, P., J. Liebergott, and M. Schultz. *Early Language Development in Full Term and Premature Infants*. Hillsdale, NJ: Erlbaum, 1995.

Messer, D. *The Development of Communication: From Social Interaction to Language*. New York: Wiley, 1994.

Moon, C., and W. P. Fifer. "Newborn Response to a Male Voice." Paper presented at the annual meeting of the International Conference on Infancy Studies, Washington, D.C., 1988.

———. "Syllables as Signals for 2-Day-Old Infants." *Infant Behavior and Development*, 13: 377–90, 1990.

Moon, C., R. Panneton-Cooper, and W. P. Fifer. "Two-Day-Olds Prefer Their Native Language." *Infant Behavior and Development*, 16: 495–500, 1993.

Nazzi, T., J. Bertoncini, and J. Mehler. "Language Discrimination by Newborns: Towards an Understanding of the Role of Rhythm." *Journal of Experimental Psychology: Human Perception and Performance*, 1998, in press.

Panneton, R. K., and A. J. DeCasper. "Newborns Prefer Intrauterine Heartbeat Sounds to Male Voices." Paper presented at the annual meeting of the International Conference on Infancy Studies, New York: New York, 1984.

Rosenblith, J., and J. E. Sims-Knight. *In the Beginning: Development in the First Two Years*. Belmont, CA: Brooks/Cole, 1985.

Saffran, J. R., R. N. Aslin, and E. L. Newport. "Statistical Learning by 8-Month-Old Infants." *Science*, 274: 1926–28, 1996.

Vihman, M. *Phonological Development*. Cambridge, MA: Blackwell, 1996.

Walker, D., J. Grimwade, and C. Wood. "Intrauterine Noise: A Component of the Fetal Environment." *American Journal of Obstetrics and Gynecology*, 109: 91–5, 1971.

Chapter 2: Yada-Yada-Yada

Adamson, L. B., and R. Bakeman. "The Development of Shared Attention During Infancy." In *Annals of Child Development*, edited by R. Vasta, Vol. 8, 1–41. London: Kingsley, 1991.

Bakeman, R., and L. B. Adamson. "Coordinating Attention to People and Objects in Mother-Infant and Peer-Infant Interaction." *Child Development,* 55: 1278–89, 1984.

Bloom, K., A. Russell, and K. Wassenberg. "Turn-Taking Affects the Quality of Infant Vocalizations." *Journal of Child Language,* 14: 211–27, 1987.

Boysson-Bardies, B. de, L. Sagart, and C. Durand. "Discernible Differences in the Babbling of Infants According to Target Language." *Journal of Child Language,* 11: 1–15, 1984.

Boysson-Bardies, B. de, and M. M. Vihman. "Adaptation to Language: Evidence from Babbling and First Words in Four Languages." *Language,* 67: 297–319, 1991.

Fernald, A. "Prosody in Speech to Children: Prelinguistic and Linguistic Functions." In *Annals of Child Development,* edited by R. Vasta, Vol. 8, 43–80. London: Kingsley, 1991.

Gogate, L. J., and L. E. Bahrick. "Intersensory Redundancy Facilitates Learning of Arbitrary Relations Between Vowel Sounds and Objects in Seven-Month-Old Infants." *Journal of Experimental Child Psychology,* 69: 133–49, 1998.

Gogate, L. J., L. E. Bahrick, and J. D. A. Watson. "A Cross-Cultural Study of Maternal Multimodal Motherese: The Use of Temporal Synchrony in Maternal Communication with Infants." Manuscript submitted for publication.

Hirsh-Pasek, K., D. G. Kemler-Nelson, P. W. Jusczyk, K. Wright Cassidy, B. Druss, and L. Kennedy. "Clauses Are Perceptual Units for Young Infants." *Cognition,* 26: 269–86, 1987.

Jusczyk, P. W., K. Hirsh-Pasek, D. G. Kemler-Nelson, L. Kennedy, A. Woodward, and J. Piwoz. "Perception of Acoustic Correlates of Major Phrasal Units by Young Infants." *Cognitive Psychology,* 24: 252–93, 1992.

Jusczyk, P. W., and N. Aslin. "Infants' Detection of Sound Patterns of Words in Fluent Speech." *Cognitive Psychology,* 29: 1–23, 1995.

Jusczyk, P. W. *The Discovery of Spoken Language.* Cambridge, MA: MIT Press, 1997.

C. L. Krumhansl, and P. W. Jusczyk. "Infants' Perception of Phrase Structure in Music." *Psychological Science,* 1: 70–3. 1990.

Klein, S. K., and I. Rapin. "Intermittent Conductive Hearing Loss and Language Development." In *Language Development in Exceptional Children,* edited by D. Bishop and K. Mogford, 96–109. Hillsdale, NJ: Erlbaum, 1993.

Locke, J. L., and D. M. Pearson. "Linguistic Significance of Babbling: Evidence from a Tracheotomized Infant." *Journal of Child Language,* 17: 1–16, 1990.

Locke, J. L. *The Child's Path to Spoken Language.* Cambridge, MA: Harvard University Press, 1993.

Mandel, D. R., P. W. Jusczyk, and D. B. Pisoni. "Infants' Recognition of the Sound Patterns of Their Own Names." *Psychological Science,* 6: 314–17, 1995.

Masataka, N. "Perception of Motherese in Japanese Sign Language by 6-Month-Old Hearing Infants." *Developmental Psychology,* 34: 241–46, 1998.

———. "Motherese in a Signed Language." *Infant Behavior and Development,* 15: 453–60, 1992a.

Oller, D. K., and R. E. Eilers. "The Role of Audition in Infant Babbling." *Child Development,* 59: 441–49, 1988.

Osofsky, J., and B. Danzger. "Relationships Between Neonatal Characteristics and Mother-Infant Interaction." *Developmental Psychology,* 10: 124–30, 1974.

Pettito, L. A., and P. F. Marentette. "Babbling in the Manual Mode: Evidence for the Ontogeny of Language." *Science,* 251: 1493–96, 1991.

Vihman, M. M. *Phonological Development: The Origins of Language in the Child.* Cambridge, MA: Blackwell Publishers, 1996.

Chapter 3: Point-ilism

Bates, E., L. Camaioni, and V. Volterra. "The Acquisition of Performatives Prior to Speech." *Merrill-Palmer Quarterly,* 21: 5–226, 1975.

Baumwell, L., C. S. Tamis-LeMonda, and M. H. Bornstein. "Maternal Verbal Sensitivity and Child Language Comprehension." *Infant Behavior and Development,* 20: 247–58, 1997.

Bell, S., and M. Ainsworth. "Infant Crying and Maternal Responsiveness." *Child Development,* 43: 1171–90, 1972.

Benedict, H. "Early Lexical Development: Comprehension and Production." *Journal of Child Language,* 6: 183–200, 1979.

Bloom, L. *The Transition from Infancy to Language: Acquiring the Power of Expression.* New York: Cambridge University Press, 1993.

Bruner, J. "The Acquisition of Pragmatic Commitments." In *The Transition from Prelinguistic to Linguistic Communication,* edited by R. M. Golinkoff, 27–42. Hillsdale, NJ: Erlbaum, 1983.

———. *Child's Talk: Learning to Use Language.* New York: Norton, 1983.

Butterworth, G., and L. Grover. "Joint Visual Attention, Manual Pointing, and Preverbal Communication in Human Infancy." In *Attention and Performance XIII,* edited by M. Jeannerod, 605–24. Hillsdale, NJ: Erlbaum, 1990.

Fogel, A., and T. E. Hannan. "Manual Actions of Nine- to Fifteen-Week-

Old Human Infants During Face-to-Face Interaction With Their Mothers." *Child Development,* 56: 1271–79, 1985.

Friederici, A. D., and J. M. I. Wessels. "Phonotactic Knowledge and Its Use in Infant Speech Perception." *Perception and Psychophysics,* 54: 287–95, 1993.

Gleitman, L., and E. Wanner. "Current Issues in Language Learning." In *Developmental Psychology: An Advanced Textbook,* edited by M. Bornstein and M. Lamb, 297–356. Hillsdale, NJ: Erlbaum, 1988.

Golinkoff, R. M. "The Preverbal Negotiation of Failed Messages: Insights into the Transition Period." In *The Transition from Prelinguistic to Linguistic Communication,* edited by R. M. Golinkoff, 57–8. Hillsdale, NJ: Erlbaum, 1983.

———. " 'I Beg Your Pardon?': The Preverbal Negotiation of Failed Messages." *Journal of Child Language,* 13: 455–76, 1986.

———. "When Is Communication a 'Meeting of Minds'?" *Journal of Child Language,* 20: 199–207, 1993.

Golinkoff, R. M., and L. Gordon. "What Makes Communication Run?: Characteristics of Immediate Successes." *First Language,* 8: 103–24, 1988.

Halle, P. A., and B. Boysson-Bardies. "Emergence of an Early Receptive Lexicon: Infants' Recognition of Words." *Infant Behavior and Development,* 17: 119–29, 1994.

Harding, C. G. "Acting with Intention: A Framework for Examining the Development of Intention." In *The Origins and Growth of Communication,* edited by L. Feagans, R. M. Golinkoff, and C. Garvey, 123–135. New York: Ablex, 1982.

Harding, C. G., and R. M. Golinkoff. "The Origins of Intentional Vocalizations in Prelinguistic Infants." *Child Development,* 50: 33–40, 1979.

Jusczyk, P. W., A. D. Friederici, J. Wessels, V. Y. Svenkerud, and A. M. Jusczyk. "Infants' Sensitivity to the Sound Patterns of Native Language Words." *Journal of Memory and Language,* 32: 402–20, 1993.

Jusczyk, P. W., P. A. Luce, and J. Charles-Luce. "Infants' Sensitivity to Phonotactic Patterns in the Native Language." *Journal of Memory and Language,* 33: 630–45, 1994.

Karzon, R. G. "Discrimination of a Polysyllabic Sequence by One-to-Four-Month-Old Infants." *Journal of Experimental Child Psychology,* 39: 326–42, 1985.

Ratner, N. K., and J. S. Bruner. "Games, Social Exchange and the Acquisition of Language." *Journal of Child Language,* 5: 391–401, 1978.

Sachs, J., B. Bard, and M. S. Johnson. "Language Learning with Restricted Input: Case Studies of Two Hearing Children of Deaf Parents." *Applied Psycholinguistics,* 2: 33–54, 1981.

Schaller, S. *A Man Without Words*. London: Ebury Press, 1992.

Schieffelin, B. B., and E. Ochs. "A Cultural Perspective on the Transition from Prelinguistic to Linguistic Communication." In *The Transition from Prelinguistic to Linguistic Communication*, edited by R. M. Golinkoff, 115–31. Hillsdale, NJ: Erlbaum, 1983.

Shotter, J. "The Cultural Context of Communication Studies: Theoretical and Methodological Issues." In *Action, Gesture, and Symbol: The Emergence of Language*, edited by A. Lock, 43–78. New York: Academic Press, 1978.

Stager, C. L., and J. F. Werker. "Infants Listen for More Phonetic Detail in Speech Perception Than in Word-Learning Tasks." *Nature*, 388: 381–2, 1997.

Werker, J. F., and R. C. Tees. "Developmental Changes Across Childhood in the Perception of Non-native Speech Sounds." *Canadian Journal of Psychology*, 37: 278–86, 1983.

Chapter 4: First Words

Acredolo, L., and S. Goodwyn. *Baby Signs*. Chicago: Contemporary Books, 1998.

Adams, M. *Learning to Read: Thinking and Learning about Print*. Cambridge, MA: MIT Press, 1990.

Bloom, L. *The Transition from Infancy to Language*. Cambridge, UK: Cambridge University Press, 1993.

Feitelson, D., and Z. Goldstein. "Patterns of Book Ownership and Reading to Young Children in Israeli School-Oriented and Nonschool-Oriented Families." *Reading Teacher*, 39: 924–30, 1986.

Golinkoff, R. M., C. Mervis, and K. Hirsh-Pasek. "Early Object Labels: The Case for a Developmental Lexical Principles Framework." *Journal of Child Language*, 21: 125–55, 1994.

Hirsh-Pasek, K., and R. Golinkoff. *The Origins of Grammar*. Cambridge, MA: MIT Press, 1996.

Hoff-Ginsberg, E. *Language Development*. Pacific Grove, CA: Brookes/Cole, 1997.

Lakoff, G. *Women, Fire, and Dangerous Things*. Chicago: University of Chicago Press, 1987.

Mandel, D. R., P. Jusczyk, and D. Pisoni. "Infants' Recognition of the Sound Patterns of Their Own Names." *Psychological Science*, 6: 314–17, 1995.

Markman, E. M. "Constraints on Word Learning: Speculations about Their Nature, Origin, and Domain Specificity." In *Minnesota Symposium on Child Psychology*, edited by M. R. Gunnar and M. P. Maratsos, 59–103. Hillsdale, NJ: Erlbaum, 1992.

Nelson, K. "Individual Differences in Language Development: Implications for Development and Language." *Developmental Psychology,* 17: 170–87, 1981.

Piaget, J. *The Language and Thought of the Child.* London: Routledge & Kegan Paul, 1926.

Pullum, G. K. *The Great Eskimo Vocabulary Hoax, and Other Irreverent Essays on the Study of Language.* Chicago: Chicago University Press, 1991.

Quine, W. V. O. *Word and Object.* Cambridge, MA: MIT Press, 1960.

Roberts, J., and I. Wallace. "Language and Otitis Media." In *Otitis Media in Young Children,* edited by J. E. Roberts, I. F. Wallace, and F. W. Henderson. Baltimore: Brookes, 1997.

Rosch, E., C. B. Mervis, W. D. Gray, D. M. Johnson, and P. Boyes-Braem. "Basic Objects in Natural Categories." *Child Development,* 8: 382–439, 1976.

Vihman, M. *Phonological Development.* Cambridge, MA: Blackwell, 1996.

Whitehurst, G., D. Arnold, J. Epstein, A. Angell, M. Smith, and J. Fischel. "A Picture Book Reading Intervention in Day Care and Home for Children from Low-Income Families." *Developmental Psychology,* 30: 679–89, 1994.

Wilke, K. *Helen Keller.* Indianapolis: Bobbs-Merrill, 1969.

Chapter 5: Vocabulary Takes Wing

Aslin, R., J. Woodward, N. LaMendola, and T. Bever. "Models of Word Segmentation in Fluent Maternal Speech to Infants." In *Signal to Syntax,* edited by E. J. Morgan and K. Demuth, 117–86. Cambridge, MA: MIT Press, 1996.

Baldwin, D. "Infants' Contribution to the Achievement of Joint Reference." *Child Development,* 62: 875–90, 1991.

———. "Infants' Ability to Consult the Speaker for Clues to Word Reference." *Journal of Child Language,* 20: 395–419, 1993.

———. "Understanding the Link Between Joint Attention and Language." In *Joint Attention: Its Origins and Role in Development,* edited by C. M. and P. J. Dunham, Hillsdale, NJ: Erlbaum, 1995.

Bloom, L. *The Transition from Infancy to Language.* Cambridge, UK: Cambridge University Press, 1993.

Brown, R. *A First Language.* Cambridge, MA: Harvard University Press, 1973.

Carey, S. "The Child as Word Learner." In *Linguistic Theory and Psychological Reality,* edited by M. Halle, J. Bresnan, and G. A. Miller, 264–93. Cambridge, MA: MIT Press, 1978.

———. "Semantic Development." In *Language Acquisition: The State of the*

Art, edited by E. W. and L. Gleitman, 347–89. Cambridge, MA: MIT Press, 1982.

Coplan, J. *Early Childhood Milestone Scale: Examiner's Manual* (2nd ed.). Austin, TX: Pro-ed, 1993.

———. "Normal Speech and Language Development: An Overview." *Pediatrics in Review,* 16: 91–100, 1995.

Fenson, L., P. Dale, S. Reznick, E. Bates, D. Thal, and S. Pethick. "Variability in Early Communicative Development." *Monographs of the Society for Research in Child Development,* 59 (Serial No. 242), 1994.

Goldfield, B., and J. Reznick. "Early Lexical Acquisition: Rate, Content and the Vocabulary Spurt." *Journal of Child Language,* 17: 171–84, 1990.

Golinkoff, R. M., C. Mervis, and K. Hirsh-Pasek. "Early Objects Labels: The Case for a Developmental Lexical Principles Framework." *Journal of Child Language,* 21: 125–55, 1994.

Gopnik, A., and A. Meltzoff. "The Development of Categorization in the Second Year and Its Relation to Other Cognitive and Linguistic Developments." *Child Development,* 58: 1523–31, 1987.

Harris, M. *Language Experience and Early Language Development: From Input to Uptake.* London: Erlbaum, 1992.

Hart, B., and T. Risley. *Meaningful Differences in the Everyday Experience of Young American Children.* Baltimore: Brookes, 1995.

Hirsh-Pasek, K., and R. Golinkoff. *The Origins of Grammar.* Cambridge, MA: MIT Press, 1996.

Hoff-Ginsberg, E. "Mother-Child Conversation in Different Social Classes and Communication Settings." *Child Development,* 62: 782–96, 1991.

———. *Language Development.* Pacific Grove, CA: Brookes/Cole, 1997.

Hoff-Ginsberg, E., and M. Shatz. "Language Input and the Child's Acquisition of Language." *Psychological Bulletin,* 92: 3–26, 1982.

Hollich, G., K. Hirsh-Pasek, and R. Golinkoff. "Introducing the 3-D Intermodal Preferential Looking Paradigm: A New Method to Answer an Age-Old Question." *Advances in Infancy Research,* 13: 355–73, 1998.

Huston, A., and J. Wright. "Mass Media and Children's Development." In *Handbook of Child Psychology,* edited by W. Damon. New York: Wiley, 1998.

Menyuk, P., J. Liebergott, and M. Schultz. *Early Language Development in Full Term and Premature Infants.* Hillsdale, NJ: Erlbaum, 1995.

Naigles, L., D. Singer, J. Singer, B. Jean-Louis, D. Sells, and C. Rosen. "Barney Says, 'Come, Go, Think, Know': Television Input Influences Specific Aspects of Language Development." (In preparation).

Nelson, K. "Concept, Word and Sentence: Interrelations in Acquisition and Development." *Psychological Review,* 81, 267–95, 1973.

Oshima-Takane, Y., E. Goodz, and J. L. Derevensky. "Birth Order Effects on Early Language Development: Do Secondborn Children Learn from Overheard Speech?" *Child Development,* 67: 621–34, 1996.

Piaget, J. *The Language and Thought of the Child.* London: Routledge & Kegan Paul, 1926.

Rescorla, L. "Overextension in Early Language Development." *Journal of Child Language,* 7: 321–35, 1980.

Rosenblith, J., and J. E. Sims-Knight. *In the Beginning: Development in the First Two Years.* Belmont, CA: Brooks/Cole, 1985.

Tomasello, M., and M. Barton. "Learning Words in Non-Ostensive Context." *Developmental Psychology,* 30: 639–50, 1994.

Tomasello, M., and J. Farrar. "Joint Attention and Early Language." *Child Development,* 57: 1454–63, 1986.

Tomasello, M., S. Mannle, and A. C. Kruger. "Linguistic Environment of 1- to 2-Year-Old Twins." *Developmental Psychology,* 22: 169–76, 1986.

Waxman, S. R. "The Development of a Linkage Between Count Nouns and Object Categories: Evidence from 15- to 21-Month-Old Infants." *Child Development,* 64: 1224–41, 1993.

Wells, G. C. *Language Development in the Pre-School Years.* Cambridge: Cambridge University Press, 1985.

Whitehurst, G. "Language Learning in Children Reared in Poverty." In *Research on Communication and Language Disorders: Contribution to Theories of Language Development,* edited by L. B. Adamson and M. Romski, 233–35. Baltimore: Brookes, 1997.

Chapter 6: *"More Juice!"*

Bloom, L. *One Word at a Time.* The Hague: Mouton, 1973.

Bloom, P. "Syntactic Distinctions in Child Language." *Journal of Child Language,* 17: 343–56, 1990.

Braine, M. "Length, Constraints, Reduction Rules and Holophrastic Processes in Children's Word Combinations." *Journal of Verbal Learning and Verbal Behavior,* 13: 448–56, 1974.

Brown, R. *A First Language.* Cambridge, MA: Harvard University Press, 1973.

Chapman, R. S., and J. F. Miller. "Word-Order in Early Two- and Three-Word Utterances. Does Production Precede Comprehension?" *Journal of Speech and Hearing Research,* 18: 355–71, 1975.

Cook, V. *Chomsky's Universal Grammar: An Introduction.* New York: Blackwell, 1989.

Fraser, C., U. Bellugi, and R. Brown. "Control of Grammar in Imitation,

Comprehension, and Production." *Journal of Verbal Learning and Verbal Behavior,* 2: 121–35, 1963.

Gerken, L., and B. J. McIntosh. "The Interplay of Function Morphemes in Young Children's Speech Perception and Production." *Developmental Psychology,* 27: 448–57, 1993.

———. "The Interplay of Function Morphemes and Prosody in Early Language." *Developmental Psychology,* 27: 204–16, 1993.

Gleitman, L. R., and E. Wanner. "Current Issues in Language Learning." In *Developmental Psychology: An Advanced Textbook,* edited by M. H. Bornstein and M. E. Lamb, 297–356. Hillsdale, NJ: Erlbaum, 1988.

Golinkoff, R., K. Hirsh-Pasek, and M. Schweisguth. *A Reappraisal of Young Children's Knowledge of Grammatical Morphemes.* (In preparation).

Hirsh-Pasek, K., and R. Golinkoff. *The Origins of Grammar.* Cambridge, MA: MIT Press, 1996.

Hirsh-Pasek, K., D. Kemler Nelson, P. Jusczyk, K. Wright Cassidy, B. Druss, and L. Kennedy. "Clauses Are Perceptual Units for Young Infants." *Cognition,* 26: 269–86, 1987.

Hoff-Ginsberg, E. "Mother-Child Conversation in Different Social Classes and Communication Settings." *Child Development,* 62: 782–96, 1991.

———. *Language Development.* Pacific Grove, CA: Brookes/Cole, 1997.

Jusczyk, P., and R. N. Aslin. "Infants' Detection of the Sound Patterns of Words in Fluent Speech." *Cognitive Psychology,* 29: 1–23, 1995.

Katz, N., E. Baker, and J. MacNamara. "What's in a Name?: A Study of How Children Learn Common and Proper Names." *Child Development,* 50: 1–13, 1974.

Menyuk, P., J. Liebergott, and M. Schultz. *Early Language Development in Full-Term and Premature Infants.* Hillsdale, NJ: Erlbaum, 1995.

Pinker, S. *The Language Instinct: How the Mind Creates Language.* New York: William Morrow, 1994.

Pye, C. "The Acquisition of K'iche' Mayan." In *Cross-Linguistic Studies of Language Acquisition,* edited by D. Slobin, 221–308. Hillsdale, NJ: Erlbaum, 1992.

Roberts, S. "Comprehension and Production of Word Order in Stage 1." *Child Development,* 54: 443–49, 1983.

Sachs, J., and L. Truswell. "Comprehension of Two-Word Instructions by Children in the One-Word Stage." *Journal of Child Language,* 5: 17–24, 1978.

Savage-Rumbaugh, E. S., J. Murphy, K. Sevcik, S. Brakke, S. L. Williams, and D. Rumbaugh. *Language Comprehension in Ape and Child.* Chicago: University of Chicago Press, 1993.

Schieffelin, B. "The Acquisition of Kaluli." In *The Cross-Linguistic Study of Language Acquisition: Vol. 1. The Data,* edited by D. I. Slobin, 525–94. Hillsdale, NJ: Erlbaum, 1985.

Shipley, E., C. Smith, and L. Gleitman. "A Study in the Acquisition of Language: Free Responses to Commands." *Language,* 45: 322–42, 1969.

Chapter 7: The Language Sophisticate

Ben-zeev, S. "The Influence of Bilingualism on Cognitive Strategy and Cognitive Development." *Child Development,* 48: 1009–18, 1977.

Berko, J. "The Child's Learning of English Morphology." *Word,* 14: 150–77, 1958.

Bloom, L. *Language Development from Two to Three.* New York: Cambridge University Press, 1990.

Bloom, P. "Syntactic Distinctions in Child Language." *Journal of Child Language,* 17: 343–56, 1990.

Bowerman, M. "The 'No Negative Evidence' Problem: How Do Children Avoid Constructing an Overly General Grammar?" In *Explaining Language Universals,* edited by V. A. Hawkins, 73–101. Oxford: Blackwell, 1988.

Chomsky, C. *The Acquisition of Syntax in Children from 5 to 10.* Cambridge, MA: MIT Press, 1969.

Curtiss, S. *Genie: A Psycholinguistic Study of a Modern Day "Wild Child."* New York: Academic Press, 1977.

DeVilliers, J. G. "Why Questions?" In *The Acquisition of Wh,* edited by T. Maxfield and B. Plunkett, University of Massachusetts Occasional Papers in Linguistics. Amherst, MA: University of Massachusetts, 1991.

Gleitman, L. R., and E. L. Newport. "The Invention of Language by Children: Environmental and Biological Influences on the Acquisition of Language." In *An Invitation to Cognitive Science: Vol. 1. Language,* edited by D. N. Osherson (series ed.), L. R. Gleitman and M. Liberman (vol. eds.), 2nd ed., 1–24. Cambridge, MA: MIT Press, 1995.

Hakuta, K. *Mirror of Language: The Debate on Bilingualism.* New York: Basic Books, 1986.

Hirsh-Pasek, K., and R. M. Golinkoff. "Language Comprehension: A New Look at Some Old Themes." In *Biological and Behavioral Determinants of Language Development,* edited by N. A. Krasnegor, D. M. Rumbaugh, R. L. Schiefelbusch, and M. Studdert-Kennedy, 301–20. Hillsdale, NJ: Erlbaum, 1991.

————. *The Origins of Grammar: Evidence from Early Language Comprehension.* Cambridge, MA: MIT Press, 1996.

Hirsh-Pasek, K., R. Treiman, and M. Schneiderman. "Brown and Hanlon Revisited: Mothers' Sensitivity to Ungrammatical Forms." *Journal of Child Language,* 11: 81–8, 1984.

Johnson, J. S., and E. L. Newport. "Critical Period Effects in Second-Language Learning: The Influence of Maturational State on the Acquisition of English as a Second Language." *Cognitive Psychology,* 21: 60–90, 1989.

Karmiloff-Smith, A. *A Functional Approach to Child Language.* Cambridge: C.U.P., 1979.

Kegl, J. "The Nicaraguan Sign Language Project: An Overview." *Signpost,* 7: 1994, Spring.

Klima, E. S., and U. Bellugi. "Syntactic Regularities." In *Psychological Papers,* edited by J. Lyon and R. J. Wales, 183–207. Edinburgh: University Press, 1967.

Marcus, G. F., S. Pinker, M. Ullman, M. Hollander, T. J. Rosen, and F. Xu. "Overregularization in Language Acquisition." *Monographs of the Society for Research in Child Development,* 57 (4, Serial No. 228), 1992.

Peal, E., and W. E. Lambert. "The Relation of Bilingualism to Intelligence." *Psychological Monographs,* 76 (27, Whole No. 546), 1962.

Pinker, S. "Language Acquisition." In *Language: An Invitation to Cognitive Science: Vol. 1,* edited by D. N. Osherson and H. Lasnik, 199–242. Cambridge, MA: MIT Press, 1990.

————. *The Language Instinct: How the Mind Creates Language.* New York: Morrow, 1994.

————. *Language Learnability and Language Development.* Cambridge, MA: Harvard University Press, 1984.

Rymer, R. *Genie: A Scientific Tragedy.* New York: HarperCollins, 1993.

Senghas, A. "Conventionalization in the First Generation: A Community Acquires a Language." *Journal of Contemporary Legal Issues,* 6: 501–19, 1995.

————. "The Development of Nicaraguan Sign Language Via the Language Acquisition Process." In *Proceedings* of the 19th Boston University Conference on Language Development, edited by D. MacLaughlin and S. McEwen. Boston: Cascadilla Press, 1995.

Strohner, H., and K. E. Nelson. "The Young Child's Development of Sentence Comprehension: Influence of Event Probability, Nonverbal Context, Syntactic Form and Strategies." *Child Development,* 45: 564–76, 1974.

Chapter 8: *"Please" and "Thank You"*

Bates, E. *Language and Context: The Acquisition of Pragmatics.* New York: Academic Press, 1976.

Becker, J. "Pragmatic Socializations: Parental Input to Preschoolers." *Discourse Processes,* 17: 131–48, 1994.

Bellinger, D. "Changes in the Explicitness of Mothers' Directives as Children Age." *Journal of Child Language,* 6: 443–58, 1979.

Blank, M., M. Gessner, and A. Eposito. "Language Without Communication: A Case Study." *Journal of Child Language,* 6: 329–52, 1979.

Bloom, L., L. Rocissano, and L. Hood. "Adult-Child Discourse: Developmental Interaction Between Information Processing and Linguistic Knowledge." *Cognitive Psychology,* 8: 521–52, 1976.

Ely, R., and J. B. Gleason. "Socialization Across Contexts." In *The Handbook of Child Language,* edited by P. Fletcher and B. MacWhinney, 251–70. Cambridge, MA: Blackwell, 1995.

Engel, S. "Learning to Reminisce: A Developmental Study of How Young Children Talk about the Past." Unpublished Ph.D. dissertation, University of New York Graduate Center, 1986.

Fivush, R., and N. R. Hamond. "Time and Again: Effects of Repetition and Retention Interval on Two-Year-Olds' Event Recall." *Journal of Experimental Child Psychology,* 47: 259–73, 1989.

———. "Autobiographical Memory Across the Preschool Years: Toward Reconceptualizing Childhood Amnesia." In *Knowing and Remembering in Young Children,* edited by R. Fivush and J. A. Hudson, 223–48. New York: Cambridge University Press, 1990.

Garvey, C. "An Approach to the Study of Children's Role Play." *Quarterly Newsletter of the Laboratory of Comparative Human Cognition,* 1: 69–73, 1979.

———. "Play with Language and Speech." In *Child Discourse,* edited by S. Ervin-Tripp and C. Mitchell-Kernan, 27–47. New York: Academic Press, 1977.

Gleason, J. B., and S. Weintraub. "The Acquisition of Routines in Child Language." *Language in Society,* 5: 129–36, 1976.

Gleason, J. B., R. Y. Perlmann, and E. Greif. "What's the Magic Word: Learning Language Through Politeness Routines." *Discourse Processes,* 7: 493–502, 1984.

Grice, H. P. "Logic and Conversation." In *Syntax and Semantics (Vol.3): Speech Acts,* edited by P. Cole and J. L. Morgan, 41–58. New York: Academic Press, 1975.

Horgan, D. "Learning to Tell Jokes: A Case Study of Metalinguistic Abilities." *Journal of Child Language,* 8: 217–27, 1981.

Hulit, L. M., and M. R. Howard. *Born to Talk: An Introduction to Speech and*

Language Development (2nd ed.). Needham Heights, MA: Allyn & Bacon, 1997.

Lawson, C. "Request Patterns in a Two-Year-Old." Unpublished manuscript. Berkeley, CA, 1967.

Nelson, K. *Language in Cognitive Development.* New York: Cambridge University Press, 1996.

Ochs, E. *Culture and Language Development.* New York: Cambridge University Press, 1988.

Reese, E., and R. Fivush. "Parental Styles of Talking about the Past." *Developmental Psychology,* 29: 596–606, 1993.

Reese, E., C. A. Haden, and R. Fivush. "Mother-Child Conversations About the Past: Relationships of Style and Memory over Time." *Cognitive Development,* 8: 403–30, 1993.

Sachs, H. "On the Analyzability of Stories by Children." In *Direction in Sociolinguistics,* edited by J. Gumperz and D. Hymes. New York: Holt, Rinehart & Winston, 1972.

Sachs, J. "Children's Play and Communicative Development." In *The Acquisition of Communicative Competence: Language Intervention Series,* edited by R. L. Schiefelbusch and J. Pickar, 109–35. Baltimore: University Park Press, 1984.

———. "The Role of Adult-Child Play in Language Development." In *Children's Play,* edited by K. H. Rubin. San Francisco: Jossey-Bass, 1980.

Schieffelin, B. B. "Getting It Together: An Ethnographic Approach to the Study of the Development of Communicative Competence." In *Developmental Pragmatics,* edited by E. Ochs and B. B. Schieffelin, 73–108. New York: Academic Press, 1979.

Shatz, M. "On the Development of Communicative Understanding: An Early Strategy for Interpreting and Responding to Messages." *Cognitive Psychology,* 3: 271–301, 1978.

Stern, D.N. *The Interpersonal World of the Infant.* Cambridge: Harvard University Press, 1977.

Epilogue: Tying It Up

Hirsh-Pasek, K., and R. Golinkoff. *The Origins of Grammar.* Cambridge, MA: MIT Press, 1996.

Pinker, S. *The Language Instinct: How the Mind Creates Language.* New York: Morrow, 1994.

Rice, M. "Cognitive Aspects of Communicative Development." In *The Acquisition of Communicative Competence: Language Intervention Series,* edited by R. L. Schiefelbusch and J. Pickar, 141–89. Baltimore: University Park Press, 1984.

Williams, G. C. *Adaptation and Natural Selection: A Critique of Some Current Evolutionary Thought*. Princeton, NJ: Princeton University Press, 1966.

Index

Acredolo, Linda, 97–98
Action words, 102, 120
Adaptive environments, 148
Adjectives, 102
Adverbs, 102
Ainsworth, Mary, 80
Ambiguity of word meanings, 118
Analogical overextensions, 124
Animal noises, 91, 93
Animal studies, 27
Articles, 178
Asynchrony, 58
Autism, 145

Babbling period (four to eight months),
    39–61
  absence of, 113
  defined, 43–44
  reason for, 44–46
Baby Signs (Acredolo and Goodwyn), 97–99,
    113–14
Baby talk (infant-directed speech), 31–34,
    41, 60–61, 112, 121–22
Baldwin, Dare, 129
Basic-level words, 100–101, 123
Bates, Elizabeth, 212
Bell, Silvia, 80
Bellinger, David, 207
Bertrand, Jacqueline, 134
Bilingual children, 196
"Biological siren" cry, 20
Birth order, 5–6, 140–41
Bloom, Lois, 104–5, 131, 153, 217

Bloom, Paul, 186
Books. *See* Reading aloud
Boys vs. girls
  and grammatical elements, 169–70
  and milestones, 5
  and vocabulary learning, 139–40
Brain
  and language stimulation, 10
  and pruning, 78
  see also Mental advances
Brown, Roger, 177, 178, 187

Caregiver, 36, 174
Carroll, Lewis, 161, 176
Categories, 95–96, 100–101
  as building blocks of language, 131
  of early words, 119–21
  novel, and novel names, 133–36
  overextensions, 124
  two-category sorting, 132
Categorization, 131–32, 146
Cause and effect, 65–67, 232
Characterizing signs, 97
Child care, 9–10, 147
Chomsky, Noam, 7–8
Clark, Herb, 205
"Cocktail party phenomenon," 52
Commonalitites, 100–101
Communicating
  animal vs. human, 94–96
  and crying, 20–21
  and first real word, 94–97
  honoring attempts at, 80–83

Communicating (*cont.*)
  lack of interest in, 144–45, 192
  and two-month boundary, 28
  without words, 64–72
Communicative devices, 65
  pointing, 67–69
  testing, 65–67
Comprehension vs. production
  and first sentences, 154–56
  and overextensions, 126
  and sentences and grammar, 170–71
  and words, 110–12
Context-bound words, 92–93
Contingency, 184–85
Conventional word, 93
Conversation
  and babbling, 42–43
  and books, 227–28
  child rarely joins, 144
  and critical period, 191
  and imitation, 31
  and incomplete utterances, 204–10
  and newborn, 35–36
  and social class, 142–43
  and social rules, 215–19
  turns, 70
  and two-word sentences, 151
Cooing, 28, 42, 43–44
Cooperation principle, 215
Coordinated sentences, 184–85
Correction, 173, 188, 194
Critical period, 190–91
Crying, 20–21, 80–81
Culture, 96, 202–204, 231–32

Deaf children, 36–37, 97, 189–90
Deaf parents, 40, 41, 147–48
Directives, 207–10
Disrupted speech, 50–52

Ear infections, 59–60, 106–7, 144, 193
Eighteen- to twenty-four-month-olds, 115–74
Eimas, Peter, 8, 23–24
Embedded sentences, 184
Emotion, and first words, 105, 106
"Expansion," 173
"Expressive" children, 108
Eye contact or gaze, 113
  and babbling, 47
  and communication, 71, 81
  and intentional communication, 66–67
  and language delay, 145, 192
  and learning new words, 130
  start of, 28
  and vocalizing, 42

Fast mapping, 135–36, 146–47
Fetal alcohol syndrome, 145

Fetus, 4, 13–19
Fifer, William, 14–15
Fillmore, Charles, 218
First words, 87–114
  diary, 94, 117
  difficulty of saying, 6–7, 104–106
  individual differences in, 106–109, 112
  types, 100–103
  see also Protowords; Real words
Foreign (second) language, 8–9, 46, 74–78
  and babbling, 46, 51
  recognizing own vs., 23–25
  when to start learning, 194–97
Function, and basic-level words, 101
Function words and particles, 176–79, 188–89
  and overgeneralization, 179–80

Games, 72, 79, 80, 118–23, 223
Gavagai problem, 103
Gender, and articles, 186–87
Generativity, 154
Gestational learning, 17–18
Gestures, 81
Gleason, Jean Berko, 178
Goffman, Erving, 200
Goodwyn, Susan, 97–98
Grammar, 175–97, 231
  and attention to grammatical elements,
      164–69
  comprehension vs. production, 170–71
  and correction, 173
  critical period for, 191
  and early speech, 185–87
  emergence of, 175–76
  and expansion, 173–74
  "glue," 176–79, 193
  particles, 158
  sensitivity to part of speech, 186
  source of, 187–91
  spurt, 184–85
  and understanding sentences, 156–57
  and "with," 169–70
Grice, Paul, 215

Hair-blow test, 66–67
Harding, Carol, 65
Hart, Bety, 142, 143, 146
Headturn Preference Procedure, 49–51, 55,
    161–62
Hearing problems, 144, 192
Heart-rate monitoring method, 14–16
"Home signs," 97
Human faces, 25–28

Imitation
  and conversation, 31
  and newborn, 30–31
  and sentences, 187–88

Immersion, 56
Imperatives, 208
Indicators, 97
Individual differences
    and first words, 106–109, 112
    and milestones, 5–6
    and word learning, 137–43
Infant-directed speech. *See* Baby talk
Infants
    mouth shape, 138
    studying language in, 8–9
Inferences, 205–10
-*ing* particle, 166–67, 177
Intelligence, 106–107, 143
Intentional communication, 65–66, 80–82, 94
Interactive environments, 148
Intermodal Preferential Looking Paradigm
    (IPLP), 159, 162, 167, 169
Intersubjectivity, 30
Intonation, 46, 151

James, William, 19
Jargon, 43–44
Johnson, Jacqueline, 194
Jokes, 91, 222–24
Jusczyk, Peter, 75

Keller, Helen, 87, 133
Kennedy, John, 161
Koppel, Ted, 10

Language
    finding word, phrases, and clauses in
        stream of, 157–58
    foreign vs. native, 8–9, 23–24, 46, 74–76,
        77–78
    "instinct," 8, 189–90
    mapping to unique events, 160–61
    and mental advances, 131
    and realizing words describe events,
        158–59
    and temporal freedom, 95
    three underpinnings of, 157–64
    as unique to humans, 230–31
Language delay, 143–46
    and autism, 145
    and hearing problems, 144–45
    and mental retardation, 145
    six warning signs, 144
    when to worry about, 192–93
Language development
    and baby talk, 32
    and caregiver, 174
    and deaf parents, 40
    how children learn, 2–3
    how parents can promote, 193–94
    and interacting with newborn, 35–36
    and nature vs. nurture, 3–4

observing in your child, 10
    pervasiveness of, 1
    scientific studies of, 1–4
    and TV, 147–48
Language sounds
    ability of infants to produce, 40
    and development of mouth, 138–39
    see also Foreign language
Linkletter, Art, 199
Locke, John, 45
Lorenz, Konrad, 27

MacArthur Communicative Development
    Inventory, 110–12, 119, 139, 140, 143
Manner principle, 217
Markers, 177
Mead, Margaret, 203
Meaning, 231
    and word order, 161–64
    of words, 103–4
Meltzoff, Andrew, 30
Memories of womb, 18–19
Memorization, 192
Mental advances
    first sentences, 150–54
    and vocabulary spurt, 130–33, 136–37
Mental retardation, 145–46
Mervis, Carolyn, 134
Milestones, 4–7
    and comparing children, 5–6
    and delayed development, 192–93
    vocabulary spurt, 143
Modeling communication, 83
Moon, Chris, 14–15
Moore, Keith, 30
Mother
    face, 26–27
    voice, 14, 17, 21–23
    see also Parents
Mouth, 28–29, 137–38
Musical recognition, 16

Name
    novel, and categories, 133–37
    recognizing own, 52–54
Name callers, 108–109
Naming insight, 119
Narratives, 219–21, 225–28
National Institute of Child Health and
    Human Development Study of Early
    Child Care, 9
Negotiation, preverbal, 70–73, 82–83
Nelson, Katherine, 108, 221
Neurological imperialism, 78
Newborns, 4, 18–34
Newport, Elissa, 194
Nine- to twelve-month-olds, 63–85
Nixon, Richard, 201

Nonlanguage symbols, 91
Noun types, 186–87

Object words, 101–102, 119–20, 186–87
Ochs, Elinor, 203
Overextensions, 124–27
Overgeneralizations, 179–80

Parents
    and babbling, 47–48
    and crying, 20–21
    and first sentences, 172–74
    intrusive, 85
    and narratives, 220–21
    and pointing, 68
    and preverbal signals, 70–72, 81–82
    and promoting language growth, 193–94
    repetive vs. elaborative, 224–26
    responsiveness, 83–85
    and scientific knowledge, 9–10
    and social rules, 204
    social vs. object namers, 109
    talking to newborn, 31–34
Past tense, 178, 179–80
Patterns in language
    detecting, 74–77
    and fetus, 15–16
    and infant-directed speech, 33–34
    and newborns, 19
Pettito, Laura, 39–40
Piaget, Jean, 65, 91, 131
Pinker, Steven, 3, 8, 229–30
Play, language and, 222–23. *See also* Games
Plural marker, 177–78
Pointing, 65, 67–69, 71, 144
Polite speech, 201–202, 212–13
Pragmatic aspects, 201–202
Pre-intentional communicative attempts, 81
Prenatal calls, 17–18
Pretense, 223–24
Preverbal communication, 64–74
Pronouns, 152
Pronunciation, 79, 137–39
    when to worry about, 193
Proper names, 120
Protowords, 92, 93, 94
Psammetichus, King of Egypt, 3

Quality principle, 216–17
Quantity principle, 216
Questions, 180–84
    comprehending, 156–57
    indirect, 205–10
    indirect directive, 208
    parent asking child, 193
    wh-, 180, 181–82
    why?, 182–84
    yes/no, 180–81
Quine, Willard, 103

Reading aloud, 121
    and fetus, 16
    and language problems, 144, 193
    and narratives, 227–28
    and picture books, 112–13
    recognizing words in, 54–56
    and word learning, 122–23
Real word learning, 90, 93–94
    first ten, 96–97
"Referential" group, 108
Rejection, signaling, 71–72
Relational overextension, 124
Relationship between objects, 124, 160
Relevance principle, 216
Representation, 131, 146
Requests
    inferences and indirect, 205–10
    and signaling, 72
    and social distinctions, 210–13
Rescorla, Leslie, 124
Responsive environment, 80–81, 84–85
Rhythm, 46, 74–75
Rice, Mabel, 232
Risley, Todd, 142, 143, 146
Roberts, Steven, 163
Rosch, Eleanor, 100
Rymer, Russ, 190

Sarcasm, 232
Scaffold, 218, 226
Schaller, Susan, 63
Scheiffelin, Bambi, 203
Scientific findings
    and baby talk, 112
    and deafness in newborn, 36–37
    and ear infections, 59–60
    and first words, 112
    and honoring communicative attempts,
        80–83
    how to use, 5, 9–11
    and interpretation vs. correction, 172–74
    and language input, 146–47
    and language problems, 143–46
    methodological breakthroughs, 8–9
    and narrative development, 224–26
    and overestimating capabilities, 37
    and picture book reading, 112–13
    and putting thoughts into words, 83–85
    and silence, 35–36, 61
    and theoretical breakthroughs, 7–8
    and TV, 147–48
Segmentation, 74–76
Senghas, Ann, 189–90
Sentences, 149–74
    and grammatical spurt, 184
    leap in capability, 175–76
    two-word, 150–54
    when to worry about lack of, 192
Sesame Street (TV show), 148

Sharing experience, 72–74
Shatz, Marilyn, 209, 210
Shotter, John, 82
Signals, 64–65, 70–73, 97–99
Situational context, 151
Situations, labeling, 109
Smiling, 27–28, 34–35
Social class, 141–43, 146–47
Social conventions, 201–202
Social cues
    and autism, 145
    and sentence comprehension, 155–56
    and vocabulary spurt, 127–30
Social distinctions, 211–13
Social interaction, 231–32
Socialites, 108, 109
Social routines, 213–15
Social skill
    and language growth, 193–94
    and vocabulary spurt, 136–37
Social theorists, 140
Social understandings, 232–33
Social use of language, 199–224
Social words, 109
Sounds
    babbling and world languages, 46, 51
    and fetus, 14–17
    memories of, 145
    and newborns, 19–20
    non-native, 78
    opposite, 58–59
    order of, 74
    proportions of, 46
    sequence of, 75–77
Specificity, 100
Specific Language Impairment (SLI), 145
Stationary group, 58
Stern, Daniel, 28
Subordinate level, 100
Sucking reflex experiments, 21
Superordinate-level words, 100, 123
Symbols, 90–92, 131, 136
Synchrony, 58
Systematic omissions, 152

Talking to baby
    and babbling stage, 40–41, 60–61
    about faraway objects, 47–48
    as newborn, 31–34
Television, 36, 147–48
Temporal relationships, 232
Tongue placement, 138
Toys, 119
"Try this" experiments
    babbling and real words, 44
    baby signs, 99
    baby talk, 34
    categorizing and vocabulary spurt, 133

charting smiles, 28
conversational rules, 219
conversation with baby, 42–43
cues and sentences, 155–56
diary and vocabulary spurt, 117
diary of protowords and first words, 94
disrupted speech, 51–52
emotion and talking, 106
fetal hearing, 16–17
finding objects near and far, 48
first ten words, 96–97, 102
foreign language, 24–25
imitation, 30
intentional communication, 67
grammatical elements, 168–69, 178–79
indirect requests, 209–10
jokes, 224
language maps to events, 160–61
name caller vs. socialite, 109
name recognition, 54
narratives, 221
negotiating, 72
newborn reactions to sound, 19
overextensions, 127
playing games, 80
pointing, 69
reading for word learning, 122–23
social cues and new words, 130
symbols in play, 92
two-word sentences, 153
word order and meaning, 163–64
Twelve- to eighteen-month-olds, 87–114
Twenty-four- to thirty-six-month-olds
    and grammar, 175–97
    and social use of language, 199–228
Twins, 141

Verbs, 102
    endings, 167–68
Vocabulary
    and birth order, 140–41
    and book reading, 122–23
    and boys vs. girls, 139–40
    and categorization, 132
    defined, 116–17
    delay in, 144–46
    and fast-mapping, 135–36
    flowering of, 88–90
    and infant-directed speech, 121–22
    and mental advances, 130–33, 136–37
    and misapplying words, 123–27
    and number of words heard, 146–47
    and social class, 141–43
    and social cues, 127–30, 136–37
    spurt, 115–48
    and TV, 148
Vocalizing, as intentional communication,
    65, 81, 83

Vocal tract, 40, 42, 45
Von Frisch, Karl, 95
Vowel sounds, 29, 33
Vygotsky, Lev, 218

Wilke, Katharine, 87
Williams, George, 229
Word(s)
    and babbling, 44, 48–52
    and birth order, 140–41
    and boys vs. girls, 139–40
    calling, 125
    combinations, 150–53
    comprehension vs. production, 110–12
    and events in world, 158–59

finding, in language stream, 157–58
and individual differences, 137–43
learning first, 88–99
learning to pronounce, 79
and meaning, 56–59, 103–104
misapplying, 123–27
order, 161–64, 169–70
and own name, 53–54
and preverbal communication, 72–74
remembering meanings of, 78–80
and social class, 141–43
and stories, 54–56
when to worry about lack of, 113–14
see also First words; Protowords; Real
    words; Vocabulary